To D

D0592830

HISTORY AS ART AND AS SCIENCE

WORLD PERSPECTIVES

Volumes already published

WORLD PERSPECTIVES · *Volume Thirty-two*

Planned and Edited by **RUTH NANDA ANSHEN**

HISTORY AS ART AND AS SCIENCE

Twin Vistas on the Past

BY H. STUART HUGHES

HARPER & ROW, PUBLISHERS
New York, Evanston, and London

FIRST EDITION

LIBRARY OF CONGRESS CATALOG CARD NUMBER: 63–20291

M-N

Contents

9-22-80 Editions 6.50

World Perspectives

What This Series Means

IT IS the thesis of *World Perspectives* that man is in the process of developing a new consciousness which, in spite of his apparent spiritual and moral captivity, can eventually lift the human race above and beyond the fear, ignorance, and isolation which beset it today. It is to this nascent consciousness, to this concept of man born out of a universe perceived through a fresh vision of reality, that *World Perspectives* is dedicated.

Only those spiritual and intellectual leaders of our epoch who have a paternity in this extension of man's horizons are invited to participate in this Series: those who are aware of the truth that beyond the divisiveness among men there exists a primordial unitive power since we are all bound together by a common humanity more fundamental than any unity of dogma; those who recognize that the centrifugal force which has scattered and atomized mankind must be replaced by an integrating structure and process capable of bestowing meaning and purpose on existence; those who realize that science itself, when not inhibited by the limitations of its own methodology, when chastened and humbled, commits man to an indeterminate range of yet undreamed consequences that may flow from it.

This Series endeavors to point to a reality of which scientific theory has revealed only one aspect. It is the commitment to this reality that lends universal intent to a scientist's most original and solitary thought. By acknowledging this frankly we shall restore science to the great family of human aspirations by which men hope to fulfill themselves in the world community as thinking and sentient beings. For our problem is to discover a principle of differentiation and yet relationship lucid enough to justify and to purify scientific, philosophic and all other knowledge, both discursive and intuitive, by accepting their interdependence. This is the crisis in consciousness made articulate through the crisis in science. This is the new awakening.

Each volume presents the thought and belief of its author and points to the way in which religion, philosophy, art, science, economics, politics and history may constitute that form of human activity which takes the fullest and most precise account of variousness, possibility, complexity and difficulty. Thus *World Perspectives* endeavors to define that ecumenical power of the mind and heart which enables man through his mysterious greatness to re-create his life.

This Series is committed to a re-examination of all those sides of human endeavor which the specialist was taught to believe he could safely leave aside. It interprets present and past events impinging on human life in our growing World Age and envisages what man may yet attain when summoned by an unbending inner necessity to the quest of what is most exalted in him. Its purpose is to offer new vistas in terms of world and human development while refusing to betray the intimate correlation between universality and individuality, dynamics and form, freedom and destiny. Each author deals with the increasing realization that spirit and nature are not separate and apart; that intuition and reason must regain their importance as the means of perceiving and fusing inner being with outer reality.

World Perspectives endeavors to show that the conception of wholeness, unity, organism is a higher and more concrete conception than that of matter and energy. Thus an enlarged meaning of life, of biology, not as it is revealed in the test tube of the laboratory but as it is experienced within the organism of life itself, is attempted in this Series. For the principle of life consists in the tension which connects spirit with the realm of matter, symbiotically joined. The element of life is dominant in the very texture of nature, thus rendering life, biology, a transempirical science. The laws of life have their origin beyond their mere physical manifestations and compel us to consider their spiritual source. In fact, the widening of the conceptual framework has not only served to restore order within the respective branches of knowledge, but has also disclosed analogies in man's position regarding the analysis and synthesis of experience in apparently separated domains of knowledge suggesting the possibility of an ever more embracing objective description of the meaning of life.

Knowledge, it is shown in these books, no longer consists in a manipulation of man and nature as opposite forces, nor in the reduction of data to mere statistical order, but is a means of liberating mankind from the destructive power of fear, pointing the way toward the goal of the rehabilitation of the human will and the rebirth of faith and confidence in the human person. The works published also endeavor to reveal that the cry for patterns, systems and authorities is growing less insistent as the desire grows stronger in both East and West for the recovery of a dignity, integrity and self-realization which are the inalienable rights of man who may now guide change by means of conscious purpose in the light of rational experience.

Other vital questions explored relate to problems of international understanding as well as to problems dealing with prejudice and the resultant tensions and antagonisms. The growing perception and responsibility of our World Age point to the new reality that the individual person and the collective person supplement and integrate each other; that the thrall of totalitarianism of both left and right has been shaken in the universal desire to recapture the authority of truth and human totality. Mankind can finally place its trust not in a proletarian authoritarianism, not in a secularized humanism, both of which have betrayed the spiritual property right of history, but in a sacramental brotherhood and in the unity of knowledge. This new consciousness has created a widening of human horizons beyond every parochialism, and a revolution in human thought comparable to the basic assumption, among the ancient Greeks, of the sovereignty of reason; corresponding to the great effulgence of the moral conscience articulated by the Hebrew prophets; analogous to the fundamental assertions of Christianity; or to the beginning of a new scientific era, the era of the science of dynamics, the experimental foundations of which were laid by Galileo in the Renaissance.

An important effort of this Series is to re-examine the contradictory meanings and applications which are given today to such terms as democracy, freedom, justice, love, peace, brotherhood and God. The purpose of such inquiries is to clear the way for the foundation of a genuine *world* history not in terms of nation or race or culture but in terms of man in relation to God, to himself, his fellow man and the universe, that reach beyond immediate self-interest. For the meaning of the World Age consists in respecting man's hopes and dreams which lead to a deeper understanding of the basic values of all peoples.

World Perspectives is planned to gain insight into the meaning of man, who not only is determined by history but who also determines history. History is to be understood as concerned not only with the life of man on this planet but as including also such cosmic influences as interpenetrate our human world. This generation is discovering that history does not conform to the social optimism of modern civilization and that the organization of human communities and the establishment of freedom and peace are not only intellectual achievements but spiritual and moral achievements as well, demanding a cherishing of the wholeness of human personality, the "unmediated wholeness of feeling and thought," and constituting a never-ending challenge to man, emerging from the abyss of meaninglessness and suffering, to be renewed and replenished in the totality of his life.

Justice itself, which has been "in a state of pilgrimage and crucifixion" and now is being slowly liberated from the grip of social and political demonologies in the East as well as in the West, begins to question its own premises. The modern revolutionary movements which have challenged the sacred institutions of society by protecting social injustice in the name of social justice are here examined and re-evaluated.

In the light of this, we have no choice but to admit that the *un*freedom against which freedom is measured must be retained with it, namely, that the aspect of truth out of which the night view appears to emerge, the darkness of our time, is as little abandonable as is man's subjective advance. Thus the two sources of man's consciousness are inseparable, not as dead but as living and complementary, an aspect of that "principle of complementarity" through which Niels Bohr has sought to unite the quantum and the wave, both of which constitute the very fabric of life's radiant energy.

There is in mankind today a counterforce to the sterility and danger of a quantitative, anonymous mass culture; a new, if sometimes imperceptible, spiritual sense of convergence toward world unity on the basis of the sacredness of each human person and respect for the plurality of cultures. There is a growing awareness that equality may not be evaluated in mere numerical terms but is proportionate and analogical in its reality. For when equality is equated with interchangeability, individuality is negated and the human person extinguished.

We stand at the brink of an age of a world in which human life presses forward to actualize new forms. The false separation of man and nature, of time and space, of freedom and security, is acknowledged, and we are faced with a new vision of man in his organic unity and of history offering a richness and diversity of quality and majesty of scope hitherto unprecedented. In relating the accumulated wisdom of man's spirit to the new reality of the World Age, in articulating its thought and belief, *World Perspectives* seeks to encourage a renaissance of hope in society and of pride in man's decision as to what his destiny will be.

World Perspectives is committed to the recognition that all great changes are preceded by a vigorous intellectual re-evaluation and reorganization. Our authors are aware that the sin of *hubris* may be avoided by showing that the creative process itself is not a free activity if by free we mean arbitrary, or unrelated to cosmic law. For the creative process in the human mind, the developmental process in organic nature and the basic laws of the inorganic realm may be but varied expressions of a universal formative process. Thus *World Perspectives* hopes to show that although the present apocalyptic period is one of exceptional tensions, there is also at work an exceptional movement toward a compensating unity which refuses to violate the ultimate moral power at work in the universe, that very power upon which all human effort must at last depend. In this way we may come to understand that there exists an inherent independence of spiritual and mental growth which, though conditioned by circumstances, is never determined by circumstances. In this way the great plethora of human knowledge may be correlated with an insight into the nature of human nature by being attuned to the wide and deep range of human thought and human experience.

In spite of the infinite obligation of men and in spite of their finite power, in spite of the intransigence of nationalisms, and in spite of the homelessness of moral passions rendered ineffectual by the scientific outlook, beneath the apparent turmoil and upheaval of the present, and out of the transformations of this dynamic period with the unfolding of a world consciousness, the purpose of *World Perspectives* is to help quicken the "unshaken heart of well-rounded truth" and interpret the significant elements of the World Age now taking shape out of the core of that undimmed continuity of the creative process which restores man to mankind while deepening and enhancing his communion with the universe.

RUTH NANDA ANSHEN

Et Jehanne, la bonne Lorraine,
Qu'Anglois bruslèrent à Rouen;
Où sont-ils, Vierge souveraine? . . .
Mais où sont les neiges d'antan!

—FRANÇOIS VILLON, *Ballade des Dames du Temps jadis*

Preface

THESE ESSAYS gradually grew out of informal talks I have given over the past four years to groups of Harvard and Radcliffe students particularly concerned with the nature of historical writing. Some of them I subsequently worked into more formal shape for the Phi Beta Kappa visiting lecture program during the academic years 1961–1962 and 1962–1963. Three have contributed to the continuing interchange with my colleagues in the social sciences which I began with my article "The Historian and the Social Scientist" published in the *American Historical Review* in October 1960: Chapter I was originally part of a colloquium series at the Harvard Center for Cognitive Studies; Chapter II was delivered as a paper at the 1962 meeting of the American Anthropological Association and subsequently published in *Current Anthropology;* Chapter III, after first being presented to the psychiatric training group at the Beth Israel Hospital in Boston in early 1961, was delivered the following year as the Stimson Lecture at Goucher College. The concluding chapter has appeared in *The American Scholar.*

Such reflections lay claim neither to completeness nor to total originality. They represent an attitude, rather, which I think is steadily gaining ground in the theory and practice of historical study.

I.

What the Historian Thinks He Knows

WHEN ONE first approaches the study of history, it does not look particularly forbidding. To judge by outside appearances, it is a tranquil business, pursued through the leisurely digestion of masses of books and documents. It may demand steady work, long hours, those qualities of scholarly doggedness which the Germans lump together under the ineffable word *Sitzfleisch*. Its rewards may be slow in coming. It may seldom reveal a genius at the age of twenty. But over the long pull it seems safe and sure enough. It requires little prior preparation, no specialized vocabulary or knowledge of mathematics. At its learned gatherings, the amateur scholar finds himself quite at home. Little wonder that in undergraduate programs history figures along with English literature as the favorite study of those whose intellectual interests are still unfixed; even Henry Adams in a moment of characteristic self-denigration could refer to the "mental indolence" of his chosen pursuits.

All this, however, is rapidly changing: in the past generation the writing of history has become less invertebrate than it used to be. Philosophers have subjected its methods and assumptions to rigorous logical analysis. Historical scholarship has begun to establish firm ties with such neighboring intellectual disciplines as economics and sociology.[1] In short, after talking about the matter for more than a century, historians have finally become a rather special breed of scientists. And in so doing, they have begun to recognize that art and science are not so far apart as they used to suppose. As E. H. Carr has written: "Scientists, social scientists, and historians are all engaged in different branches of the same study: the study of man and his environment, of the effects of man on his environment and of his environment on man. The object of the study is the same: to increase man's understanding of, and mastery over, his environment."[2]

Or—to cite a scientist's view of intellectual method—"The two processes, that of science and that of art, are not very different. Both science and art form in the course of the centuries a human language by which we can speak about the more remote parts of reality, and the coherent sets of concepts as well as the different styles of art are different words or groups of words in this language."[3] Both the scientist and the artist communicate what they have understood through the language of metaphor. If a scientific hypothesis is a metaphor, so is a plastic design or a phrase of music. At the same time as metaphors they are radically incommensurate. "The elegant rationality of science and the metaphoric non-rational-

[1] I have tried to analyze these new trends in my essay "The Historian and the Social Scientist," *American Historical Reciew,* LXVI (October 1960), 20–46.

[2] *What Is History?* (New York, 1961), p. 111.

[3] Werner Heisenberg, *Physics and Philosophy: The Revolution in Modern Science* (New York, 1958), p. 109.

ity of art operate with deeply different grammars."[4] One conveys its meaning through precise structures of thought—the other by suggestion and indirection. Their procedures are complementary rather than identical. And the writing of history partakes of the nature of both. Perhaps more than in any other field of study, these two aspects of man's intellectual quest are inextricably entangled in the pursuit of knowledge about the human past.

Hence the study of history offers living proof of the complementary nature of art and of science. One might think that this would be a source of pride to historians. And I suspect that my fellow historians do take pride in the mediating character of their own discipline more frequently than they explicitly proclaim it. All too often, however, the half-scientific, half-artistic nature of their pursuits figures as a source of puzzlement and of difficulty in explaining to their colleagues in other fields what they are about. In particular, the growing affiliation of history with social science seems more of a threat than an opportunity. In the minds of historians wedded to the tradition of history as a branch of literature, the new emphasis on methodological rigor suggests the abandonment of something infinitely precious. The fear of scientific attachments may be rooted in unfortunate early experience: it may go back to college days, when a young scholar with a strongly literary bent found himself inept in the laboratory. It may reflect an aesthetic distaste for scientists as cultural barbarians with no feeling for language. It may mask a sense of inferiority: after all, scientists have no trouble in understanding what historians write, but the reverse is far from true. In any

---

[4] Jerome S. Bruner, *On Knowing: Essays for the Left Hand* (Cambridge, Mass., 1962), p. 74.

case, a great many historians seem to feel that if their subject should become too scientific it would forfeit its soul—it would lose the quality of color and adventure that first inspired them to embark on historical studies at all.

Here I strenuously object. I have never argued—and I do not propose to argue now—that history should strive for the exactitude of the more precise sciences. I resist any notion that historians should alter their characteristic vocabulary and mode of presentation, that they should cease to think of their subject as a branch of literature. The dilemma, I believe, is quite false. History can become more scientific—more conscious of its assumptions and its intellectual procedures—without losing its aesthetic quality. Indeed, an explicit recognition of history's place among the sciences may enhance the intellectual excitement it conveys. It may add a new dimension to the old sense of historical adventure.

It is some of these new adventures, far out on the boundaries of investigation where history as art and as science blend, that I wish to chart in the present series of essays. And I think I can best begin by recalling the peculiarities of historical knowledge, the philosophical pitfalls that lie hidden under the deceptive smoothness of historical prose.

Historians—in contrast to investigators in almost any other field of knowledge—very seldom confront their data directly. The literary or artistic scholar has the poem or painting before him; the astronomer scans the heavens through a telescope; the geologist tramps the soil he studies; the physicist or chemist runs experiments in his laboratory. The mathematician and the philosopher are abstracters from reality by definition and do not pretend to empirical competence. The historian alone is both wedded to empirical reality and condemned to view his subject matter at second remove. He alone must accept the word of others before he even begins to devise his account.

This, at least, is true of the conventional historiography based on records or documents—and a type of historical writing that is bound to remain in honor no matter how many experimental approaches may be tried. Of course, there is the tangible evidence of archaeological remains, and of these I shall have more to say later on. There are also one or two celebrated examples of historians who have performed a kind of laboratory experiment by reenacting episodes from the past. We may recall the learned German who checked the classical accounts of Thermopylae by staging a mock battle in a Prussian armory. More recently Samuel Eliot Morison proved the accuracy of Columbus' original log by sailing a ship himself from Spain to the West Indies. But these are the dramatic exceptions to the general rule. I think there should be many more of them, and that historians should stretch their imaginations to find new ways of coming closer to the stuff of historical experience itself. Yet no matter how hard they try, historians will seldom have the luck to find methods of proof as neat as those in the examples I have cited. (Few great battles have involved so small a number of men and have occurred in so confined and clearly delimited a space as the Spartans' defense of the pass at Thermopylae.) Most of the time, historians will continue to be thrown back on the uncontrolled evidence of written records.

Moreover, even if we were deluged with artifacts and could run retrospective experiments at will, the problem of historical knowledge would still be with us. For merely to identify something—to label it accurately or to locate it in chronological

sequence—is not to *know* it in the historian's usual meaning
of the term. Historical knowledge involves *meaning*. Most
contemporary historians follow the Italian philosopher and
historian Benedetto Croce in arguing that without an imputa-
tion of meaning historical prose is simply barren chronicle.

I shall not tarry over the multifold meanings of the word
"meaning." To do so would be to burden the argument with
an intolerable semantic overload. I shall merely do what historians are so often blamed for doing and say that in this
case the meaning of meaning will gradually emerge from context. Historians are by nature wary of precise definition; they
hate to be confined within tight terminological boundaries, and
they are ever alert to the fallacy of misplaced concreteness;
they much prefer to write ordinary words in their common-
sense usage and then let the reader little by little become aware
of how these words have subtly changed their significance
through time. For present purposes, let us say that "meaning"
is the connectedness of things.

To find meaning, then, involves understanding. In the historian's mind the problems of knowing and of understanding
are so close as to be almost identical. I suspect that this is
true of other fields of knowledge as well. Anyone who has had
some experience with free association realizes that the mind
does not identify objects in isolation—they always come into
view or into memory imbedded in a thick tissue of relatedness
and correspondence. And since history approaches closer to
everyday experience than any other branch of knowledge, it
is only natural that it should be more particularly the realm
of inextricable connectedness. What we conventionally call an
"event" in history is simply a segment of the endless web of

experience that we have torn out of context for purposes of clearer understanding.

All this has been explained in sophisticated detail by a number of contemporary analyses of historical thinking.[5] Most of these studies, however, have dealt with "micro-history"—with the problems of delimiting and understanding a succession of relatively small events. At this level, we can be rather precise about what we are doing. At the level of "macro-history," things are quite otherwise. When it comes to establishing long-range "trends," the rules of historical logic begin to give way, and the investigator is cast adrift in a sea of incommensurate possibilities. Yet this is the level on which history must be written if it is ever to approach the understanding of man's wider relationship to his environment. Here the question of historical knowledge becomes baffling in the extreme: it ends as a matter of metaphysics—and even of faith.

We can find at least four classic answers. The first—and still the basic one—came out of the German nineteenth-century school of historical writing, whose leading figure was Leopold von Ranke. This we may term the old idealist position. Ranke's most frequently quoted dictum—that he proposed to write history *"wie es eigentlich gewesen,"* "as it really was"—should not be taken quite so literally as it came to be

[5] For example: William Dray, *Laws and Explanation in History* (Oxford, 1957); Patrick Gardiner, *The Nature of Historical Explanation* (Oxford, 1952); H.-I. Marrou, *De la connaissance historique* (Paris, 1954); Hans Meyerhoff, editor, *The Philosophy of History in Our Time* (Garden City, N.Y., 1959); W. H. Walsh, *An Introduction to Philosophy of History* (London, 1951); Morton G. White, "Historical Explanation," *Mind,* LII (July 1943), 212–229.

by most of his successors. I do not believe Ranke was so naïve as to think that he could produce in his writing a facsimile of the past; like any practicing historian, he must have been dimly aware of the role played by selection and personal judgment in establishing his account. Yet he and his co-workers did have a simple faith that was religious in its intensity and that was grounded in a fervent Protestantism. They believed that if they could penetrate to the central *idea* of an event or personality, they would have grasped its essence and the rest would naturally follow. The old idealist position implied a "most sympathetic, most flexible, and most reverent attitude towards the great variety of original creations in the past." It meant nothing less than a search for the "hand of God" through a method of "intuitive approximation." For Ranke and his disciples, the study of history was not really analysis at all; it was *contemplation* rather—"a source of 'unspeakable sweetness and vitality.' Knowing and worshipping were one and the same experience."[6]

Such was the implicit epistemology of the creators of *Historismus*—the founders of the school of research that first established history as a fully self-conscious discipline. Despite its high-flown language, it was basically unphilosophical. It simply took over the misty rhetoric of German idealism and Romanticism without subjecting these terms to critical examination. And the same can be said of its enemy and successor—nineteenth-century positivism. The characteristic positivist historian did not even lay claim to philosophical competence: he scorned metaphysics and regarded the problem of historical

[6] Theodore H. Von Laue, *Leopold Ranke: The Formative Years* (Princeton, N.J., 1950), pp. 43–44, 116.

knowledge as no problem at all. His goal was simply "applying to the history of Man those methods of investigation which have been found successful in other branches of knowledge"[7] —that is, in the natural sciences. Like the original idealist historians, the early positivists adopted somebody else's epistemology. They also had a faith—the faith that history could become a science, and for this, at the very least, they deserve our respect. Yet their notion of science was simple-minded and unidimensional; they absorbed from the natural scientists of their day an unquestioning confidence that the search for "causes" and "laws" was the sole and proper occupation of the up-to-date investigator. Fittingly enough, it was the natural scientists themselves who pulled the rug from under positivist historiography. The great revolution in scientific thinking at the turn of the century deprived the science-minded historians of their philosophical base—although it took some of them another generation to wake up to what had happened.

These first two answers to the problem of historical knowledge are now little more than intellectual curiosities. But each of the main nineteenth-century schools has had its twentieth-century offshoot, and idealism and positivism in their new form inevitably provide the starting point for the speculations of the philosophically inclined among contemporary historians.

The neoidealist position, whose most influential exponents were Wilhelm Dilthey in Germany and Benedetto Croce in Italy, began as an effort to ward off the threat from positivism and natural science by re-establishing the study of history as

[7] Henry Thomas Buckle, *History of Civilization in England,* new edition (London, 1891), I, 227.

an intellectual discipline with its own characteristics and procedures. The neoidealists were well aware of the philosophical inadequacies of their nineteenth-century forebears. They knew that in a science-minded age it would not suffice simply to repeat with Ranke that ultimate reality lay in "idea" or "spirit." And so they labored to refine the logic of historical discourse; they tried to chart the operations the historian's mind actually performs in putting together a coherent account of the past. Most of this work has proved of permanent value: few historians today would deny the neoidealists' central contention that historical understanding is a subjective process— a mighty effort to recall to life what is irrevocably over and done with.[8]

Yet on the central question of historical knowledge the neoidealist answer is far from satisfactory. If the historian does not seek out causes and laws in the fashion of the natural scientist, what then does he do? The usual idealist response has been some variation on the theme provided by the German verb *"verstehen"*: the historian arrives at "inner understanding." But to a skeptical and empirically oriented Anglo-Saxon mind, this sounds like begging the question: one understands —because one understands. Perhaps the best we can do with the concept of *verstehen* is to turn to the rare variety of Frenchman who has struggled through the morass of German historical terminology and emerged with his intellect intact. "We speak of understanding," Raymond Aron explains, "when *knowledge shows a meaning which, immanent to the reality,*

---

[8] For a comparative analysis of neoidealism, see my *Consciousness and Society* (New York, 1958), Chapter 6. A useful selection from Dilthey's writings has finally appeared in English translation: *Pattern and Meaning in History,* edited by H. P. Rickman (New York, 1962).

has been or could have been thought by those who lived and realized it."[9]

Such a definition is both profoundly true and profoundly unhelpful. It suggests what every historian worthy of his trade thinks he is doing when he tries to recapture the meaning of past occurrences. It conveys the faith that sustains him in his arduous quest—the faith that by an effort of sympathetic imagination he can embrace with his own mind what the men of another time actually thought and felt. If a historian did not have some such faith, he would not have the courage to write at all; he would succumb to the depressing suspicion that history, as Voltaire put it, is no more than "tricks we play on the dead." At the same time, to define an activity of the mind as *verstehen* tells us very little about the process itself. Here the neoidealists are quite at a loss. Croce himself could come up with no better figure of speech than a "lightning flash" to convey the nature of historical understanding. And even in England, at the hands of Croce's disciple R. G. Collingwood, the doctrine acquired overtones of mysticism different perhaps but at least as intellectually troubling as those that enveloped it in Germany.

Moreover, to speak of historical understanding in terms of some kind of "re-thinking" or "re-experiencing" does not give an entirely accurate sense of what the historian is in a position to perform. He cannot summon back to life a past that is irretrievably finished. He cannot give the full sense of events as reality in the process of becoming—*because he knows the out-*

[9] Raymond Aron, *Introduction to the Philosophy of History: An Essay on the Limits of Historical Objectivity,* translated by George J. Irwin (Boston, 1961), p. 47. The original French edition of Aron's book was published in 1938.

come. By no literary device or trick of false innocence can he recapture his historical virginity; it is idle for him to pretend to an unsophistication of judgment which fools nobody. Hence the historian cannot possibly pose—as he sometimes tries to—in the guise of a contemporary of the events he describes. His actual position is far more precarious. Like Proust finally reaching the end of his search for time past, the historian is "perched" on the "vertiginous summit" of the whole long perspective of events he has tried to recapture.

From this standpoint, the study of recent history appears more difficult than the investigation of the remote past, rather than the simpler matter that it is frequently said to be. For the historian who writes about the latest events in man's experience must presuppose in his mind all that went before. And similarly, when he turns his thoughts back to these earlier eras, his understanding is colored by everything that has happened since. He knows not only the outcome but the sequels: however much he may try to divest himself of his privileged position, however much he may screen out what is not strictly relevant to his account, it is still lurking in the back of his consciousness. And such is the case even when the subsequent events are never mentioned. I was forcibly struck by this simple truth in reading over with a small group of my students two of the most influential novels coming out of the First World War. One had been published in 1928, the other exactly a decade later. Both dwelt with hatred and revulsion on the horrors of combat, both spoke from a common ideological standpoint of human solidarity transcending national frontiers. But in the second a subtle shift of emphasis had taken place; the loathing for war was still present, yet it was a loathing tempered by distance and by the sense that Europe was once more girding for conflict; it was no longer possible to write in terms of something that must never be allowed to happen again.

Thus these sequels of which the historian himself may not be consciously aware are of all types and levels of specificity. They are not only actions or events—they are also thoughts and sentiments. They form part of the endless reciprocity between present and past—between the historian and his subject matter—whose full complexity the idealist metaphor of "re-enactment" is powerless to convey.[10]

Still worse, however, is the quicksand of philosophical relativism to which the logic of subjective epistemology eventually carries us. On the outer reaches of idealist thought, the grounding for historical truth becomes spongy indeed. If the procedure known as *verstehen* can seldom be subjected to empirical check—if the very "internal" character of such understanding excludes the customary methods of scientific verification—how is it possible for us to know the truth of these insights or even to communicate them in an unambiguous fashion? How are we to assess whether one historian's judgment is better than that of another? In the end we are reduced to a flip of the coin—"You pay your money and you take your choice."

It took a full century for historical idealism to reach this pass. The problem of the relativity of individual judgments troubled Ranke scarcely at all; he had his religious faith to sustain him. Two generations later the neoidealists saw very clearly the chasm that was opening before them; they had lost the serene faith of a simpler age, and although most of them

[10] For all the foregoing, see Marrou, *De la connaissance historique,* pp. 43–46, and Carr, *What Is History?* p. 35.

still recognized the existence of something resembling a God, they were far from certain of finding the traces of his handiwork in the record of history. Yet still they clung to the fragments of certitude, a residual faith in some inexplicable consensus of the "spirit." No European historian of the early twentieth century was willing to throw in his hand and confess the total relativity of historical judgments. It was an American, Carl Becker, who finally had the bravery—or the sense of intellectual defeat—to affirm that "everyman" was "his own historian."

Such a verdict did not deny, of course, that there were some judgments which were more expert than others. Yet it did suggest quite clearly that on the larger questions of historical interpretation, criteria for comparative evaluation were almost totally lacking. And here the problem rested. In idealist terms, the limits of skepticism had been reached: historical thought could go no farther.

The other contemporary refurbishing of a nineteenth-century position—neopositivism—has been formulated far less explicitly than has neoidealist thought. Its adherents have been practicing historians of a severely professional bent, who have spoken more of techniques and methods than they have of the ultimate philosophical grounding of their researches. Indeed, I am not sure whether the term "neopositivist" would be acceptable to them, but I can find none better. Moreover, it has the advantage of associating this most influential school of contemporary historical study with the leading twentieth-century bodies of thought in philosophy and natural science which quite consciously apply the positivist label to their own work.

In a word, the new historical positivists—and I am thinking more particularly of the contemporary French school of economic and social historians—while implicitly accepting the subjective epistemology of neoidealism, have resumed under more favorable circumstances the old positivist task of creating a science of historical study. No longer do they think of science in terms of a simple scheme of causes and laws: the natural scientists themselves would not give sanction for that. I referred earlier to the vast upheaval in scientific thinking which after the turn of the century deprived the original positivists of their intellectual justification. When the natural scientists themselves had redefined nature's laws as mere hypotheses, when they had begun to substitute relativity, plural explanations, and eventually even indeterminacy for the earlier certitudes of a consistent universe, the science-minded historians had no recourse but to follow. Some of them continued to employ the old scientific language as though nothing had happened. Most of the more sophisticated concluded with Croce that history would never be a science at all. Only a few tried to see what could be salvaged from the intellectual wreck; like the logical-positivist philosophers in Austria and England, a handful of courageous historians in France set out to discover whether there were any fixed points still remaining in the fluid universe to which relativity in natural science and relativism in historical judgment had so cruelly consigned them.

The chief of these was Marc Bloch—a medievalist and economic historian by training but one whose mind roamed at will over the whole vast terrain of historical method. Bloch found salvation from the nightmares of late idealist skepticism by changing the metaphor in which he wrote of his own profession. Where Dilthey and Croce had spoken almost exclusively of an internal process of thought, Bloch shifted the emphasis to what was external and tangible. He did not deny the subjective character of historical judgment. He simply drew attention once again—and far more systematically than had been true of his nineteenth-century forebears—to the realities that the historian can actually see or hear or touch: archaeological remains, languages, folklore, and the like. These, he argued, provided the fixed points on which the thought of the historian could come to rest, and from which it could also take a new start—much as the surveyor makes his first reading from a metal plaque on the ground of whose accuracy of elevation he can be fairly certain.

It is no surprise, then, to find that Bloch wrote of his chosen endeavor as a *métier*. He viewed himself as a craftsman, not merely "re-enacting" the past in his mind, as the classics of the idealist tradition taught, but tracing with a technician's precision the basic processes of past eras, whether in patterns of settlement or in the tilling of the soil. And these, he found, since they were tangibly present—since they could actually be confronted by the historian rather than just "re-thought" from the dubious evidence of documents—were by their very nature less subject to debate. "What is most profound in history," he declared, "may also be the most certain."[11] Artifacts and the attitudes they betokened came closer to some bedrock of history than what we conventionally call events: mentality, technique, social and economic structure were far less likely than was a narrative sequence to suffer concealment or deformation. And the historian who was more a reconstructor than a narrator, Bloch argued, would be more

[11] *The Historian's Craft,* translated by Peter Putnam (New York, 1953), p. 104.

likely to reach something to which he could confidently give the name of truth.

Indeed, the very deformations of these basic evidences could serve the cause of truth. A legend may be patently absurd, a popular credence in flagrant contradiction with the data of science, but the character and direction of such distortions can often tell us more about the emotional assumptions of a given society—about its collective expectations and strivings—than any amount of direct description. Beyond that:

Physical objects are far from being the only ones which can be . . . readily apprehended at first hand. A linguistic characteristic, a point of law embodied in a text, a rite . . . are realities just as much as the flint, hewn of yore by the artisan of the stone age— realities which we ourselves apprehend and elaborate by a strictly personal effort of the intelligence. There is no need to appeal to any other human mind as an interpreter. . . . It is not true that the historian can see what goes on in his laboratory only through the eyes of another person. To be sure, he never arrives until after the experiment has been concluded. But, under favorable cir- cumstances, the experiment leaves behind certain residues which he can see with his own eyes.[12]

Bloch did not "solve" the problem of historical knowledge. But he made it more manageable than it had previously been. When the historian of today asks himself what he thinks he knows, he can speak with a little more confidence than was possible a generation ago.

There is a theory of "truth" in historical writing which parallels the neopositivist restatement of the question of his- torical knowledge. Historians have been arguing for genera-

[12] *Ibid.*, p. 54.

tions over the nature of truth in their own craft. Broadly speaking, traditional positivists have advanced a "correspondence" theory—that is, they have maintained that a historical account can be considered true if it corresponds with "the facts." The usual idealist rejoinder has been a variety of "coherence" theory: the account is to be judged on the basis of its internal logic and consistency. Neither of these positions has proved very satisfactory. The correspondence theory has the advantage of down-to-earth good sense: the quixotic alone will deny the existence of "hard" data in history or dispute the contention that the historian should try to make his account conform to them. But this assurance holds good only for micro-history; at the level of the grand generalization, it is nearly impossible to say what the facts are. As for the coherence theory, it has the defect of all idealist thought in emphasizing logic and aesthetics at the expense of common sense. If the criterion of judgment is almost exclusively internal—if an account is to be accepted or rejected primarily for its artistic and philosophical elegance —then it is difficult to see where the writing of history differs from the strictly imaginative exercises of the human spirit.[13]

Here once again, as Bloch saw when he redefined the nature of his own pursuits, the way out of the philosophical fog is by reversing the usual statement of the problem. A more encouraging line of inquiry opens up if one shifts the emphasis from what is true to what is false. According to this process of reasoning, it is too much to ask of the historian that he write only what is true; for the more conscientious, such a requirement would put intolerable fetters on the creative imagination. One should demand, rather, that the historian say nothing

[13] For all the foregoing, see Walsh, *Introduction to Philosophy of History,* Chapter 4.

that he knows to be contrary to the facts. (And if this seems too modest an injunction, one has only to review a small portion of the vast literature of polemical and partisan history to realize how often it has been flouted.) On the larger issues evoked by past events, the historian can seldom be sure of what is true. But he has a pretty good idea of what is radically false. There are certain boundary stones or markers—frequently those direct evidences of which Bloch wrote—that set the limits to his imaginative flights.

This boundaries or limits theory is fully in accord with contemporary procedures in natural science and analytic philosophy. In this sense it can properly be called neopositivist. Just as in physics or semantics one can disprove something far more readily than one can establish it beyond question, so in the logic of historical discourse, one can at last get a firm footing by demonstrating which of two conflicting interpretations is patently untenable. From there, the way lies open to theoretical reconstruction. Once the historian has rejected the impossible, once he has established the limits within which his creative urge is free to wander, then he can set out with a good conscience on the boldest quests of intellectual discovery. In our own century, the natural scientists have made their great advances by throwing aside their old assumptions and striking out on new and uncharted lines of thought. The same is now beginning to be true of historians as well.

Armed thus on the one hand against intellectual naïveté and on the other against the corrosion of skepticism and self-doubt, contemporary historians are finding the courage to build structures of explanation which are both more inclusive and more logically consistent than has been conventionally true of the historian's craft. One of the exhilarating aspects of directing advanced students in today's intellectual atmosphere is the shared sense of being on the verge of great discoveries. Our students are free—and we their teachers with them—in a way that is quite new in the historical profession. When I myself began graduate studies a quarter of a century ago, the outlook appeared radically different: most of us were oppressed by the feeling that the major work had already been done—the documents had already been sifted and the canon for their interpretation established. We thought of ourselves as epigoni, working in the shadow of the great historians of the generations immediately preceding our own.

Then as the double and complementary lessons of the neoidealists and of Marc Bloch converged upon us, we caught a breath of new hope. We saw that if we turned the conventional prism of historical vision only a little, a whole new world of possibilities would come into view. Croce taught us to see the writing of history as an exercise of creative thought; the French showed how we could ground this thought in the directly perceived evidences of a vanished past. Together they released us from bondage to a type of study that had narrowed the aim of history to the systematic exploitation of documentary materials. Both demonstrated, in language that was the more helpful for its very diversity, that the historian's major task was by no means accomplished when the contents of "the documents" had been established in scrupulous order. Indeed, that task had scarcely begun. The truly exciting problems of interpretation— whose mere existence the more unsophisticated among us had scarcely suspected—nearly all lay in the future.

I think it is quite possible that the study of history today is entering a period of rapid change and advance such as characterized the science of physics in the first three decades of the twentieth century. This advance is proceeding on a number of fronts at once. The social historians are incorporating into their thought the whole stream of speculation on class and status, and on the relation of economic activities to the cultural "superstructure," that descends from Karl Marx and Max Weber. In the fields of economic and political history alike, imaginative scholars are experimenting with applications of quantitative method and the calculus of probabilities. On the boundary where the concerns of anthropology, biology, the humanities, and psychology meet and blend, the historian is at last beginning to broaden his definitions of human motivation and of psycho-physical change.

It is with the last of these lines of advance that I shall deal in the next two essays. And then in the final two I shall turn my attention to the effect of such new interpretations on the central thread of traditional historiography—the narrative itself—and on the writing of the history of our own time.

II.

History, the Humanities,
and Anthropological Change

HISTORIANS and "humanists," when they do not watch what they are doing, are temperamentally inclined to treat the raw material of their subject as forever unchanging. They take man *as a given*—and on this unyielding structure they impose or embroider the stuff of their own disciplines, literature or art, religion or politics, as the case may be. Of course they know better. Most of them have learned something of the plasticity of human instincts and have come to distrust facile generalizations about "human nature." But they either have learned these lessons incompletely or are subject to a suspicious forgetfulness about them. They cannot hold their minds for long on the notion of man as a creature whose limits may be fixed by his physiology and the size of his brain, but whose capacities for change and adaptation within these limits offer the very subject matter of history and the humanities themselves.

Such is the paradox of so much of the contemporary study of human culture. It is as though its practitioners preferred to make a sharp separation between two realms of understanding —the physiological on the one hand, the cultural on the other.

I suspect that the humanist's old distaste for the material world has helped produce this cleavage. I would also venture that a certain doctrinaire Freudianism—a lesson the literary folk have learned too well—has unwittingly reinforced the traditional belief that instincts, and more particularly sexual instincts, never change. Perhaps the idea of a mutual interaction between humanity in the raw and its "spiritual" creations has proved too difficult to manage; scholars have grown dizzy at the thought of a human being whose slow elaboration of a cultural "superstructure" at the same time—and still more slowly—has produced side effects on his own physical and emotional make-up. For the most part, the humanists have preferred to hold the animal man steady and to confine the variables to the works of his "higher" being.

Here, then, lies a largely uncharted land—the meeting point between art and biology, and between the concerns of physical and cultural anthropology. Historians and humanists have known of it for centuries; yet most have been reluctant to venture very far inside. It is here, I think, that anthropologists— to whom the notion of cultural and physiological interaction is second nature—can serve the rest of us as guides.

For a number of years now a most rewarding dialogue between historians and cultural anthropologists has been in progress.[1] In his old age the lamented dean of American anthropologists, Alfred L. Kroeber, turned to an interest in history and to a testing of such meta-historical works of speculation as Spengler's *Decline of the West*. Almost simultaneously

---

[1] Much of what follows originally derives from the informal "Biology Seminar" held at the Center for Advanced Study in the Behavioral Sciences, Stanford, Calif., in the academic year 1956–1957.

Kroeber's young British admirer, Philip Bagby, was urging his fellow historians to draw on anthropology for their basic concepts of human culture.[2] By the late 1950's a number of historians were at last ready to endorse the view that the widest and most fruitful definition of their trade was as "retrospective culture anthropology." I think it significant that although I myself was at the time unaware of Bagby's work, I had come to similar conclusions about the compatibility between the two disciplines, and was arguing that the historian and the anthropologist shared a "permissive attitude" toward their data; that they were "perfectly happy in the realm of imprecision and of 'intuitive' procedures"; and that they were both striving to find the basic patterns, the symbolic expressions of thought and emotion, that would serve to define an entire society. Beyond that, I have contended that systematic field work on the anthropological model offers "the best possible training-ground for the historian whose mind is oriented toward social and psychological synthesis."[3]

Let us grant for a moment that such views have by now become widespread among the historical profession. It is not too difficult—it does not wrench the mind too painfully—for the historian or the humanist to accept the notion of "living his way" into the totality of a culture. On the contrary, his heart may be gladdened by the new and heady sense of actuality that accompanies this type of study. With the investigation of physical or instinctual change it is quite otherwise. Here the historian's spirit rebels. The notion of such change *within his-*

[2] Alfred L. Kroeber, *Style and Civilizations* (Ithaca, N.Y., 1957); Philip Bagby, *Culture and History* (London, 1958). The historical profession has suffered a severe loss in Bagby's untimely death.

[3] "The Historian and the Social Scientist," *American Historical Review*, LXVI (October 1960), 34, 42–43.

torical time is foreign to him. He has banished it to tens of thousands of years ago, to the realm of the physical anthropologist and to the concerns of what he calls prehistory.

Yet the historian or the humanist knows perfectly well that physical and instinctual changes *have* occurred within the confines of historical time. He constantly mentions them—but in passing or in the context of events that loom larger in his mind. It is no great discovery on my part to speak of these things. It is rather a question of bringing together the elements, the scattered evidences, of a new type of historical or humanistic study that already exists, but is not yet fully conscious of what it is about.

One way to begin is to take another look at the positivist historians of the nineteenth century. On further reflection, I think that critics like myself have frequently been unfair to this whole school. We have focused on its failures—on its crudity and overconfidence—rather than on its wider goals. We have condemned its tendency toward materialist explanations without giving it credit for the rewarding lines of investigation it was the first to explore. Take as an example a passage from Hippolyte Taine:

When we read a Greek tragedy, our first care should be to picture to ourselves the Greeks, that is, the men who lived half naked, in the gymnasia, or in the public squares, under a glowing sky, face to face with the most noble landscapes, bent on making their bodies nimble and strong, on conversing, discussing, voting, carrying on patriotic piracies, but for the rest lazy and temperate, with three urns for their furniture, two anchovies in a jar of oil for their food, waited on by slaves, so as to give them leisure to cultivate their understanding and exercise their limbs, with no desire beyond that of having the most beautiful town, the most beautiful possessions, the most beautiful ideas, the most beautiful men. . . . A language, a legislation, a catechism, is never more than an abstract thing: the complete thing is the man who acts, the man corporeal and visible, who eats, walks, fights, labours.[4]

Perhaps some words of this effusion are no longer borne out by the researches of classical scholarship. But it is wholly admirable in its concreteness—the sense it conveys of men whose feeling for their own bodies and whose relationship to the natural world were radically different from what they are for most of us today.

As a Frenchman, Taine belongs in the major stream of historians who have done more than those of any other nation to situate the historical study of man in a rich environmental context. Yet the progenitor of them all is not French but Italian— Giambattista Vico, that marvelous Neapolitan of the early eighteenth century who is at the fountainhead of nearly everything that has proved fruitful in subsequent historical study. Vico fits into no neat category. A man born out of season, he sounds now medieval and now ultramodern—at once a belated scholastic and a prophet of nineteenth- and twentieth-century social thought—just as his writings oscillate between credulity and a bold defiance of accepted intellectual practice, between provincial innocence and an emancipation of mind soaring above all established frontiers, between turgid foolishness and crisp, breath-taking insight. Ethnologist, archaeologist, linguist —anthropologists may well call Vico the first practitioner of their craft. After two and a half centuries, we historians have not yet absorbed everything we can learn from his example.

[4] *History of English Literature,* translated by H. Van Laun (Edinburgh, 1871), I, 3.

Our first lessons—those that inflamed the imaginations of Jules Michelet and the other historians of the early nineteenth century who "discovered" Vico after nearly a hundred years of neglect—concerned the tangible, intact evidences of how the men of past ages lived and thought. Vico taught us to pay attention to the still-living or visible manifestations of the past as opposed to an exclusive reliance on "the documents." In his own quaint language:

Truth is sifted from falsehood in everything that has been preserved for us through long centuries by those vulgar traditions which, since they have been preserved for so long a time and by entire peoples, must have had a public ground of truth.

The great fragments of antiquity, hitherto useless to science because they lay begrimed, broken, and scattered, shed great light when cleaned, pieced together, and restored.[5]

These precepts most of us now understand, although we often fail to act on them. And we understand them largely through the mediation of the contemporary French school of social historians—led by Marc Bloch and Lucien Febvre—whose goal was to achieve a "broader and more human history" in the tradition of Vico and Michelet. During the interwar years Bloch and Febvre labored to bring into meaningful synthesis the data of geography and economics, of sociology and psychology, and to extract from them a credible, multifaceted account of past societies; in brief, they tried to study the history of their own culture much as an anthropologist would approach the understanding of a culture foreign to him. The way

[5] *The New Science of Giambattista Vico,* translated from the third edition (1744) by Thomas Goddard Bergin and Max Harold Fisch (Anchor paperback, 1961), p. 64.

to go about it, Febvre argued, was "first to catalog in detail, then put together, . . . the mental equipment which the men of that epoch had at their disposal; by a mighty effort of scholarship, but also of imagination, to reconstruct the whole physical, intellectual, and moral universe within which each generation . . . transformed itself."[6] An unattainable goal, we may say—certainly unattainable in any final sense—but one which historians have never come closer to reaching than Bloch did in his now-classic work on feudal society.

Vico himself had doubted whether the intelligence of living men could actually embrace the sentiments of primitive humanity. "It is . . . beyond our power," he wrote, "to enter into the vast imagination of those first men, whose minds were not in the least abstract, refined, or spiritualized, because they were entirely immersed in the senses, buffeted by the passions, buried in the body."[7] Behind and beyond what the French school had learned from Vico, lay the further tormenting question of how historians could truly understand the minds of men whose physical and physiological circumstances were so radically dissimilar from their own as to constitute almost a difference of kind. Vico had said the job was "beyond our power"—but still he had tried. Historians are loath by temperament ever to grant that a problem is insoluble. Toward the end of their scholarly careers, both Bloch and Febvre turned their attention to the evidences of physical adaptation and instinctual change within the limits of historical time. Subsequently their students have pursued the problem in systematic detail. This is obviously a concern that anthropologists, historians, and humanists share: it is at the same time one of

[6] *Combats pour l'histoire* (Paris, 1953), p. 218.
[7] *New Science,* p. 76.

the most enticing and one of the most baffling of the frontiers to historical knowledge today. For here the data are invariably indirect: men have taken their bodies so for granted that they have not bothered to comment on them. To learn something of how humanity in past ages saw and heard and felt and smelled, we historians must be eternally on the alert for the casual reference, the apparently trivial clue, that will suddenly open up a whole unsuspected realm of understanding.

Three approaches, I think, will help guide us into this new territory. The first and most readily apparent is the cumulative record of technological change. The second is the scattered evidence on deformations, diseases, and the adaptations of the senses that constitute the rudiments of a psycho-physiological history. The third is language—ever the most sensitive indicator for all types of human investigation—the tangible link between body and mind, between biology and symbolic expression.

Here once again we may start with Vico—and with the great Neapolitan's single most influential dictum:

In the night of thick darkness enveloping the earliest antiquity, so remote from ourselves, there shines the eternal and never failing light of a truth beyond all question: that the world of civil society has certainly been made by men, and that its principles are therefore to be found within the modifications of our own human mind.[8]

That is, men are capable of understanding the history of human culture, *because they made it.* While God alone—the eternal creator—can comprehend the natural world *He* made,

[8] *Ibid.,* pp. 52–53.

mere men can come to know "the civil world" that was their own creation.

For the past two and a half centuries historians have been periodically forgetting Vico's teaching. Each generation has had to relearn, frequently with pain, what should have been part of its common inheritance. And this forgetfulness has not simply been because historians, as literary men, have scorned and distrusted technology and its ways. It has arisen from a basic misunderstanding both of the past and of the historical craft itself.

In other languages than our own, the verbs "to make" and "to do" are close or even identical. The mere word "fact"— the cornerstone of conventional historiography—betrays this near identity. But for most historians the concepts of what is done and of what is made exist in two different spiritual worlds. The one partakes of the autonomy of free and individual human life. The other belongs to the dead world of the material, the mechanical, the repetitive, and the anonymous. These are caricatures, of course; yet I think it undeniable that a profession which has cherished the "human" as its basic concern has almost instinctively found something "inhuman" in the processes of technology. It is curious that the very writer who did more than anyone else to restore the influence of Vico to the contemporary world of thought—Benedetto Croce—rejected technological explanations as throwing open the spiritual citadel of historiography to its positivist assailants.

What Croce—and before or after him, the whole idealist school of historians—denied was the "spiritual" character of technology. They forgot that every new device had at some time had an inventor, and that this invention was an authentic act of creation belonging to the same world of human autonomy and of the spirit which seemed to them alone worthy of the historian's attention. They lost sight of the fact that mechanical innovation, no matter how modest, was an event in the history of man's self-realization which deserved the same kind of sympathetic attention—of inner participation by the historian—as the enunciation of a new religious dogma or the promulgation of a new constitutional enactment.

Undoubtedly a further difficulty arose from the fact that technology was largely anonymous—that for most of history the technical innovators were unknown figures or collective entities who did not lend themselves to historical "re-living" as readily as statesmen, artists, or religious leaders. But surely historians—at least since Michelet—have known how to write of collectivities and of the anonymous prime movers of great perturbations. They have known that history is individual only in the sense that both its acting and its understanding are ultimately reducible to the play of a single human consciousness. Yet precisely here lies the confusion. The play of the individual consciousness —whether of past actor or of present writer—has fascinated the historian to the exclusion of nearly everything else. It has led him to forget that men have *made* their history quite literally as workers with their own hands, and that this cumulative construction has of necessity been a process more anonymous than personal.

Now what is the relevance of all this for physiological and instinctive adaptation? It is that in earlier ages—down to the nineteenth century at least—the physical equipment of Western men was more differentiated by their technical pursuits than it is today. Some (by our standards) enjoyed too little physical exercise—most of them far too much. The peasant or laborer developed enormous muscles, but he became stooped from toil;

the cobbler who sat all day—and a working day longer than ours—in a cramped position, might have spindly or atrophied legs and failing eyesight. The soldiers performed miracles of endurance: the record of forced marches in the eighteenth century is beyond dispute. Yet many of them were deformed, and would have been rejected for service out of hand by a medical examiner today. In early modern times, men's bodies themselves revealed their trades. They looked less impressive than those of contemporary men, but as specialized human machines they were perhaps more efficient. As one historian—again of the French school—has surmised, the very deformities of the body which were taken for granted then and would shock us today, were the direct result of intense and unbalanced physical exertion.[9]

When I was a boy, I was puzzled by the fact that the suits of armor I saw in museums were so small. Surely, I thought, the men of the Middle Ages were at least as big as the men I knew—indeed, they loomed in my mind as giants of prowess. How was it possible for the heroes of whose exploits I had read with delight to wedge themselves into such diminutive iron clothing? If they were really that small, how could they have wielded so dexterously the massive swords and battle-axes which the museums also displayed and which my own male relatives could lift only with awkwardness and difficulty? The paradox, of course, was only apparent. The knights and yeomen *were* tiny in stature—but they were physically tough to a degree that we can scarcely imagine today. Who among our friends and contemporaries would be capable of carrying on his back *that* weight of metal under a blazing summer sun?

[9] Charles Morazé, *La France Bourgeoise* (Paris, 1946), pp. 36–37.

In tracing the paradox of enormous strength combined with small stature and bodily deformities, I have imperceptibly passed to the second road to psycho-physical understanding—the evidence of disease, the use of the senses, the functioning of the glands. How has the human animal adapted itself within the confines of historical time? Again I shall draw my examples largely from Europe and from the late Middle Ages and early modern times—a period which has the advantages of being both well documented and close enough to us so that the disparities we find with our contemporary experience strike us more forcibly than they would in the case of a remote era or an exotic society. The cultural tradition is our own; the difference in space is negligible; the span of time is no more than half a millennium. Were we seeking a still closer and more dramatic confrontation, we could point to present-day Israel, where within a single generation the physique and mental set of the sons have become almost unrecognizable to the fathers.

I should like to begin in very general terms with the reflections of a psychiatrist who has specialized in the observation of human beings under intense stress. He is speaking of the glandular "mobilizations" that represent the organism's response to fear or anger:

With man's increasing mastery over his environment, these anticipatory mobilizations have less and less often been followed by vigorous activity. With the development of efficient food production, mastery over predators, machines for transportation, communication, and heavy work . . . the need for intensive physical activity has greatly diminshed. Moreover, even the possibility for intensive activity is sharply restricted by many circumstances of modern living—e.g., industrial and professional settings in which personal tensions cannot readily be relieved by taking action.

The net effect seems to be that the contemporary human organism frequently gets mobilized for exertion but ends up doing little or nothing—preparation for action, without action.

What difference, if any, does this make? . . . I want only to draw attention to the possibility that these stress responses may be less useful than they once were, and in some circumstances may actually be harmful. To illustrate how this evolutionary shift might work, let me briefly call attention to one clinically important problem area: atherosclerosis. The secretion of adrenal hormones under psychological stress may, in the context of many contemporary circumstances, produce a mobilization of fat without subsequent utilization. Perhaps some of the fat that used to be burned in the process of exertion now gets deposited in the intimal lining of the arteries—at least in predisposed individuals.

In this view, the susceptibility to development of atherosclerotic pathology would be increased by: (a) frequent and/or prolonged stress responses and (b) circumstances or life styles that inhibit muscular exercise. These conditions would favor a high level of fat mobilization with a low level of fat utilization. Such a formulation helps to integrate two sets of observations pertinent to incidence of atherosclerotic heart disease: both chronic psychologic stress and sedentary way of life seem to be predisposing factors. In research and clinical discussions, these factors are often set in opposition to each other. Perhaps these are two sides of the same coin that can be viewed whole in light of human evolution.[10]

The evidence forcibly suggests that an increase in heart disease has come as a direct consequence of the changed physical

[10] David A. Hamburg, "Relevance of Recent Evolutionary Changes to Human Stress Biology," mimeographed publication of the National Institute of Mental Health, 1959, pp. 11–12.

conditions of contemporary life. Perhaps the same will prove true for other diseases as well. What about cancer? Although it is difficult to judge from early medical accounts, which may actually be describing cancer under a variety of vague expressions, it seems likely that here also we find a drastic rise in the incidence of suffering within the span of very recent history—although the cause remains unknown to us. Tuberculosis offers an equally telling example: this was primarily a disease of the nineteenth century, and its ravages bear a clear relation to the unprecedented increase in crowded living and working conditions in the industrial cities, where defective hygiene was no longer compensated for, as it had been in the countryside, by the possibility of escape and restoration in the open fields. What about the massive onslaught of syphilis three centuries earlier? It takes a mighty effort of imagination to picture to ourselves the horror of men and women who found the age-old fulminations of moralists against lechery suddenly and inexplicably reinforced by a deadly physical danger.

It is not just that the relative weight of different diseases—the prime causes of death in each era—by their variations from century to century have slowly altered the definition of "normal" bodily functioning. It is also that the emotional attitude of men has changed, as their fears have fixed now on one scourge, now on another. "The plague" has vanished from Western society: it took the genius of a novelist—Albert Camus—to suggest in a parable of its reappearance the resurgence of barbarism in our own time. Most of us today are accustomed to being well fed—indeed, all too often to being excessively fed. We can scarcely appreciate what it means to live in constant fear of famine. "This obsession of death through hunger

. . . is the first and most striking mark" of men's basic attitudes at the dawn of modern times.[11] To be chronically underfed, to live on an ill-balanced cereal diet, to suffer from all sorts of diseases of malnutrition—these conditions we are well aware of from our studies of "underdeveloped" societies in the present era. What we have mostly failed to do is to apply this knowledge to an understanding of the biological and emotional make-up of our own remote ancestors.

With such terrors ever before their minds—to which we must add the fear of ghosts and goblins and supernatural beings of all kinds, plus the more realistic dangers against which we are now accustomed to take out insurance policies—it is no wonder that the Europeans of early modern times were more "passionate" than we. I mean this quite seriously. Their "humors" changed more suddenly; they spoke more rapidly; they sprang more quickly to love or to anger. As Vico said of primitive man, they were still "immersed in the senses, buffeted by the passions, buried in the body." Or, to put it more precisely, the frustration and sublimation of the instincts were not so common as they are today. The men of the sixteenth century heard and touched more readily than they saw; the sense that for us has become primary—the sense of sight, which is central to science, to all ordering and classifying and rationalizing—for them came in third rank behind the senses of the ears and hands.[12] Reading was still in its infancy: I am persuaded that the early humanists read more slowly than we do, perhaps following the words with their fingers and moving their lips, defying all the principles of remedial reading which now would relegate them without ap-

[11] Robert Mandrou, *Introduction à la France moderne: Essai de psychologie historique 1500–1640* (Paris, 1961), p. 35.
[12] *Ibid.,* pp. 69–70.

peal to the category of retarded school children. Language was still far more a matter of oral usage than of the written or the printed word: in church, in the universities, at the theater, people heard the message *and remembered it.* Their memories may well have been more effective than ours, and it is certain that they had a better capacity to hear out a complex argument or a passage of involved syntax—witness any number of sermons and the dense rhetoric of Shakespeare's plays.

And so to the third path—language. What does it mean for human instincts and emotions that the oral should predominate over the written tongue? For one thing, it means that during most of European history, language has been a protean and uncertain tool of communication, that it has been a plastic product of the mouth and ears—even of the hands—rather than something eternally fixed in the dead print of grammars and dictionaries. Until very recently, bilingualism or even tri- or quadrilingualism was the norm rather than the exception. As late as the sixteenth century in the south of France it was not uncommon for educated men to speak four varieties of the basic Romance tongue: Latin, of course, although its hold was weakening; the French of Paris, which was the language of royal administration; the old literary *langue d'oc,* now clearly in decay; and the particular patois of the local area. Each language was alive: each was struggling to supplant its rivals, and their vocabularies overlapped and "corrupted" each other in a bewildering medley of transitional expressions.

The underground struggle of competing languages—a psycho-physical struggle, if there ever was one—is difficult to document in coherent sequence. We can date approximately the moment of "victory" of one language over another. But the stages of the conquest are less clearly marked. For a long time it was thought that the language of northern France simply overwhelmed the Midi after the ruthless Albigensian crusade of the thirteenth century; subsequent studies have revealed that the process took a full three hundred years.[13] In Middle English—in the poetry of Chaucer—we have rare and precious evidence of a transitional, hybrid tongue: we can literally see and hear the French words, still recognizable as such, being grafted onto a Germanic stem. In this case, it was the language of the common people, the older inhabitants, which triumphed; at other times—as in the Western part of the Roman Empire— it was the speech of the conquering rulers which gradually won predominance. But how long the process took, and what were the decisive elements, material or emotional, that went into the victory—on these the evidence is both scanty and uncertain. Here the combined efforts of linguists and archaeologists have finally begun to clear away the confusions and mutual misunderstandings which had enveloped the whole subject.[14]

Strange mixed languages can be found in the royal records of such borderland and much fought-over states as Hungary and Naples. They suggest a situation in which an emotional attachment to one form of speech or another is ill-defined, and self-identification by language may be weak or almost nonexistent. We are so accustomed to such an identification—our linguistic ties are so firmly fixed—that it may strike us as odd that Europeans could ever have lived otherwise. But if we begin to think of language as something more sensual than intellec-

[13] *Ibid.*, pp. 87–88; Febvre, *Combats pour l'histoire,* pp. 169–181.
[14] See, for example, Hugh Hencken, *Indo-European Languages and Archeology,* American Anthropological Association, Memoir No. 84, December 1955; Mario Pei, *Voices of Man: The Meaning and Function of Language* (New York, 1962), Problems V, VII, IX, XI.

tual, something neither systematically learned nor grammatically policed, but rather taken for granted as were the senses of taste or touch, then the attitude toward language of the men of earlier centuries suddenly becomes clear to us. Words existed in the context of the tangible transactions of the day: the suitable expression rose to mind depending on whether one was talking to a priest or a royal official, a merchant or a peasant. It was of no great moment that the language varied from one conversation to another; the individual in question might be quite unconscious, as the bilingual often are today, of which among the various languages at his command he was actually speaking. It was up to the men of learning to tidy up the jumble as best they could.

Now for a concluding reflection or two on the role of language in contemporary industrial society. Once more, as at the dawn of modern times, linguistic usage is becoming fluid and pragmatic. The rules are breaking down: the firm traditions that the major European languages—more especially French and English—established in the seventeenth century are slowly dissolving. The strictures of the purists are helpless to stem the flood of neologisms and grammatical simplifications. Unquestionably this loosening of linguistic usage forms part of a wider process of psychic adaptation to altered circumstances. The three centuries in which fixed literary languages ruled supreme were the same centuries that saw the triumph of rationalism, of individualism, of capitalism, of the nation-state—of all the familiar features that mark the classic era of European world dominance. The literary prestige of the great languages was central to the whole process: one of the defining characteristics of the ruling races (as of the rare natives who received the privilege of assimilation) was their ability to speak correctly the language of administration and commerce; the rest were mocked for their bizarre accent and limited vocabulary.

Today all this is changing. The languages have remained; French and English between them account for the public speech of nearly all the new nations of Africa. But the linguistic distinction between masters and natives is narrowing. Just as those for whom English is a learned language are beginning to outnumber those born into such speech, so the question of proprietary rights is becoming unclear. Whose language is it anyway—does it belong to the majority, or to the minority of those whose ancestors spoke it more or less correctly? Perhaps the very question is losing its importance, as both claimants join in a happy fraternity of permissive usage.

I am suggesting, then, that a change in attitude toward language may form part of a vast alteration in the physical and instinctual adaptation of Western man. We are familiar with its intellectualized aspects—with the end of colonial domination and, more generally, the weakening of the institutions and practices associated with an individualistic society. Only a few commentators, however, have ventured to suggest that these political and social changes may mark a return to an earlier attitude toward the senses and the instincts. The educated man in our industrial society reads less than his grandfather and listens to music more; he is less squeamish about indulging his sensual appetites; he is probably less reflective. His body has grown larger, his posture more relaxed. His walk, his gestures subtly reflect the new character of his physical and psychological environment: we have only to revisit a film of twenty years back to be struck by oddities of manner and expression that seemed quite natural to us when we originally saw it.

And so we return to the puzzle of stress responses in our contemporary society. Modern industrialism has imposed on our bodies a curious and unprecedented rhythm. It is not so much its frenetic "pace" that has revolutionized our patterns of existence. It is rather the alternation of a dominant attitude of passivity and receptiveness with moments of feverish activity. Most of the time we merely wait our turn—watching the machines that regulate our existence carry out their prescribed tasks. Then suddenly from one moment to the next we shift to an intense concentration: the operations we perform are precise; a single mistake can mean disaster. This is the rhythm of living that takes its toll in our anxiety and stress responses. And for most of what we do, language—in its discursive or purist sense—is simply irrelevant.

Man's psycho-physical evolution today is at least as rapid as it has been in the immediate past. I suspect that like technological change, it has actually accelerated. Yet most of the time we are scarcely aware of it. I suggest that we humanists and historians begin to awaken to this particular manifestation of the facts of life.

III.

History and Psychoanalysis: The Explanation of Motive

IN THE WRITING of history "how" and "why" are inseparable questions. In the theory and practice of psychoanalysis the same is true. With both disciplines, the prime quest is for human motives: the historian and the analyst alike seek out the reasons for which individuals and groups did what they did, and in each case the method of the search is itself part of the process of understanding. Both strive for a precise, detailed reconstruction of the circumstances surrounding an action: both operate on the assumption that the patience of the investigator will bring its appropriate reward—that from a rich context of experience recalled to consciousness, there will eventually emerge the inner logic of a single decision, an "insoluble" dilemma, or an entire human life. In history as in psychoanalysis, understanding implies the pursuit of what is hidden or only imperfectly known: both distrust the ready explanation that springs first to mind. The connection between the two seems obvious, but it has only recently been explicitly recognized.[1] Why have historians and analysts taken so long to see what they have in common?

[1] Most notably by William L. Langer in "The Next Assignment," *American Historical Review*, LXIII (January 1958), 283–304, and by Bruce Mazlish, Editor, *Psychoanalysis and History* (Englewood Cliffs,

A first explanation lies in the one-sided character of the two "revolutions" in historical writing that have produced our contemporary attitude toward our own craft—the creation of modern historical study in Germany by the school of Ranke, and its neoidealist restatement a century later at the hands of Dilthey and Croce.[2] Both of these movements of thought were radically subjectivist. Both viewed the historian's goal in terms of an "inner understanding" which would transcend the mere accumulation of factual data. In this sense—from our present-day vantage point—the state of mind in which the old and the new idealists approached their labors appears close to the concerns of psychology. But that is to view the matter anachronistically. At the time of the two revolutions in question, neither history nor psychology was ready for an alliance. Indeed, in the springtide of *Historismus,* psychology as a science scarcely existed. And even at the time of the second historiographic revolution, in the 1890's and the opening years of the twentieth century, psychology's most visible proponents seemed to deny everything the idealist school of historical writing held most precious. The mechanistic, naturalistic, materialist, and positivist language (in the polemics of neoidealism the terms are almost interchangeable) that characterized late-nineteenth-century psychology suggested a deadly threat to man's freedom of will and the autonomy of his spirit.

Thus the most sensitive minds among the European histori-

N.J., 1963), Hans Meyerhoff, "On Psychoanalysis as History," *Psychoanalysis and the Psychoanalytic Review,* XLIX (Summer 1962), 3–20, and Fritz Schmidl, "Psychoanalysis and History," *The Psychoanalytic Quarterly,* XXXI (1962), 532–548.

[2] For general interpretations of this double revolution, see Friedrich Meinecke, *Die Entstehung des Historismus,* 2 vols. (Munich and Berlin, 1936), and my own *Consciousness and Society* (New York, 1958), Chapter 6.

ans saw no reason to concern themselves with experimental or clinical psychology. On the contrary, they felt it imperative to defend their profession against the inroads of scientific naturalism. For by the 1870's and 1880's, the dominant positivist mentality was affecting even the writing of history. While the master was still alive, the heirs of Ranke were forgetting his religious principles and the sympathetic exercise of imagination which he believed to be the sovereign goal of the historian's art, and were restricting themselves to a documentary verification of past events: perhaps only half consciously, they were admitting the positivist enemy into the citadel of historiography itself. Indeed, it was for this reason that Dilthey found it necessary to restate the old idealist canon to take account of the progress in natural science during the previous half century, to reassert the independence of historical study in full knowledge of a new intellectual force that the original school of *Historismus* had ignored.

Dilthey himself tried to grapple with psychology of the more speculative sort. But in this openness of mind his successors among the neoidealists refused to follow him. Far from regarding such trafficking with science as an example to be imitated, they dismissed it as the pardonable aberration of an otherwise great man. Rather than picking up the helpful, if fragmentary suggestions that Dilthey had offered, they returned to the intellectual world of Goethe or Ranke—or even, as in Croce's case, to a quasi-Hegelianism. In brief, they retreated to a bald assertion that "the spirit" alone held the key to historical understanding.

What did they mean by "spirit"? What has idealism, old and new, tried to convey by a term whose ring may be exalted but whose message is far from clear? Initially we should note that the German word *Geist* has connotations which in English we render by two such distinct terms as "mind" and "soul": to us the one sounds intellectual, the other mystical and very likely religious. The first is commonly employed in science, the second only occasionally, and then with embarrassment. (I recall a conversation with a psychiatrist who objected to my use of the word "spiritual"; as soon as I redefined it as "mental," he professed himself satisfied.) In a strict sense, *Geist* or "spirit" may mean no more than the subjective aspect of human behavior: in that usage, there is nothing about it at which a man of science need cavil. But among the idealist school of historians, it has surrounded itself with an aura of lofty abstraction which has both alienated the scientists and obscured the work of history itself. As applied by idealist historiography, the concept of spiritual explanation became so vague as to be of little practical use.

It is here that a second explanation for the long delay in the alliance between history and psychoanalysis needs to be introduced—a historical explanation, like the first, deriving from the way in which Freudian psychology came into being. The intellectual world of Sigmund Freud, the bent of his education, the attitude with which he approached his labors were all rooted in the scientific positivism of the late nineteenth century. To the end of his life, Freud's basic vocabulary of explanation remained mechanistic. Similarly, just as the historians among Freud's contemporaries scorned the claims of natural science, so Freud himself manifested little direct interest in history: it was not until the latter part of his life, in the series of anthropological fantasies extending from *Totem and*

Taboo to *Moses and Monotheism,* that he began to enrich his theory with a conscious dimension of time.[3] Thus the misunderstanding was mutual. The historians knew science only in its nineteenth-century guise, and could find little relevance for their own studies in an external and formalistic psychology. The psychoanalysts similarly thought of history as a dry search for "facts" which could never explain anything really important. They had no concept of the present-day phenomenon of the eternally curious historian who with a blithe methodological agnosticism would reach out for help from all quarters—including those same late works of Freud which the analysts themselves frequently tried to explain away. From the nineteenth century, history and psychoanalysis inherited a common canonical language: it took them until the middle of the twentieth century to realize that the fact that their masters wrote in German was only the outward sign of a much deeper intellectual compatibility.

Once the first hurdles of mutual incomprehensibility have been surmounted—once the obvious differences in vocabulary, in training, in professional approach have been confronted and understood—the most extraordinary parallels between the two disciplines spring to mind. In both cases, a certain tentativeness and imprecision adhere to the intellectual method itself: historians, like analysts, have sustained unending reproaches from their colleagues in neighboring fields on the grounds that their explanations are impossible to verify by the usual empirical criteria. And historians and analysts alike have all too often allowed themselves to be thrown on the defensive. They have apologized for their "pre-scientific" conclusions, stressing the

[3] *Consciousness and Society,* Chapter 4.

uncertain and conflicting character of their evidence rather than the imaginative boldness of their interpretations. Isolated from one another, they have separately faced the attacks of the literal-minded devotees of science. If they were to pool their intellectual resources, each would find precious reinforcement: together they could assert the validity of a method whose very lack of a conventional scientific grounding constitutes its peculiar strength.

For the historian as for the psychoanalyst, an interpretation ranks as satisfactory not by passing some formal scientific test but by conveying an inner conviction. For both, plural explanations are second nature. The former speaks of "multiple causation"; the latter finds a psychic event "overdetermined." Indeed, for both of them the word "cause" is admissible only if defined with extreme flexibility: most of the time they prefer to express their interpretations in terms more clearly suggesting the possibility of alternative ways of looking at the matter. Both deal in complex configurations, searching for a thread of inner logic that will tie together an apparent chaos of random words and actions. The analyst knows that this is what he is doing: his theoretical works proclaim it. The historian is less conscious of his own theory—indeed, he sometimes behaves as though he had no theory at all. Yet what else has the historian been doing ever since Hegel first inaugurated the quest for the guiding finger of the *Weltgeist?*

Psychoanalysis *is* history—or possibly biography. The analyst recognizes this although he seldom gives it explicit expression. What is more, his professional and moral goal is the same as that of the historian: to liberate man from the burden of the past by helping him to understand that past. Similarly the historian's classic problem—the explanation of human motives—is one for which psychoanalysis provides a fund of understanding richer than that afforded by any other discipline. And it offers it in a form peculiarly congenial to the mind of the historian: its rules of evidence and of relevance are permissive in the extreme, and it is alert to the symptomatic importance of the apparently trivial; what a less imaginative method might dismiss out of hand, the analyst (or the historian) may well put at the center of his interpretation. In this sense, history in its turn is psychoanalysis: in their study of motive the two share the conviction that everything is both relevant and random, incoherent and ordered, in the all-inclusive context of a human existence.

Where to date history has notably failed is in its explanation of the "irrational." And here again the reason lies in the deficiencies of the idealist tradition. The original goal of Ranke and the others was to correct the rationalist simplifications of Enlightenment historiography by making room for the spontaneous in human behavior: in polemic contrast with Voltaire or Gibbon, the German nineteenth-century school stressed personal individuality and development. In so doing, it was quite prepared to admit the claims of the irrational: indeed, to the extent that historical idealism coincided with the Romantic movement, the idealist historians welcomed the violence and passion of the past that would not fit into a conventional rational framework. But they had no suitable categories of thought in which to express their new understanding. For Ranke, what was individual remained "ineffable": his reverence for the unique in history withheld him from subjecting it to searching analysis. And similarly his love for the emotional richness of the past blurred his ethical perceptions.

Although a strict moralist in his personal life, Ranke was far more forgiving when it came to the sins of the great figures of earlier centuries: as Lord Acton complained, he wrote of "transactions and occurrences when it would be safe to speak of turpitude and crime."[4]

In Ranke's mind the cruelty and incoherence of the past were sublimated into wonderment at the infinite variety of God's handiwork. With his more tender-minded successors, this love became terror. I do not know exactly when the word "demonic" first entered the German historical vocabulary.[5] But certainly by the twentieth century it was firmly ensconced there. By "demonic" the Germans meant a sudden welling-up of passion—whether creative or destructive or both together— that exceeded the bounds of "normal" human behavior. Its ravages they found peculiar to their own national spirit, as opposed to the more rational tradition of the Latin and Mediterranean world. Ambiguity was of its essence. It exercised a deadly attraction that was a source both of pride and of fear. It marked the Germans off from their neighbors as a people destined to special greatness and subject to unusual temptations; what was catastrophic and what was life-giving about it teetered in uneasy balance in the Teutonic soul. Not until the advent of Hitler did such contemporary German historians as Friedrich Meinecke and Gerhard Ritter come to the regretful conclusion that the negative elements predominated and that the demonic must at all costs be purged from their spiritual tradition.

To Croce's limpid Mediterranean mind, something as vague

4 "German Schools of History," *Historical Essays and Studies* (London, 1907), p. 355.
5 See Note at the end of this chapter.

as this was not an acceptable historical category. For Croce, what could not be expressed in logical form was not worth saying at all: it was in this sense that he deviated from the main stream of historical idealism and revived the teaching of Hegel. The result was to dismiss whole eras of history as the realm of mere incoherence. It was characteristic of Croce and his school to favor epochs of civic tranquility and consensus, or—as in the history of the philosopher's native Naples—to follow the wavering line of intellectual, constructive achievement that alone could give logic to a succession of tragic errors in administration and statesmanship.

Thus the idealist historians recognized the irrational without knowing what to do with it. They could subsume it under the love of God; they could quake in holy terror before an inexplicable force whose echoes, muffled by dutiful lives of scholarship, resounded within their own breasts; they could extract from it the scattered elements that were capable of logical categorization. But they were unable to enfold it in the sympathetic understanding which they thought of as their supreme professional skill; they found it impossible to embrace the precise contours of behavior and emotion which remained foreign to them.

More specifically, historians of all schools have not known how to deal with contradictions. The gap between word and deed, the emotional tone that belies the overt ideal allegiance, the apparently careless phrase or gesture betraying an unrecognized intention—these have usually left historians at a loss. And this disorientation has been reinforced by the scholar's tendency to accept the message of official documents at its face value. It has been the same with the shifts and dodges of "double-think" or the sealing off of the mind into closed compartments. Historians know that these pitfalls exist: the self-observant among them are aware that they themselves sometimes react in similar fashion. But when it comes to the prime movers of history, they have been reluctant to recognize the simultaneous presence of motives that seem to be in radical opposition. As Erik Erikson has complained, "Historical dialectics refuses to acknowledge the principle that a great revolutionary's psyche may also harbor a great reactionary; but psychological dialectics must assume it to be possible, and even probable."[6]

(In this connection, I recall one of my colleagues expressing surprise at the martial enthusiasms of my young son, which struck him as in flagrant contradiction with my own involvement in the cause of peace. "But don't you see," I answered, "this is just the point." That is, the unconscious logic of understanding between my son and me was clear, if unexpressed. We had parceled out the roles—each could serve as a foil to the other—with the boy permitted to enact in all innocence what the responsible man could no longer sanction in his own behavior. A longing for harmony, a passionate advocacy of peace, may well emerge from the sublimation of deep-seated aggression. I doubt whether there has ever been a strenuous pacifist who has not been fascinated by war and violence.)

Such is the entering wedge for a psychoanalytic interpretation of motive. If the historian—like the analyst—finds conviction in the "fit" of an explanatory line of thought, so his discovery of a discrepancy, of a lack of fit, is the clue that something must be wrong with the explanation that has first sprung to mind. If he comes to recognize that an unconscious or half-conscious motive can alone bring into a clear pattern

[6] *Young Man Luther* (New York, 1958), p. 231.

the pieces of a hopelessly jumbled puzzle, the historian has reached the threshold of a psychoanalytic interpretation, whether he knows it or not. And in this context "threshold" is the proper expression. Our goal as historians is not always to *assign* a motive; frequently the exact determination of the thought and emotion that went into a specific series of actions is beyond our powers. We may prefer to suggest no more than the *preparatory* elements in the spiritual biography of a historical actor that years later will narrow his range of choice. We may simply try to find the bent of character, the thwarted emotion, the hidden *trauma* limiting his possibilities of future achievement. If we can do that, we shall already have contributed mightily to historical understanding, even though our formulation of the motive that finally triggered a crucial decision may remain forever subject to debate.

A few examples from my own teaching experience may serve to illuminate what I mean by locating the preparatory elements in an individual's emotional make-up. I first recall my own excitement—and I trust that of my students—when one of them in seminar accidentally stumbled on the psychological understanding that was eluding him. The seminar report had begun rather tentatively: soon the student was deep in quicksand, and by the end of half an hour he was foundering in a mass of contradictions. Finally he confessed in some desperation that he could make no sense of his protagonist's behavior. The figure in question was a war hero and an expert on armament. At the same time he was a man of the Left, he hated war, and he hoped that his country could avoid having to fight another one. In view of his previous experience and competence, he had been appointed to a ministry directing one of the technical branches of the military establishment. Into this work he threw himself with zeal; he labored conscientiously to develop arms of the highest proficiency. Yet somehow nothing got done—he bogged down in fussy detail, and little progressed beyond the stage of the drawing board and the prototype. Meantime his enemies were beginning to accuse him of administrative sabotage and even of treason.

My student—who was convinced of his subject's personal integrity—was at a loss for an explanation. As he wrestled with his problem and finally confessed his inability to solve it, the solution lay right before him—like justice in Plato's *Republic*, kicking around our feet unnoticed. For the student had quite unwittingly run up against a classic case of inner conflict. His protagonist's technical and military pride was locked in hidden combat with his leftist and pacifist leanings. The minister could not permit himself to recognize this openly— he could not allow the struggle that was tearing him apart to rise to full consciousness. To do so would have been to betray one or the other, either his ideological allegiance or his professional and administrative responsibility. So the only way he was able to settle the issue was by letting his unconscious do the work; his hidden preference eventually revealed itself through the peculiarly insidious device of sabotage masking as an ultrascrupulous performance of duty.

Few cases are as neat as this. Yet it suggests a whole approach to the study of one particular form of incoherent behavior—that is, the contradictions arising from a simultaneous allegiance to two incompatible ideals or ideologies, one of which has not yet reached full consciousness. I think this is especially true of the type of social and cultural change that is felt as devastating to the emotional life of the community.

Contradiction and conflict are inevitable when the prevalent modes of expression fail to keep pace—as they usually do—with an unfamiliar social reality. In such cases ritual is often the only recourse: traditional words and gestures give comfort when the external features of life have become charged with a threat which is all the more terrible for being only half understood. I think that one of the great strengths of Johan Huizinga's beautiful book, *The Waning of the Middle Ages,* is the way it demonstrates how in the fourteenth and fifteenth centuries the elaboration of protocol and of ritualistic behavior served as a reassurance against unbearable anxiety: here on a wider scale we find the same kind of compulsive meticulousness that we observed just now in an isolated individual's response to ideological distress.

I recall another student—this time at the Ph.D. dissertation stage—who underwent a crisis of self-doubt in the course of his research. His subject was again biographical: a historian and literary figure, not himself of first rank, but a close observer and even an intimate of the great. Having outlived nearly all his contemporaries, he had leisure for reflection on his own past and was flattered when my student wrote that he was already engaged in tracing his career and influence. Soon the two became personally acquainted: as their talks progressed and the student ransacked his subject's personal papers, he gradually came to feel that he understood the "old boy" pretty well. But what he found disconcerted him. Here once more the problem arose from conflicting ideological statements: as another contemporary put it, the old littérateur was "a man of the Right who thought himself to be of the Left" (or was it the other way around?). My student had penetrated to the earliest evidences of these contradictions: he had discovered that the familiar revolt against parental ideals had in this case been transmuted into close identification with the father's cultural values; the result had been a lack of self-confidence and a tendency to dilettantism—perhaps even a deficiency in what the French call *sérieux*. The psychological pieces fitted together in the student's mind. Yet the conclusion seemed too trivial to stand muster as a creditable research performance.

Actually the conclusion was not trivial at all, and the final results were admirable. My student's puzzlement derived from his own scruples about the apparent simplicity of his findings —a common complaint in an academic tradition which likes to see a few drops of sweat still adhering to a job well done. What he had discovered had been neither easy nor obvious. It simply appeared so once he had successfully carried it through: now that he had finally understood his problem, he could not imagine his readers or his professors failing to reach the same results with ridiculous ease. (I am reminded of a friend who on the completion of his own psychoanalysis wondered whether it had really been necessary to go through "all that" in order to arrive at some rather platitudinous convictions about his personal behavior.) In both instances, the investigators forgot that what in the end looked like platitude at the start had been a great riddle. It appeared simple *only because they had understood it*—indeed, its very simplicity was a sign that, *from their standpoint,* they had understood it correctly. One of the most grievous deceptions encountered in teaching or writing is the sense that the very theme of one's work is dissolving into nothingness just at the moment in which one is beginning to encompass it. As the analyst well knows, it is often harder to deal with triumph than with disaster.

In the case of the elderly man of letters, there was much in the student's own origins and cultural associations which could help in establishing mutual comprehension. There was a good fit between the subject and the mind approaching it. This, I think, is a criterion often forgotten in the selection of a Ph.D. topic. Unless there is some emotional tie, some elective affinity linking the student to his subject of study, the results will be pedantic and perfunctory; the writer will succumb to the tedium of which those in graduate school so often and so justly complain. Croce and his fellow idealists recognized the importance of "spiritual" commitment to a specific scholarly endeavor: it was at the basis of their celebrated distinction between true history and "chronicle." But they were not equipped to handle the trickier problem of an emotional pull that has not yet reached consciousness. A case of religious doubt, for instance, may become manifest only when a student finds himself drawn to the historical investigation of co-religionists who in their own time hovered on the edge of heresy, and the very study of the heterodox may prove to be the means of resolving the unsuspected crisis of faith.

A final example of the sort of historical research I have in mind is more strictly psychoanalytic. It is an account of the early career of the Nazi propaganda chief, Joseph Goebbels, drawing heavily on the subject's own youthful literary efforts.[7] The author's psychoanalytic competence is almost professional: it is quite apparent that he knows intimately whereof he speaks. And it is significant that his interpretation does not fasten on his protagonist's obvious handicap—a clubfoot—

---

[7] Richard MacMasters Hunt, *Joseph Goebbels: A Study of the Formation of his National-Socialist Consciousness* (unpublished dissertation: Harvard University, 1960).

which a cruder psychological study might have made the showpiece of a melodramatic story. It focuses rather on Goebbels' uncertain, marginal class position and on the loss of his ancestral Catholic faith. The result, the author finds, was an agonizing questioning of personal identity and the need to give himself over completely to a loved savior (Goebbels' vocabulary, as in the case of so many other professed atheists, remained religious and Christian), a redeemer who in the end proved to be Adolf Hitler.

In broader terms, this study draws attention to the fact that by far the greater part of the high-ranking Nazi leaders, like Goebbels and Hitler himself, came from originally Catholic families who had fallen away from the faith of their fathers. Here once more it is so simple a matter to make the count that in doing so one may be accused of underlining the obvious. But in fact the historians of the period have done little with the evidence that lay ready to hand: few have seen the importance of religion—and more particularly the sense of a religious void which cried out for a substitute belief—in the formation of an authoritarian ideology. Indeed, this account of Goebbels' youth sketches an entire configuration of personal motives that to date has been relatively unexplored. In common with Erikson's book on the young Luther—whose example it follows—the work attempts to untangle an emotional and social interlocking which is more elusive than the economic-religious configuration defined by Weber two generations ago. It suggests that the simultaneous and reinforcing pressures of thwarted sexual impulse, religious yearning, and class uncertainty together produce an explosive complex—and a complex characteristic of the twentieth century. From such an interpretation of the emotional history of a single individual, we may derive a more general understanding of our own era as an age of desperate search for identity.

Up to now I have spoken almost exclusively of personal biography. It may be objected that psychoanalytic interpretations have long since been established in this field, and that I have been trying to force a door which already stands open. It is quite true that in the past two or three decades the psychoanalytic biography has become a recognized historical and literary genre. But it is by no means sure that the results have been fortunate: far too many efforts of this sort are over-ambitious and betray the hand of the amateur in stretching a few scraps of emotional data far beyond their interpretative capacities. Many of them read like poor imitations of Freud's *Leonardo da Vinci*—itself a tour de force exploiting scanty evidence to the full, but scarcely a model for lesser men to follow.

What is chiefly wrong with the conventional psychoanalytic biography is its crude unilateralism. It suggests a one-to-one relationship, arguing that the protagonist did this or that *because* of some painful experience in early childhood. The explanation comes out too pat, and the trauma in question is almost invariably viewed as a handicap and no more. It took a literary critic—Edmund Wilson—to give us "the conception of superior strength as inseparable from disability, . . . the idea that genius and disease . . . may be inextricably bound up together."[8] And subsequently Erikson has deepened the same insight in his depiction of Luther's struggles with his early scruples, his triumph over his emotional vulnerability in

[8] *The Wound and the Bow* (Cambridge, Mass., 1941), pp. 287, 289.

his middle period, and the return of psychopathic symptoms in the authoritarian behavior of his last years.

Yet the image of Luther that abides with us is of a man who has transformed his weakness into spiritual power and the gift of speaking directly to the emotional needs of his fellow men. For this understanding we historians are greatly in Erikson's debt. We are likewise indebted to him for his stress on the years of adolescence and early manhood—roughly from the age of fifteen to thirty—as decisive in the careers of the great men of the past. Here again Erikson has corrected the one-sidedness of the more usual psychoanalytic biography. In line with the emphasis on personal identity and the ego in post-Freudian analytic practice, he has shifted the focus from childhood trauma to youthful struggle for self-definition. Such an approach is far more congenial to the historian's mind than the earlier (and almost exclusive) stress on the first six or seven years of life. Almost by definition, history prefers to deal with epochs of full consciousness, whether in the evolution of peoples or in the career of an individual. Moreover, an emphasis on adolescence and early manhood facilitates the historian's task. Reliable evidence on childhood is usually scanty, even in the lives of very prominent men, and if the biographer is told that this alone is decisive, he is in effect forced to choose between equally unpalatable alternatives. He may either renounce a psychoanalytic interpretation entirely, or make a highly risky extrapolation, in which his lack of clinical experience is almost sure to lead him astray. In contrast, the years from fifteen to thirty are often well documented—the problem has simply been that historians have not quite known what to do with the data at their disposal.

If we historians, then, accept these two working assumptions—that the individual trauma itself may well be the spur to major thought and action, and that the years of early maturity are decisive in the establishment of permanent ideal allegiances—we shall be in a better position to go beyond biography to a more general analysis of leading groups in society. In the course of setting the individual psychoanalytic study on firmer ground, we shall have found interpretative principles capable of wider application. I have already suggested this in referring to the fact that Goebbels' apostasy from Catholicism was an experience common to the higher Nazi leadership. One of the virtues of the psychoanalytic approach is the possibility it offers of simultaneously extending and testing a hypothesis about the motives of a single historical figure by seeing how it fits other men placed in similar circumstances.

Arnold J. Toynbee—with his customary talent for coining historical terminology that is awkward and at the same time manages to stick—has referred to the emergence in the past generation of a new type of history which he calls "prosopographical," that is, a historical approach which personifies abstractions: churches, parliaments, and the like. He is particularly impressed with the study of institutions through close biographical analysis of the elites that have controlled them. Such an approach, he maintains, can bridge "the gap between human beings and institutions, the most favorable situations" being "those in which a relatively small minority of the participants in a society, constituting a more or less strictly closed social circle, control between them one or more of their society's more important institutions, or even the society's whole life."[9] Where Toynbee finds this method most successful is in

[9] *Reconsiderations, A Study of History,* vol. XII, (London, 1961), p. 122.

the study of well-defined oligarchies such as those which ruled eighteenth-century England or late republican Rome. He is less sure that the "prosopographical" technique will work in situations of broad democratic participation in public affairs.

It is precisely here that psychoanalytic evidence is relevant. I quite agree with Toynbee that one of the major problems historians face is bridging the gap between human beings and institutions—finding the link between personal and group experience. And I also grant that psychoanalytic interpretations to date have dealt more successfully with individual historical figures than with the lives of communities. Or—at the other end of the scale—they have offered imaginative suggestions for understanding a mass emotional phenomenon such as the pervading sense of despair following the Black Death, or a widely ramifying aesthetic movement such as Romanticism. In contrast, the middle level—interpretations of the thought and action of groups small enough to be clearly identified and studied in some detail—has mostly been lacking. There has been nothing quite corresponding to the statistically based analyses of oligarchies to which Toynbee refers.

More closely considered, however, the psychoanalytic approach offers advantages for this type of study which a conventional statistical assessment cannot match. The latter almost necessarily rests on *external* evidence—on common criteria that are readily apparent and hence easily compared, such as membership in an elite. A psychoanalytic interpretation may also use external criteria in defining its problem group: high-ranking Nazi leadership is a case in point. But it will go beyond this to inquire about common *emotional experience*—about shared anxieties and aspirations which may be all the more decisive for being only partially conscious. And it will find that experiences such as these cut across the conventional delimitations of class or elite groups. Thus they point to a way of understanding motivations in a democratic or quasi-democratic community in which elites are ill-defined.

I suggest that historians might experiment with drawing up rosters of personalities from specified periods for whom biographical evidence is sufficient and in whom they suspect the existence of an emotional common denominator; by subjecting these biographies to detailed comparative scrutiny they may arrive at valid generalizations about the deep-seated fears and ideal strivings of the era or eras in question. (I mean "valid" in the sense that their interpretations rest on the experience of verifiable men and women, rather than being impressionistic constructions which skeptical colleagues can so easily dismiss as figments of the imagination.) I have in mind the application to past ages of comparative biographical techniques such as Robert Jay Lifton has devised for assessing the experience of the victims of thought control in Communist China.[10] Other examples will doubtless occur to any historian who has grappled with the agonizing difficulty of expressing the "spirit" of an era in terms specific enough to carry conviction to his readers.

Here we arrive at the nub of our whole problem. If psychoanalysis can help history to cope with its supreme difficulty—the motivation of the great historical actors of the past—it can also suggest a way of linking the emotional experience of the individual to that of the wider group. Although this latter contribution has so far produced fewer results than has the isolated biographical study, its major lines of inquiry are beginning to be defined. The pioneer work of men like Erikson and

[10] *Thought Reform and the Psychology of Totalism* (New York, 1961).

Lifton has given us new guideposts for pursuing a very old task. In particular, it has shown us that we historians have been right all along in stressing individuality and the unique quality of personal experience. But it turns out that we have been right for rather different reasons from those alleged by the idealist school. It is not that there is something "ineffable" about the individual—it is not that human personality is too sacred a matter to be meddled with by the scientific and the profane: with human motives, as with anything else, systematic (or, if one will, scientific) generalization is indispensable to understanding and communication. It is rather that the individual consciousness is our final datum, the bedrock of what we know. The major tradition of modern Western philosophy—whether springing from Locke or from Descartes—has always known this; it has asserted again and again that we must go back to the individual's own mind (and ultimately to that of the investigator himself) in order to find ourselves on solid ground.

This conviction the historian shares with the psychoanalyst. Neither is metaphysically inclined. Both try to keep up the pretense that they can go about their professional labors without inquiring too deeply into ultimate philosophical matters. Yet in fact they have a common metaphysic. Both believe in the radical subjectivity of human understanding. At the same time—and for similar reasons—both yearn to escape from the prison of the individual consciousness, or rather, to break out of the double confinement of the investigator's mind and of that other mind (whether of historical actor or analysand) with which he is trying to bring his own consciousness into sympathetic response. Both know that the way to individual understanding lies through the almost imperceptible alterations that the historian's or the psychoanalyst's mind itself undergoes in the course of groping its way toward its subject. And both are beginning to realize that the same holds for the effort to escape from the conventional tête-à-tête of two isolated psyches: they have found that the study of the individual is notably enriched by its association with one directed toward a wider group. Together the historian and the psychoanalyst have discovered the overriding importance of locating and exploiting such a group; they have finally realized that the individual can be understood in his full cultural context only if his spiritual biography is viewed in relation to the lives of others with whom he has deep-seated emotional affinities.

So in history as in psychoanalysis we may conclude that the path to the fuller understanding of the individual lies through the group—and vice versa. In both cases, the explanation of motive runs from the single human being to others comparable to him, and then back to the individual once more, as the ramifying thought and action of both are gradually illuminated. This reciprocal method is the ultimate concern that history and psychoanalysis share. In both cases, its systematic development has barely begun.

The individual consciousness is likewise the training ground of the two professions. In the one case, this is fully recognized: a psychoanalyst's experience of his own analysis forms a central element in his education. With the young historian, precedent and protocol are less clear: in his graduate training there is no conscious effort to encourage or to direct the student's sympathetic imagination which corresponds to the discipline in the handling of documents that he receives in seminar. I think this is a grave error. The exercise of "intuition" is at least as important to the historian as his sureness of touch in documentary interpretation. By now it must be apparent that a major polemical purpose of these essays is to stimulate the release of historical study from its bondage to libraries and documents. I have mentioned field work as one way of letting in fresh air. Some variety of psychoanalytic training would be another.

I am far from clear as to what form this training might best take. A full psychoanalysis would certainly be too long and expensive for most Ph.D. candidates—and some would be temperamentally unfitted for it. In a few cases, however, it might be precisely what was called for, and I trust that foundation funds would be forthcoming to finance such a venture. I hope that in the coming years a significant minority of young historians, particularly those most concerned with the psychological aspects of historical interpretation, will be going through personal analysis under the guidance of experienced clinicians. For the others, it may be possible to work out a shorter program in consultation with the Psychoanalytic Institutes established near some of our major universities.

Nothing less, I believe, will be adequate to the needs of historical understanding in the second half of the twentieth century. I see no other approach—in the contemporary intellectual setting—that remotely matches psychoanalysis in cultivating that "feel" which has always been the particular mark of the born historian, as of the analyst. But I do not claim that such a course of training will do the job in itself. It should not be thought of as a substitute for the self-education—the gradual growth in personal awareness—which is the historian's own lonely task. Psychoanalysis can contribute mightily to this process; it cannot take over the assignment entirely. As Theodor Mommsen reminded us almost ninety years ago: "If a professor of history thinks he is able to educate historians in the same sense as classical scholars and mathematicians can be educated, he is under a dangerous and detrimental delusion. The historian . . . cannot be educated, he has to educate himself."[11]

Note

Certainly one of the earliest definitions of the "demonic" is that given by Goethe in *Dichtung und Wahrheit*:[12]

He [Goethe] thought that he discovered in Nature, animate and inanimate, with soul and without soul, something which was only manifested in contradictions, and therefore could not be grasped under one conception, still less under one word. It was not godlike, for it seemed unreasonable; not human, for it had no understanding; not devilish, for it was beneficent; not angelic, for it often showed malicious pleasure. It resembled chance, for it exhibited no consequence; it was like Providence, for it hinted at connection. Everything which limits us seemed by it to be penetrable; it seemed to sport in an arbitrary fashion with the necessary elements of our being; it contracted time and expanded space. Only in the impossible did it seem to find pleasure, and the possible it seemed to thrust from itself with contempt.

This principle, which seemed to step in between all other principles, to separate them and to unite them, I named Demonic, after the example of the ancients, and of those who had become aware of something similar. I sought to save myself before this

[11] Rectoral Address (1874) at the University of Berlin: quoted in Ernst Cassirer, *An Essay on Man* (New Haven, 1944), p. 257.
[12] *Goethe's Autobiography: Poetry and Truth,* translated by R. O. Moon (Washington, D.C., 1949), pp. 682–684).

fearful principle, by fleeing, as was my custom, behind an image. . . .

Although that Demonic element can manifest itself in all corporeal and incorporeal things, indeed even in animals expresses itself most remarkably, yet it stands especially in the most wonderful connection with man, and forms a power which, if not opposed to the moral order of the world, yet crosses it so that one may be regarded as the warp and the other as the woof.

For the phenomena which are hereby produced there are numerous names; for all philosophies and religions have endeavoured in prose and poetry to solve this riddle, and finally to settle the thing which still remains for them henceforward unassailed.

But the Demonic element appears most fearfully when it comes forward predominatingly in some man. During my life I have been able to observe several, partly near and partly at a distance. They are not always the most excellent men either as regards intelligence or talents, and they seldom recommend themselves by goodness of heart; but a tremendous power issues from them, and they exercise an incredible dominion over all creatures, indeed, even over the elements, and who can say how far such influence will extend. All united moral powers are of no avail against it; in vain all the more enlightened part of mankind make them suspect as either deceivers or deceived, the mass will be attracted by them. Seldom or never do contemporaries find their equals, and they are to be overcome by nothing but by the universe itself with which they began the struggle, and from such remarks that strange but monstrous proverb may have arisen: *Nemo contra Deum, nisi Deus ipse.*

IV.

The Sweep of the Narrative Line

THOSE OF us who advocate experiment in historical writing may quite plausibly be charged with neglecting or denigrating the central thread of the historian's tradition. When we argue for a schematic account of the past—for the establishment of precisely delineated processes or structures that will give to history a more clearly scientific frame—we may be accused of forgetting that historical prose has always consisted primarily of narrative. When we see suggestive virtue in the "meta-historical" flights of a Spengler or a Toynbee[1]—a type of writing which despite its scientific trappings is actually far out on the poetic limits of our craft—we may similarly be told that these vast speculations have little to do with the historian's main business. Whether we try to bring history closer to social science or to give greater scope to the wanderings of

[1] See particularly the concluding chapter and Appendix II, pp. 183–187 (on Toynbee), of my *Oswald Spengler: A Critical Estimate,* revised edition (New York, 1962); also Frank E. Manuel, "In Defense of Philosophical History," *The Antioch Review,* XX (Fall 1960), 331–343. Manuel and I reached our positive judgment on meta-history quite independently of each other.

its artistic fancy—in either case our knuckles are rapped. The main business, we are reminded, is narrative: that is what distinguishes the writing of history from all other intellectual pursuits. As its very name keeps recalling to our minds, history is a story. Alone of the learned disciplines, it tries to recapture how things happened. Others may abstract from reality to their heart's content, to select what particular aspect of man's experience they choose to analyze. History alone aspires to give a full *and real* account.

Hence history faces a problem confronted by no other discipline. It is all very well, my contradictors will say, to defend the meta-historians or to urge the merits of a schematic, quasi-scientific treatment. These may seem to be new and exciting pursuits. Yet there is another side to their apparent novelty and difficulty of execution. In one respect at least the more experimental types of history are easier to compose than the historical writing of tradition. For like science or art, they are *partially arbitrary* abstractions from reality. Such abstractions have never fully satisfied the historian and probably never will. A true historian yearns to grasp reality itself, to convey the nature of "becoming," to plunge, as the philosopher Bergson aspired to do, into the flux of human experience. If he is born to his craft, he will settle for nothing less.

Is this an impossible goal? Is the historian's effort to convey, through narrative, a sense of how it felt to participate in the great events of the past—is this in any sense feasible? Or is it perhaps one of those generous illusions essential to men embarked on a futile but magnificent quest? I myself am of two minds on these questions. And I think that the best way to try to answer them is to examine first what historians actually do when they undertake to write narrative prose and then

to see how these narratives relate to the more experimental
types of historical writing that I have discussed in the earlier
essays.

I have never meant to belittle narrative history. We who
have argued the merits of other historical genres have no intention of substituting a new type of writing for an old. We do
not want to displace narrative history from its traditional central role: we recognize that most of the classics of history as
literature are cast in the narrative mold, and that the telling of
a story will continue to be an indispensable feature of our endeavor. After all, it is chronological sequence that most sharply
distinguishes the writing of history from all other intellectual
pursuits. What we are after, rather, is an enrichment of historical understanding; we want to find out what sort of understanding can be reached through prose that is primarily narrative and in what respects our subject matter can benefit from
a more analytic or schematic type of study. At the very least,
if we look once again at history's traditional storytelling function from the standpoint of twentieth-century historians with a
primarily analytic emphasis, we may be able to assess with
greater accuracy the scope and limitations of the narrative
method.

One generalization immediately springs to mind—narrative
history is far less simple a matter than it appears to be. On
this, both its defenders and its detractors will agree. As the
primary vehicle for historical literature through two and a half
millennia of writing, the narrative has been refined and polished to a highly professional finish. Historians have developed
a myriad of literary devices for gliding over what they do not

adequately know or understand. With more schematic history, the gaps yawn embarrassingly wide: in narrative prose, they can be artfully concealed. Moreover, if the analytic historian makes a judgment, he is usually explicit about it: the story-teller can slip such a judgment into a highly colored adjective or a subordinate clause without alerting the reader to what he is doing. Thus most narrative history does not quite live up to its advance billing: it is neither as comprehensive nor as "objective" as it is popularly supposed to be.

Let us take a look at the typical accounts of times past and see what in fact they "cover." In most of such accounts the method is actually closer to that of the novel or the drama than the author explicitly recognizes. Just as in fiction told in the third person, we find on closer inspection that there is often a leading character whose point of view is dominant—who might as well be the "I" by whom the story is told—so in history we can detect the figure or figures through whose eyes the historian witnesses the events he describes. He may think of himself as an omniscient quasi-deity serenely viewing human affairs from an altitude of lofty detachment. In fact, he is condemned to be a mere mortal and is obliged to pick from among his cast of characters those to whom he will extend his imaginative sympathy. And these will almost of necessity be from the higher ranks—statesmen, commanding generals, or perhaps an occasional wise intimate of the great. It is hard to find a political history written from the stand-point of the ordinary voter or the account of a battle which reflects the sentiments of the suffering enlisted man. And this is not through any snobbery or hard-heartedness on the part of the historian. It is simply that the voter or the common soldier has a "worm's eye view" of the matter. He cannot possibly provide the range of vision that the historian requires in order to carry out his task.

But is even the view of the statesman or the general as comprehensive as it seems to be? Of course not—it is limited in all sorts of ways, and most obviously by locale. In devising his account, the historian finds himself obliged to proceed like a dramatist. He cannot be everywhere at once (in this respect also, he is only a mortal); he must shift his action from one place to another, as his own judgment or feel tells him how to focus his story. And these theaters or stages are once again of the loftier sort—the halls of parliament, a cabinet meeting, a staff headquarters. Concentrated thus, the account becomes detailed and specific; sometimes even snatches of dialogue find a place. Here the historian behaves almost like a participant himself, as he strives to recreate the reality and to convey the excitement of the meeting in question. Just as only a few characters enjoy the historian's inner sympathy—can have some actuality breathed into them as the author pauses for a moment to catch a glimpse of events through their eyes—while the others are relegated to the rank of what the French call mere *figurants,* so it is only on an infinitesimal minority of the vast welter of human experiences that the historian can turn his full narrative power; the rest must remain background, externally viewed, for which a lifeless summary has to suffice.

The narrative, then, proceeds on two levels: out in front, the great scenes; behind, the vast anonymity of all the rest of the living and acting and dying. It is hard to see how the historian can do otherwise. Yet what starts as a technical necessity is reinforced by personal preference and mental sloth. Where "the documents" lead, the historian follows; and if these documents are official in nature, his account becomes that much easier, for it is as guides to the major scenes that official records chiefly function. With this observation, we land right in the middle of one of the historian's most cherished illusions —the myth of the eyewitness account.

Eyewitness of what? The manuals tell us that the accounts of participants rank directly after official documents as prime "sources," since the authors are writing of events they saw with their own eyes. But how much did they actually see (leaving quite aside the question of how much they could accurately remember)? This can be only a small segment of the large events on which their word commands authority, the rare occasions on which they were both physically present and mentally alert. For most of what figures in participants' accounts, the authors are no better off than the rest of us: they know it only at second hand. I have found it a useful exercise for my students to subject to critical examination such a celebrated work by a great participant as Winston Churchill's *The Second World War*. Surely here is a series of volumes whose authoritative character no one will question. Yet when we ask how much of the war Mr. Churchill truly "saw," the answer is a very small portion indeed. Only a few fragments of his six volumes are really at firsthand—and these again are the great scenes, the set pieces which the narrative historian has always adored.

If the historian did not permit hearsay evidence, how could he possibly piece together his story? Here the parallel between history and a court of law, dear to the philosophers of our craft, is quite misleading. The historian does not really proceed in the fashion either of a judge or of an attorney. "The lawyer aims to make a case; the historian wishes to understand a situation. The evidence which convinces lawyers often fails to satisfy us; our methods seem singularly imprecise to them."[2] I had the misfortune once to be a witness in a court of law, and I recall my frustration at the judge's constantly ruling out of order the points that I regarded as most significant. "Fact is fact," he scolded me, "and hearsay is hearsay"; presumably in the judge's mind the two neither met nor overlapped. In my own experience, whether as historian or as participant, I had found no such clear line of demarcation.

Personal experience can serve as a useful check on how far the knowledge of participants—or the record of their doings— actually extends. Fabrice in *La Chartreuse de Parme* was puzzled as to whether he had or had not fought in the Battle of Waterloo. Veterans of the Second World War may recall a similar puzzlement when they found themselves unaccountably awarded battle stars for service in which they had never heard a shot fired in anger; they simply happened to be inside the conventional lines in time and space with which the higher headquarters had defined the limits of a battle. At the center of a historical phenomenon, those directly involved may have a reasonably clear idea of what is going on. On the periphery, bewilderment takes over.

And what of a mass phenomenon in which there is no identifiable center or point of direction? How is the narrative historian to tell the story of a mob action in which it is impossible to distinguish leaders from led? Even in the less amorphous case of an election, it is one thing to record the activities of the candidates, quite another to trace how the voters came to a series of individual decisions that eventually added up to the

---

[2] A. J. P. Taylor, *The Origins of the Second World War* (New York, 1962), p. 13.

verdict of numbers. When the election is over it all seems clear: how could we ever have doubted the outcome? But just the day before, the same electoral landscape offered nothing but confusion. It is a sobering experience to cast one's thought over the thousands of dwellings in a whole sprawling constituency and to try to determine what is going on inside each voter's mind as the moment of decision approaches. Those who have made the attempt may be justly skeptical of the confident fashion in which historians pronounce on corresponding events in the past. Similarly, anyone who has followed his own activities in the current press may well be struck with wonder at the credence which historians conventionally give to newspaper articles of an earlier day. I used to know an elderly statesman who told me that in forty years of public life he had never once read an accurate newspaper account of his own doings.

Must we despair, then, of ever producing a satisfactory story of the past? If the narrative historian's sympathetic understanding extends no farther than the front of the stage or stages he has devised, if his account blurs at the edges and shakes even at the center, is he justified in claiming to have told the tale of how things came to be as they are? Not exactly—the historian does not quite perform what he says he does. But he accomplishes something else, and this is no small feat. He locates and describes the key events—what we conventionally call the turning points of history—some of which may have been visible as such to the participants themselves, others appearing in this light only with the passage of time.

Thus the historian who prides himself on the comprehensive scope of his narrative is usually unaware of what he has actually done. He fails to see how radical a selection he has been obliged to make among the number of courses open to him, and how in this respect his situation is not so very different from that of the historian who frankly fits his material into a scheme that he has himself composed. In both cases, the writer has established his own criteria of relevance; in both cases, these criteria derive, whether consciously or by implication, from the historian's own value system. However he chooses to proceed, he—the historian—is the one who is directing the show: the events will not do it for him.

Within the limits of this radical selectivity, what the narrative historian *can* convey is the direction of change through time. He can try to chart how one human situation was gradually transformed into another. But he is unable to trace the process every step of the way. Men's activities come in an uninterrupted flow, and by the very effort to describe this flow, the historian is obliged to chop it up into segments. Such are the episodes in time and space on which he chooses to focus his attention. Here the historian pauses to take a bearing, to sketch a scene, to depict an individual character, or to mount a dramatic action. But these are merely the way stations: the crucial significance lies in the points of arrival and of departure. At those points alone can the historian find some sure footing, and it is the mark of the writer who knows his trade to have chosen them with discernment. No literary device can trace the entire trajectory of an object in motion: it can specify only the beginning and the end.

More broadly, our verbal metaphors are powerless to convey the infinite richness and inextricable connectedness of human experience. We may speak of flux, texture, dense interpenetration—all these are inadequate. Yet once again, even without finding fully satisfactory words for expressing it, the historian knows whereof he speaks. And he knows also that the greatest challenge he faces is the imperative to render in one continuous sweep of prose style both the direction of events and their simultaneous occurrence. He must keep his narrative moving in the direction he has found significant; at the same time he is obliged to take account of the multiple viewpoints on the past characteristic of the modern temper. He must find a literary method which combines narrative pace with analytic richness—which holds together change through time and the vast simultaneity of human doings.

Hence the historian's supreme technical virtuosity lies in fusing the new method of social and psychological analysis with his traditional storytelling function. If he can keep the "how" and the "why" moving steadily alongside each other—if he can shift easily back and forth from the multiple doubts and hesitations of the participants to the single certainty of the historian who knows the outcome—then he is a writer who understands his business well. The trick is to follow now one, now another, of the aspects of experience—economic innovation, psychological shock, social regrouping, as the case may be—in their parallel or interacting effects, and to pick up each in turn, shifting it to the foreground as it impinges on the major human change which the central narrative is carrying, until finally all the streams of interpretation converge. The point of convergence is, of course, of the historian's own choosing, but there are some points well chosen and others that are not. The sign that it is a good choice is when the whole broad range of the original narrative or analysis, the multiple streams that the historian has been coaxing along, come together effortlessly and as though without prior design.

Such convergences have varied widely with the differing tempers of historians and the events to which they have given central importance. Michelet preferred to work with a *tableau*—a set piece of wide dimensions that would establish pictorially in the reader's mind the end result of a long historical chain. To close his account of the Middle Ages, he chose the trial and death of Joan of Arc. This tragic fragment of history, to which our contemporary dramatists have returned again and again, as though forever dissatisfied with established answers, at Michelet's hands became the individual expression of transition from the era of religious faith to the era of national states: "This last figure of the past was also the first of the time that was beginning. In her appeared the Virgin . . . and already the Fatherland."[3] In the brief career of Joan of Lorraine—half idyl and half inferno—Michelet found the ideal vehicle to convey his own sense of historical paradox and human contradiction, and with it a view of the medieval twilight that imposed itself on his successors.

Another type of convergence may be found in the single episode that brings into final focus a long and complex development. In *To the Finland Station*, Edmund Wilson, after tracing a full century of historical study exploited to revolutionary ends—and with Michelet himself figuring as a precursor—located the moment of climax with Lenin's arrival by train in Petrograd in April 1917. The Bolshevik leader's impromptu harangue from an armored car seemed to Wilson to mark the decisive moment when revolutionary thought went over into action; after Marx's decades of laborious study and writing, his ideological heirs were at last ready to put into prac-

[3] *History of France,* translated by G. H. Smith (New York, 1845), II, 168. I have altered the translation.

tice what the master had taught, through identifying their own deeds with the course of history. After that decisive April evening, the writing and the acting of history would never be quite the same again.

Such a device may strike the professional historian as too much the contrivance of a belletrist who has been insufficiently disciplined in seminar. But a close scrutiny of some highly professional contemporary writing reveals that similar techniques enjoy a perfectly respectable standing. I am thinking, for example, of a biographical study of Darwin's leading American disciple, John William Draper. The supreme moment in the life of this fervent propagator of "the religion of science" comes with his trip to England in 1860 and his reading a paper to an Oxford audience riven by the controversy over *The Origin of Species,* which had been published the previous year. The scene is a familiar one to students of English thought—once again a kind of parliament hall, this time a parliament of science, where Thomas Huxley, for the Darwinians, puts the orthodox Bishop Wilberforce to rout. Yet despite countless retellings, the role of the visitor from America has remained obscure: it is only now that we realize his individual importance in delivering the paper which precipitated the crucial exchange and thereby widened the controversy beyond the narrowly scientific limits within which the Darwinians of strict observance were trying to confine it. In this consciousness of the broader issues at stake, Draper and Wilberforce saw alike:

Both men saw, or at least sensed, that the emotions would feel the impress of the new theory. It was not for them a limited-liability enterprise, but an assault, for better or worse, on the whole intellectual, emotional, and ethical structure of the European world. The theory of evolution could not be quarantined;

it must spread its contagion from one end to the other of human thought and through the whole range of final commitments within which thought operates.

And so we find that it was the lesser figure in the debate who sensed more clearly where the controversy was heading—that it would end by shaking the entire "emotional and intellectual habitat of ordinary Victorian man."[4] Here once more, by turning the prism of his vision just a few degrees, the historian has caught familiar material in a new light and elegantly located a critical convergence. And he has done something more: as our previous specimens have suggested, it is not sufficient that the writer assemble the various strands of his account into a single climactic episode; this episode itself should ideally become the point of departure for a new sweep of historical prose. Beyond the summit point of the narrative, the succeeding paragraphs and chapters may broaden the scope of the account, in ever widening circles, until the reader discovers with delight that what seemed to be no more than an artistic summation has in fact revealed unsuspected implications from which a whole new series of explanatory sequences have taken their rise.

Those of us who define our vision of history in terms of a retrospective cultural anthropology have stressed the central importance of symbols in establishing the common values of a given culture. These symbols may be of all types and degrees of specificity—religious, aesthetic, moral—yet they have in common their power to hold together heterogeneous manifestations of the human spirit whose inner connection people sel-

[4] Donald Fleming, *John William Draper and the Religion of Science* (Philadelphia, 1950), pp. 72–73.

dom express in logical form. The symbol conveys the implicit principles by which the society lives, the shared understanding of assumptions which require no formal proof.

Most characteristically such symbols are plastic. They point their message through an image or picture. And so is it also with narrative history. As Georges Sorel was one of the first to discover, most people do not understand their history in terms of careful chronology or reasoned explanation; they *see* it rather, as images of the apocalyptic battles which have changed the world. For Christians there stands the supreme drama of the crucifixion, for revolutionaries the compelling examples of 1789 and 1917, for Americans the tragic riddle of the Civil War. These are the historical myths that bind the group together: it was Sorel again who taught us that the popular understanding of history must necessarily be in terms of myth.

But what does this have to do with the narratives composed by professional historians? Surely the trained historical craftsman can and does rise above the vulgar mythology of the populace. In a purely technical sense he does—and yet in another and perhaps more profound sense he is dependent on the popular understanding for the very origin and form of his writing. I tried to show a moment ago that the crucial passages in the best narrative histories depict dramatic episodes where time sequences converge in one tense point of concentration before sweeping out once again into a new explanatory succession. These convergences are primarily pictorial—and by psychological necessity. For in his basic mental equipment the historian is no different from his untutored readers; he also must fuse his material into a summary picture in order to get an adequate grasp upon it. This is perhaps what Croce had in mind when he coined his baffling formula of a "lightning flash" of understanding; what seemed an opaque way of describing a process of logical explanation suddenly becomes clear if we apply it to the pictorial creations of the narrative historian, a role in which Croce could also on occasion turn in a distinguished performance.

The true relationship between expert history and popular myth is neither as simple as it would be if the professionals merely set mythology straight, nor as discouraging as if trained historians did nothing more than embrace the popular belief. The real relation between the two is one of constant interaction. As Vico discovered two and a half centuries ago, historical myths have a "public ground of truth" which needs only to be "cleaned, pieced together, and restored." The historian cannot even begin to devise his account until he knows what this mythology is; unless he reckons with his readers' prior preparation, unless he starts from their half-conscious assumptions about their own past, there is not the remotest chance that he will be listened to. He may eventually choose to jar them into a new understanding; but he has to begin with what is already a familiar feature of their mental landscape.

Historians, like other people, first learned their history as children, and if they do not retain a child's curiosity and wonder about the past, they will never be able to communicate their subsequent understanding. As we saw much earlier, this popular and easily accessible character of historical prose is something that it is vital for us to preserve at a time when an increasing professionalism is closing in upon us. The historian originally takes his decisive events where he finds them—in the sense common to the culture in which he grew up. Indeed, some of his predecessors have been the first architects of the popular mythology. A few historical events shape themselves in the public mind without apparent effort: appropriate labels are almost immediately found, and the canon of episodes worth remembering is established very early; the French Revolution and our own Civil War are cases in point. Most of the time, however, the conventional delimiting of events proceeds slowly, and historians may wrangle for generations until some one of them—like Oscar Handlin with the phenomenon of immigration—finally affixes the stamp that wins general favor.

In this fashion the historian both echoes and rectifies popular belief. Sometimes he merely deepens the common understanding of a crucial turning point; at other times he argues his public into accepting a new one. Or—as in the case of the fall of France in 1940—he may show them that a familiar dramatic sequence needs to be understood in a new sense. The original view of the French military defeat—that it was the direct result of political and social "decay"—telescoped into a simple cause and effect relationship a series of events whose interlockings were much less direct. On closer study, we have concluded that the military disaster had little connection with a loss of confidence in parliamentary government; it can mostly be ascribed to the incompetence of the French generals. Its relationship to the polemics against democracy that had marked the preceding decade was parallel and catalytic; by shattering the public values by which the French lived, the military defeat precipitated out of a latent mood of ideological questioning a full-scale counterrevolution.

I sometimes suspect that in the course of correcting the old myths the historians themselves create new ones. I am thinking, for example, of the amount of speculation that has surrounded Hitler's meeting with a group of Rhine-Ruhr industrialists at the house of the banker Schroeder in early January 1933. Here we have a dramatic gathering that was supposed to be secret and hence was unknown to the general public until after the fall of the Third Reich. It was only then that historians found evidence of a tacit bargain which enabled Hitler to reach the chancellorship less than a month later: the businessmen undertook to pay the Nazis' debts; the Nazi leader for his part gave assurances that he would not touch the basic capitalist structure of the German economy.[5] I think that this assessment of the situation in early 1933 is substantially correct: some such understanding was an essential preliminary to the conservatives' acceptance of Hitler as chancellor. But I question whether a single meeting had the crucial significance which historians have subsequently ascribed to it; I think that the reassurance extended to the business classes was a more amorphous matter —that it did not go beyond hints and symptomatic gestures.

In cases like these, the historian's great temptation is to make a single episode bear too much explanatory weight. He is carried away by the power of his own narration, succumbing himself to the aesthetic preferences of his audience. Yet even in the more doubtful cases, he is also showing them something they did not know before. By casting his view forward from the "pact" of January 1933, the historian lets his readers in on the sequels and the paradoxes of the outcome. Which partner to the bargain was fooling which? Did anyone present have the slightest suspicion where an agreement so casually arrived at would lead—that it would end twelve years later in the fiery ruins of that chancellery which Hitler was now in such a hurry to enter? Or perhaps did one or two of the more sensitive

[5] George W. F. Hallgarten, "Adolf Hitler and German Heavy Industry, 1931–1933," *The Journal of Economic History,* XII (Summer 1952), 222–246.

present unconsciously long for some such *Götterdämmerung?*
The historian's most intoxicating task is to demonstrate the
irony of historical action, the day of dupes repeated in infinite
succession until only the end of humanity itself can determine
who has the last laugh. Some historical figures achieve what
they set out to do; other accomplish the opposite; perhaps the
most characteristic attain against their announced intention the
things that at a deeper level they wanted all along. And what
better way for the historian to suggest this cosmic irony than
through the constant reworking of the great myth scenes in our
common past?

Most of the examples I have presented are from political and
military history. And this for good reason. The narrative historian shares with his readers the conviction that politics and
war should carry the central narrative thread. This may seem
a depressingly old-fashioned conclusion from someone who has
undertaken to reconnoiter the frontier posts in contemporary
historical writing. Have two centuries of experiment with the
histories of all the other products of man's spirit ended only in
a return to parliaments and battles?

I am far from suggesting that this is all. But I think that the
more sophisticated historians—and readers—need to be reminded that here once more the common understanding is
basic to what they do. The public forms its notion of current
history by what it reads in the newspapers; wars and threats of
war predominate. In these the ordinary reader discerns the narrative motion within his society that seems to establish the
temporal framework for its routine activities. And the historian
also, if he wants to convey how the members of that society
themselves conceived the public dimension of their lives, is

obliged to proceed likewise. The sort of analytic history that deals in statistical aggregates—economic, demographic, and the like—cannot possibly give the sense of personal immediacy inherent in the doings of generals and statesmen. Indeed, one of the great problems of analytic history is to acquire something of this face-to-face character; hence the importance of community studies in bringing the more repetitive of men's activities into human scale.

Thus the new analytic type of history can learn from the traditional narrative as well as enrich the latter with its unorthodox techniques and insights. The narrative approach can give human warmth and actuality to economic and social generalization; analytic tools of investigation can aid in the never-ending process of correcting the popular notion of history's mythical moments—by suggesting where the activities of generals and statesmen had a truly decisive effect and where they were merely episodic or anecdotal. If we historians can do both of these things at the same time—if we can refresh the old narrative with unsuspected vistas of understanding, while losing nothing of its motion and vitality—then we shall indeed have inaugurated a new era in historical studies. To make a sharp separation between narrative and analytic method is not at all what we are after; it is rather to fuse the two in a brighter and clearer illumination of the past.

Both partake of history's twin character as art and as science. The artistic aspects of the narrative are patent: they have been the main burden of the present essay. But one feature of its scientific character may not have emerged so explicitly. To narrate is also to predict. Here once again the very nature of the historian's mental equipment dictates what he does, however much his conscious intention may deny it. The historian conventionally refuses to make predictions; he says this is not his business and leaves it to the more schematic social sciences. But in fact he *implies* predictions all the time. He cannot stop his prose in midstream.

The historian . . . is bound to generalize; and, in so doing, he provides general guides for future action which, though not specific predictions, are both valid and useful. But he cannot predict specific events, because the specific is unique and because the element of accident enters into it. This distinction, which worries philosophers, is perfectly clear to the ordinary man. If two or three children in a school develop measles, you will conclude that the epidemic will spread; and this prediction, if you care to call it such, is based on a generalization from past experience, and is a valid and useful guide to action. But you cannot make the specific prediction that Charles or Mary will catch measles.[6]

The historian will not call the shots. Yet like other types of scientists he will delimit what is possible, what is probable, and what is almost certain. Most of the time he will do it by indirection, by simply organizing his statement of past events so that they move toward other events that lie in the future. This we call retrospective prediction. For the subsequent series of events does not really lie in the future—*the historian's* future—but merely in the future of the participants in the initial series. Such predictions are by definition accurate: here we recall the historian's privileged position of knowing the outcome. But what happens when the chain of retrospection comes to an end? What is the historian to do when he reaches his own present— when he loses his special knowledge and becomes a blind participant like anyone else, peering into the future as best he may?

[6] Edward Hallett Carr, *What Is History?* (New York, 1961), pp. 87–88.

Does he give up the predictive character of his thought? Does he radically recast the structure of his narrative sentences so as to shut off their built-in motion toward the future? I do not think he does so, and I do not think he ought to do so. He can and does continue just as before. He continues to project his line of analysis into a future that is now actually, rather than merely by literary convention, unknown to him. All this will become amply apparent, I think, when we turn now to examine the perils and the joys of writing the history of our own time.

V.

Is Contemporary History Real History?

WHEN I was a student, I had the strong impression that the writing and teaching of contemporary history were not quite respectable. It was rumored that in Europe a full century had to pass before a subject was considered ripe for historical treatment, and that the whole period since the French Revolution fell into the suspect category of the contemporary. Even in my own country, I noticed, the college courses which were labeled "since" a given date and hence presumably went right to the present, in fact stopped or petered out at least a decade before the year in which they were given. There always yawned a gap, of varying dimensions, between the date at which the formal study of history stopped and the onset of the individual age of reason when I had begun to read the current news with understanding. So far as I can tell, something of this situation still persists. I have found my students' knowledge at its vaguest on the period of their own childhood: Hitler today is scarcely more real than Attila the Hun. Since the recent past seems to the young just as alien as the remote past, I have concluded that there is no good reason for not treating it as equally historical, and I have labored to eliminate the gap of ignorance that so troubled my student years by bringing my own lectures abreast of the morning newspapers.

Yet still the doubts of an earlier day have never ceased bothering me. To many—perhaps to most—of my fellow historians the history of one's own time is not "real" history. It suffers from certain irremediable insufficiencies that make it less than history—current events, perhaps, or even political science, but not history in the usual meaning of the term. These presumed insufficiencies—of documentation, of perspective, and of detachment or "objectivity"—need to be examined with some care if I am to convince myself and others that all this time I have not been embarked on a fool's errand.

The most familiar charge leveled against contemporary history is that it cannot be written since we do not yet have "the documents." It would be foolish to deny the force of this reproach. The Soviet archives are closed to scholars and seem likely to remain so; how many other important repositories are under seal I would not care to estimate. No one will quarrel with the assertion that the historian who tries to write about the mid-twentieth century is laboring under handicaps he would not suffer if he were dealing with an earlier period.

I do not think, however, that this handicap is as great as it is commonly supposed to be. The stress on documentary insufficiency derives from a corresponding overestimation of the value of documents themselves—a point that I have repeatedly touched on earlier in these essays and that should now be explained more fully. Obviously it is impossible to write most types of history without documentation to go on. But we should not ask too much of written sources. "No document," E. H. Carr reminds us, "can tell us more than what the author of the document thought—what he thought had happened, what he thought ought to happen or would happen, or perhaps only what he wanted others to think he thought, or even only what he himself thought he thought."[1]

The cult of documents, like so much else in historical writing, can itself be explained historically. It goes back to the beginnings of systematic scholarship, when Catholic and Protestant divines tried to demolish each other's arguments by assailing the validity of old canonical texts, or discovering new ones, and it was reinforced in the first half of the nineteenth century when Leopold von Ranke based his seminar training on the systematic exploitation of documentary materials. Ranke's favorite sources were the *relazioni* of Venetian ambassadors—the wide-ranging reports of cool, experienced diplomats, surveying the international scene with the poise and skepticism befitting the representatives of a small state whose disproportionate influence reflected a cultivated finesse in manipulating the European balance of power. Such an attitude suited the temperament of a young historian sensitive to nuances of policy and character. Or perhaps the long-deceased Venetian ambassadors molded the historian's mind to conform to their own. *"Der Stoff brachte die Form mit sich"*—"the material imposed the form" of his history—Ranke unguardedly remarked, thereby admitting that he was allowing his sources to ride *him* rather than guiding *them* with a firm hand. Whatever the process, in the end there came to be a close fit between the historian and the materials with which he was working.

From this elective affinity derived a number of consequences of great importance to subsequent historical scholarship. First

[1] *What Is History?* (New York, 1961), p. 16.

there was the tendency we have already observed to view events with the eyes of a statesman, simply taking for granted the great-power system and the diplomatic status quo. Along with it went the further assumption that war and diplomacy were the historian's main business—what Ranke called the primacy of foreign policy—which even in our own country won general acceptance, thereby provoking in reaction the contemporary tendency to begin with internal policy and to deal with foreign affairs as the outward reflection of internal struggles. Still more, the tidy and finite character of diplomatic dispatches persuaded historians that other types of documentation were equally manageable. The less reflective jumped to the conclusion that in every field of historical investigation there existed a body of documents as clearly delimited as these; they forgot that on certain subjects—as for administrative history—the documentation might be overwhelming in its mass and heterogeneity, while elsewhere it might be almost nonexistent. Above all, the cult of documents tended to discourage direct observation: diplomacy, as a closed and semi-secret preserve, was almost the last place where the historian would have an opportunity to do his own field work. Here the Second World War had a most fortunate by-product. Quite a number of historians, both British and American, found themselves in foreign service, and the directness and reality of their writing on diplomatic history gained immeasurably by this wartime experience.

Even for past centuries, then, the historian's conventional assumption that there is such a thing as "the documents," readily identifiable and existing in finite quantity, breaks down on closer inspection. For our own era, it becomes a near absurdity. Since the invention of the typewriter and of the more modern and flashy forms of reproducing devices, the amount of administrative paper in circulation—of typed or dittoed or multilithed material that can lay claim to the dignity of official documentation—has passed all human bounds. At the other end of the scale, the habitual use of the long-distance telephone and the practice of airplane travel have effected an equally drastic reduction: when the great chat with each other over the transatlantic wire or go long journeys for a brief personal encounter, many of their most important exchanges may never be recorded. Gone are the days when a diplomat sitting at some distant post—conscious that he might not receive instructions for weeks or see his chief for years, and that his dispatches would necessarily be read under circumstances far different from those in which they were composed—was obliged to write with something of the historian's serenity and detachment. Today we have only the urgent message—or silence in the record. The result is a vast unevenness in what the historian has to work on, an *embarras de richesse* combined with and canceled out by the most distressing lacunae. The neat coverage of eighteenth- and nineteenth-century documentation has quite vanished. In some respects, the historian of today is in the happiest situation his breed has ever enjoyed. (Yet in this too-ample pasture the honest admit that they are reduced to selective grazing.) Elsewhere, the contemporary historian may be no better off than the medievalist struggling with an almost total documentary gap.

Let us agree, then—cheerfully rather than in despair—that for the mid-twentieth century there will never come a time when "the documents" are available. Yet this history must be written; the public demands it and has a right to demand it. If we do not do the job, others less qualified will undertake it for us. Nor is the idea of writing the history of one's own time as unconventional as certain of the manuals make it appear. Historians have always done it, even in the nineteenth century when the notion of its disreputability was first established. Still more, many of the works that we honor as the classics of our craft fall into this category. I shall have occasion to comment on some of them later on. Of course, their authors wrote without adequate documentation; of course, their conclusions have been substantially corrected by subsequent scholarship. But these works still stand—at the very least as literature and as monuments of human observation.

Perhaps that is all that the writing of contemporary history can accomplish. Yet it is already a great deal. Short on documents, certain to be superseded in detail, the historian of his own time can still produce a work of art which will illuminate for posterity the perceptions and the illusions of his contemporaries. That this is no mean feat will become amply apparent when we turn to the deeper and more troubling questions of perspective and objectivity.

By now nearly all of us have accepted Croce's dictum that the writing of history necessarily changes with the standpoint of the historian, that *all* history is contemporary in the sense that its presentation reflects the circumstances and attitudes of those who write it. Each generation writes history anew. There is no such thing as a "definitive" work of historical scholarship. Or, more precisely, if there are a few books whose authority has gone unquestioned for more than a generation, it is because the events with which they deal have been temporarily removed from current controversy, and historians have heard no urgent call to take a new look at them.

From this standpoint, the second major count against contemporary history—that is, "contemporary" in the usual sense of the term—the charge that we do not as yet have sufficient perspective upon it, simply falls to the ground. It is true that some minimum of time (perhaps only a matter of months) must elapse before we consciously begin to sort out the great events from the small. But this process of evaluation has actually been taking place in our minds all along. (We knew at the time that the crisis over Cuba in the spring of 1961 was a big event; what we did not know was that it would be dwarfed by a greater Cuban crisis a year and a half later.) There is no set point at which contemporary polemics cease and historical judgment takes over; the two proceed simultaneously, in the remote past as in the present.

In any ultimate sense, the best (or the worst) that the passage of time can do to contemporary events is to make them appear smaller, to reduce their image in the mirror of eternity. But this fate may not befall them right away; a number of generations or even centuries may go by before historical minutiae that once seemed of supreme importance fall into irrelevancy. When I was a student, we pursued the history of the French Revolution in meticulous detail; we were fully informed about all the shifts of party allegiance and ideological statement that punctuated the 1790's. Today, a generation later, these matters tend to be dealt with in a more summary fashion. The reason, I think, is again a change in collective experience. My student years were the 1930's—an era of passionate ideological involvement, the decade that in retrospect looks like the Indian summer of ideology itself before the very concept was swallowed up in the amorphous blandness of contemporary political exchange. Nowadays religion or social status may strike the students as more pressing matters for historical investigation, and old controversies that to my college generation seemed trivial and stale—like the points at issue between Luther and Calvin—may unexpectedly take on a burning urgency.

More closely regarded, then, the matter of historical perspective begins to blend with the third question and the most misunderstood of all, that of detachment or objectivity. To cite once more my student experience, I remember that at one time I really believed that the writer or teacher of history could and should attain to a sublime detachment. As the French put it, he should be above the *mêlée* of human events, delivering with sovereign confidence the "verdict of posterity." Since then an intense exposure to the ideas of Benedetto Croce has cured me of such notions: I have learned that the result of the historian's efforts to be detached has usually been the very opposite of what anyone would call great history. It has been bloodless history, with no clear focus, arising from antiquarian curiosity rather than from deep personal concern, and shot through with metaphysical and moral assumptions that are all the more insidious for being artfully concealed.

This does not mean that I—and others like me—have learned from Croce to write partisan history with a good conscience. Far from it: we detest mere polemic, and we certainly know how to distinguish between fine historical writing and writing designed to serve a cause. We recognize that historians have been right in striving for serenity and the world-embracing view. But we understand this aspiration in rather a different sense from the way in which it used to be taught to us. What we have learned from Croce and his like is that "objectivity" is to be valued only if it is hard-won—only if it is the end result of a desperate *and conscious* battle to rise above partisan passion. The man who does not feel issues deeply cannot write great history about them. Unaware of his own prejudices, he cannot bring them to full consciousness and thus transcend them, nor will his prose be infused with that quality of tension and excitement which comes from strong emotion just barely held under control. Only after he has mastered his own limitations can the historian begin to make constructive use of them. "Man's capacity to rise above his social and historical situation seems to be conditioned by the sensitivity with which he recognizes the extent of his involvement in it."[2] The origin of true historical curiosity, as we have just seen, is a sense of relevance for one's own time; and the criteria of such relevance derive from a passionate attachment to one's own moral and aesthetic values. With the gradual unfolding of knowledge, this passion is finally sublimated into something that can claim the dignity of historical judgment.

The same considerations apply to another and still more troubling aspect of the objectivity question—the matter of moral judgments. Acton, we recall, reproached Ranke for failing to condemn the crimes of the great historical personalities of times gone by. Yet Acton himself fell into the opposite error by scattering praise and blame wholesale throughout the centuries. Both, I think, misunderstood the real point; the real question was one of historical imagination, in which both Ranke and Acton were in their different ways equally defective. The former—as a sheltered scholar knowing nothing of war and violence—could not feel with sufficient intensity the sufferings of the victims whose execution he narrated so coolly. (I recall the shock I experienced when I suddenly realized during a tranquil reading of his *History of the Popes* that the saintly

[2] *Ibid.,* p. 54.

Counter-Reformation pontiff whose ecclesiastical house cleaning Ranke was implicitly endorsing was actually having heretics
burned at the stake!) Acton, in contrast, had little understanding for the agonizing dilemmas of statesmanship in eras when
cruelty was taken for granted and when killing might be the
only way to avoid being killed oneself. I do not think we have
to make a choice between these eminent examples; we are not
obliged either to declare our moral indifference or to hand out
moral judgments right and left. If we simply do our job *as
historians* with both conscientiousness and imagination, the
ethical issues will emerge clearly enough. Herbert Butterfield
puts it admirably:

The truth is that . . . we need no help from the historian to
bring us to the recognition of the criminality of religious persecution or wholesale massacre or the modern concentration camp or
the repression of dissident opinions. And those who do not recog-
nise that the killing and torturing of human beings is barbarity
will hardly be brought to that realisation by any labels and nick-
names that historians may attach to these things. There is one
way in which the historian may reinforce the initial moral judgment and thereby assist the cause of morality in general; and that
way lies directly within his province, for it entails merely describing, say, the massacre or the persecution, laying it out in
concrete detail, and giving the specification of what it means in
actuality. It is possible to say that one of the causes of moral indifference is precisely the failure to realise in an objective manner
and make vivid to oneself the terrible nature of crime and suffering; but those who are unmoved by the historical description will
not be stirred by any pontifical commentary that may be super-
added.[3]

[3] *History and Human Relations* (London, 1951), pp. 122–123.

Once more, the question of objectivity—of detachment—of moral judgment—proves to be no different whether it be the remote past or the recent present with which the historian is concerned. In the classic contrast between Ranke and Acton, the incompatibility of view remained the same both in their scholarly researches and in their comments on contemporary events. The specific point at issue was the Papacy in early modern times. But when the German historian wrote about the great powers of his own day, he endorsed the status quo with as much complacency as in swallowing the crimes of an earlier age, and when the English Catholic layman reported on the Vatican Council of 1870, he denounced the machinations of the Papal lobby with the same vigor with which he had exposed the cruelties of the Inquisition. For contemporary history and for history in the more conventional sense, the criteria and the limits of "objectivity" finally sift out as much alike. The historian can do no better than write with all honesty in the perspective his own irreducible values set for him. A conservative cannot help writing as a conservative, and a radical as a radical, and they should not feel obliged to apologize for so doing.

In both cases, the qualities of great history will emerge of themselves, whatever the specific ideological commitment of the author. I much prefer to read a book well done, but with whose assumptions I disagree, than a work based on values similar to mine which is technically or philosophically sloppy. Similarly, I think all great history has a built-in ambivalence. The historian adheres to his own ideological commitments—but another part of him understands and sympathizes with those of the enemy. The Protestant Ranke made a better case for the Popes than the Catholic Acton, and Francis Parkman, although he was convinced that the triumph of the British over the

French in North America was a good thing, could not help writing of Montcalm's death with admiration and sorrow. Here again the sublimation of the cruder passions has been at work: the historian's saving ambivalence has helped him to get beyond mere journalism or partisan polemic. The undercurrent of strong emotion remains: the urgency is still there. But through the sustained application of thought, what began as noisy controversy—whether in present or in past—has been almost miraculously transmuted into history.

"Thucydides, an Athenian, wrote the history of the war between the Peloponnesians and the Athenians, beginning at the moment that it broke out, and believing that it would be a great war, and more worthy of relation than any that had preceded it." Such is the opening sentence of the first and the most famous of contemporary histories. Two millennia later Thucydides' Italian emulator, Francesco Guicciardini, started his history on a similar note. "I have decided," he tells us, "to write down the things that happened within our memory in Italy, ever since French arms, called in by our own princes, began . . . to trouble the country." Not since the time of the Roman Empire, the historian explains, "had Italy ever enjoyed such prosperity nor experienced so desirable a state of affairs as that in which it reposed so securely in the year of our lord 1490."[4] Then came the death of Lorenzo de'Medici and the French invasions—and a generation later Italian liberty was no more.

The tone is arrestingly alike. Both Thucydides and Guicciardini had lived through the events they described; both had

[4] *Storia d'Italia*, Book I.

recognized the catastrophic character of these events while they were still going on and had felt an overwhelming compulsion to explain this significance to their contemporaries while the memory was fresh in people's minds. The defeat of Athens by Sparta was for Thucydides—as it is for us—the decisive turning point in Hellenic history. For Guicciardini the French invasions, by upsetting the delicate Italian political balance, relentlessly sapped Italy's European cultural hegemony—and here once again the researches of subsequent scholars have not altered the contemporary judgment. Both Thucydides and Guicciardini combined literary distinction with an astonishingly accurate sense of the importance of their subject matter. By general assent, their creations rank as *great* contemporary history—great in theme as in execution. And the historians themselves were well aware of the extent of their own achievement; they were possessed and borne aloft by the majesty of their theme. It is worth pausing a moment over these two men to see whether from their example we can derive some clearer idea of the criteria of great contemporary history through twenty-five hundred years of historical literature.

Neither Thucydides nor Guicciardini was merely an observer. Both had been involved in responsible positions in the events they described, and both had experienced the bitterness of defeat and disgrace. Thucydides had served as an Athenian general in the early part of the Peloponnesian War; Guicciardini was a diplomat and a member of the Florentine oligarchy which had only grudgingly accepted the return of the Medici under foreign protection. Indeed both were by nature and origin traditionalist oligarchs, with a distrust of the tyrannies and popular commotions that dominated their times. Hence their sense of defeat was threefold: their personal disappointment was compounded by grief at the humiliation of their city and their own social class.

They wrote their histories, then, with a serenity born of despair. Retired from active participation, without hope for the future, they felt the call to explain to their contemporaries how these great disappointments had come to pass. The result was a special kind of detachment, a recognition that the fault did not all lie on one side: the incompetence of the historian's own party had contributed to the outcome. Thucydides was sufficiently honest to concede the Spartans' military excellence and to expose unsparingly the Athenian fecklessness which had led to disaster at the Siege of Syracuse; Guicciardini finally settled for Medicean rule as the best guarantee of "good order" after Italians of his own type had demonstrated their political incapacity. Once more we find that the historian's personal ambivalence is central to his account: the wrong side has won, but the defeated, in seeking the explanation for their own misfortunes, cannot help recognizing the ways in which the victors proved their moral and technical superiors.

As we move down to the nineteenth century, we discover a corresponding succession of the politically or ideologically disappointed who find themselves driven by inner necessity to write the history of their own time. In France the roster of these *hommes politiques manqués* is particularly distinguished: Guizot, Tocqueville, Thiers are among them. In one or two cases, the experience of public eclipse proves only temporary: after two decades of opposition, the old liberal Thiers is triumphantly vindicated by the defeat of Napoleon III in 1870. At other times, as with Tocqueville, the disappointment is permanent, and life closes on a note of deep foreboding: the European herald of American democracy does not live to see the fall of tyranny in his own country. Yet the undercurrent of sentiment remains constant. These men know public events at firsthand; they have staked their all on politics and lost. And with this loss they have attained to an understanding that would not have been theirs had they celebrated a series of victories. With all men who have played a leading role in great events, the temptation to personal apologia may at any time become overpowering. But strange as it may sound, this temptation is the more insidious when the public figure in question does not have a failure to explain away. For here "history" does the job for him—the events themselves prove him right—and he is not obliged to make the same effort of understanding or to give his vanquished enemies their due. I doubt if De Gaulle would have written so impressive a set of memoirs if he had composed them in the flush of triumph in 1945 or in the euphoria of vindication after 1958 rather than in the lean years when all his hopes seemed in ruins.

Not all great contemporary history need sound this note of elegy. Nor does it have to be written by someone who has had a direct contact with large events. I think of these merely as a kind of optimum stance toward the material. But the tone of immediacy and urgency that characterizes all major historical writing has to come from somewhere. If it does not derive from close personal experience, then there must be a vicarious human encounter that performs the same emotional function.

If we trace the biographies of those who have chosen to be historians, we almost invariably come across an early experience that made a radical change in the individual's sense of the world around him—the shock of altered circumstance that

compelled him to ask the question why. A family move to a
new and exciting scene, the unexpected arrival of an exotic
personality, the brutal discovery of status or class difference,
the awakening of religious doubt—any one of these may give
the decisive push. In my own case, a trip to France at the age
of eight shattered my childhood securities. A fragile American
illusion of tidy protectedness collapsed before the revelation
of cruelty new and old, as the still-fresh trenches of the First
World War and the horror of the forts around Verdun blended
in my mind with the gray, threatening monuments of the
Middle Ages, the gloomy mass of the Mont-Saint-Michel enveloped in interminable rain, the dungeons, the torture chambers, the burning of Joan of Arc, who, so far as a child from
across the Atlantic could tell, had never done harm to anyone.

So this child, like all the other thousands of children before
him whom history had caught in its meshes, would not rest
until he had begun to inquire how such things could have
been. Historical vocations usually come early, although they
may not be recognized at the start for what they are. Once
the imagination has been stirred, the tormenting questions may
lie dormant for years until one day a lifetime commitment
declares itself without apparent preparation.

I remember a historian of the starchier professorial type
once declaring that it was a waste of time to teach history in
school because the boys and girls would get it all wrong and
would have to relearn it when they reached college. All they
would retain would be some unconnected personal anecdotes
and hero stories. I can scarcely imagine a judgment more mistaken. It is not a question of getting things "right"—not even
the most learned historian will succeed in doing *that* in any
ultimate meaning of the term. The real point is to stir the

youthful imagination. And for this purpose anything will serve, no matter how suspect it may be from the standpoint of strict historical accuracy. With the very young we teachers should discard our professional fastidiousness. If the historical vision is caught in childhood, the corrections can be applied later on. But if we hobble the child's first flights of fancy, this vision may be blotted out or never appear at all.

It is notorious that Sir Walter Scott was an inaccurate historical novelist. If there ever was an imaginative writer of repute who "got things all wrong," it was he. Yet his novels of chivalry and "derring-do" (even his vocabulary was phoney) cradled the fancy of generations of future historians. When we inquire into the boyhood of leading historical writers of the nineteenth century, it is instructive to find how often Sir Walter is at the start of things. In Ranke's case, the Waverley novels lit a bonfire that blazed on for eighty years. Today there must be other historical romances—doubtless much better "researched" than were Scott's—which are kindling the same wild flame. And a teacher of history would be greatly in error if he should inadvertently put it out.

The Greek stories of gods and heroes, the legends of King Arthur, the battles of our own Civil War—the games of running and hiding that children play in open fields or city streets —simply a chance occurrence may provide the decisive impulse to reflection. It matters little, so long as the historical imagination awakens. This, we have seen, is true of all history, not merely of the history of our own time. But in the context of the first decisive questions, contemporary history plays a crucial part. In the triad formed by the present instant, the recent past, and the remote experience of our ancestors, it is the second that links the other two. It is the one step back that enables the imagination to take the great leap to what is almost totally strange. In my own case, if I had not witnessed the blasted relics of the slaughter that had been raging when I was born, my tortured fancy might not have jumped so early to the riddle of medieval cruelty.

Whether child or adult, whether amateur lover of historical literature or professional scholar forever at his task of scrupulous documentation, the historian is obliged to reckon with his own time. He cannot escape it: its pressures are all around him. And if his trade has more than antiquarian meaning for him, he will feel impelled to comment on the recent past. For the same dilemmas of personal loyalty and ideal allegiance, of inborn ruthlessness and good will toward men, which have troubled his mind in his study of remote ages will force themselves upon him when he rests his weary eyes for a moment on the circumstances in which he is actually living. Marc Bloch the medievalist was inspired by his experience in 1940 as a staff officer of the reserve to write a little study of the fall of France. And the power of his account—the most convincing analysis of that great defeat I have ever read—derives precisely from the fact that the tragedy is seen through the eyes of a man who has traced with affectionate attention more than a millennium of his country's history and whose unutterable sorrow can be glimpsed behind every balanced phrase and reasoned historical judgment.[5]

In Europe it is not uncommon for historians to practice two specialties, an early, strictly professional field and the history of their own time. In the United States a mistaken overemphasis on academic rigor has led the average scholar to confine his efforts to a single area of historical knowledge. Most spe-

[5] *Strange Defeat,* translated by Gerard Hopkins (London, 1949).

cialists, protesting their lack of professional qualifications, shun the writing of contemporary history. But in so doing they leave the field to others who are still less qualified. Indeed, the specialist on some remote area of man's experience, like Bloch, may have a particular aptitude for the comparative understanding of the almost-yesterday, an understanding that may long lie unsuspected until the accident of personal involvement suddenly brings it to conscious expression.

Somebody must interpret our era to our contemporaries. Somebody must stake out the broad lines of social change and cultural restatement, and he must not be afraid to make predictions or chagrined at being occasionally caught out on a limb. There was a time when universally minded social thinkers performed this function, when the fathers of sociology, from Montesquieu through Marx to Weber, freely speculated on where their age was heading. Today, the sociologists, like the historians, have grown cautious. The chair of speculative social thought is nearly everywhere without an occupant. Historians have peculiar qualifications to fill it, and they are already beginning to do so. For the historian who sees no incompatibility between his different roles—who is at least as much an artist as he is a social scientist—is uniquely equipped to lead others toward the imaginative fusion of these attributes, and thereby to illuminate the era in which we live.

A DICTIONARY OF NATURAL RESOURCES
and their principal uses

2ND EDITION

A DICTIONARY OF
NATURAL RESOURCES
and their principal uses

BY

NORA JACKSON, L.C.P., F.R.G.S.
Deputy Head, Langley Secondary School, Langley, Bucks.

AND

PHILIP PENN
Head of Geography Department, Roxeth Manor Boys' School, Harrow

PERGAMON PRESS
OXFORD · LONDON · EDINBURGH · NEW YORK
TORONTO · SYDNEY · PARIS · BRAUNSCHWEIG

Pergamon Press Ltd., Headington Hill Hall, Oxford
4 & 5 Fitzroy Square, London W.1

Pergamon Press (Scotland) Ltd., 2 & 3 Teviot Place, Edinburgh 1

Pergamon Press Inc., Maxwell House,
Fairview Park, Elmsford, New York 10523

Pergamon of Canada Ltd., 207 Queen's Quay West, Toronto 1

Pergamon Press (Aust.) Pty. Ltd., 19a Boundary Street,
Rushcutters Bay, N.S.W. 2011, Australia

Pergamon Press S.A.R.L., 24 rue des Écoles, Paris 5ᵉ

Vieweg & Sohn GmbH, Burgplatz 1, Braunschweig

First edition 1966

Second edition 1969

Library of Congress Catalog Card No. 73-91463

Printed in Great Britain by the European Printing Company Bletchley Bucks.

HF
1041
.J28
1969

08 006625 9 (flexicover)
08 006626 7 (hard cover)

PREFACE

The book is set out, as the title indicates, on the lines of a dictionary—that is, it is arranged alphabetically. Under each natural resource listed there is a general description of that plant or tree or mineral, etc., and its uses. In the case of the more important resources, e.g. cotton, tea, rubber, there is also a description of the conditions of growth and climate. Great pains have been taken to ensure that the uses of the natural resources are as up to date as possible, bearing in mind that new uses for raw materials are being continually explored.

It can be stated with confidence that no natural resource in the world that is of any real commercial value has been omitted, and that therefore the ground covered by the book is very comprehensive.

The book is written at such a level that it will be of use as a standard work in any library, public school, university or home as a book of general reference and should prove invaluable as an adjunct in the classroom, not only in the subject of geography but in any subject, as a means of quick and easy reference.

LIST OF PLATES

A

Abaca *(Manila hemp)*. A vegetable fibre obtained from the leaf sheaths and leaf stems of a plant akin to the banana plant and plantain. This plant, native to the Philippines, has been introduced to other tropical areas such as Indonesia, India, Central America and the West Indies. The term Manila hemp is derived from the town of Manila in the Philippines. The best abaca is one of the strongest and hardest of fibres. Quality depends upon the part of the leaf stalk from which the fibre is obtained, and also upon the care exercised in separating the fibre from the waste material. Because of its resistance to salt water, abaca is of particular importance in the manufacture of ropes and cables, and especially marine cordage and hawsers. In addition, it is also used for making paper, hats, and mats. The stem consists of overlapping leaf sheaths and grows to a height of about 8-20 feet.

Absinthe. A scented and highly toxic green liqueur distilled from the bitter oil of wormwood, which contains a high percentage of alcohol.

Acacia. A genus of thorny trees and shrubs of the mimosa family, consisting of many species which are widely distributed throughout the tropical, sub-tropical, and warm temperate regions of the world, especially Australia and Africa. The bark of most species is a valuable source of tannin, especially the Australian and South African wattles. Additional products derived from certain species include gum arabic, dye, perfume and cabinet woods.

Agar *(Agar-agar)*. A jelly-like substance obtained from certain types of algae and seaweeds such as Ceylon moss. It is extracted by boiling the seaweed in water to dissolve the agar which afterwards sets as a jelly. Agar is used medicinally, and as a thickening agent in food, but its best-known use is as a culture medium for bacteria.

1

Agar-agar. *See* Agar.

Agate. A variety of quartz with striped or clouded colouring which occurs mainly in volcanic rocks. Agates are found in many parts of the world but most are produced commercially in the Americas and India. It is used in some fine instruments and as a semi-precious stone.

Agave. A genus of tall flowering plants, some species of which may grow to 40 feet in height. The tall flower stem grows from the centre of a cluster of thick, narrow, fleshy leaves. One species is the Maguey, or American aloe, which is native to Mexico and Central America, and it is from the fermented sap of this species that pulque, the national drink of Mexico, is made. The leaves of various agaves are an important source of fibre. Henequen and sisal are species of agave.

Alabaster. A semi-transparent form of white, pink or yellowish gypsum that has an appearance similar to marble, but is softer. It is a stone used for statues and ornaments. Deposits occur in the Midlands and south-west of England, and also in the region of Florence, Italy.

Alfa. *See* Esparto grass.

Alfalfa *(Lucerne, Purple Medick)*. This is a deep-rooted leguminous plant of great importance as a fodder crop in the form of pasturage, hay or silage. It can withstand heat and cold, and is a good crop in regions which suffer droughts because it has tap-roots up to 40 feet long which are able to find moisture when other plants would die off. Alfalfa is a very nutritious fodder and also very quick-growing, and when conditions are particularly favourable it may be possible to obtain 10 or more croppings in a single year. Most alfalfa is grown in Argentina, the U.S.A. and Canada.

Algae. A group of primitive plants without roots, stems or leaves but which contain chlorophyll, the green colouring substance of plants which converts carbon dioxide and water into carbohydrates. They are found all over the world in both fresh and salt water as pond scum and seaweed. Some marine algae are used in preparing certain foods such as blancmange, soup and ice-cream, and in the manufacture of silk, paper and cosmetics. *(See also* Agar.)

Alizarin. A vegetable colouring matter prepared from the roots of madder, various species of which are found in north-east Asia, India, north-west Europe and the U.S.A. Since ancient times it has been used to make red dyes, such as Turkey red.

Alkanet. A red dye obtained from the roots of a plant of the same name which is cultivated in parts of southern Europe and in the Levant.

Alligator pear. *See* Avocado.

Allspice. *See* Pimento.

Almandine. A deep red semi-precious transparent stone of the garnet family found in igneous rocks. It is used in jewellery and as the jewels in watches. Deposits are found in Switzerland and Alaska.

Almond. This tree is closely related to the peach tree and is believed to be native to Asia Minor. Today it is cultivated for its nuts in many other areas, including the western Mediterranean lands, California and Australia. Inedible bitter almonds are mainly important for their oil. Sweet almonds are eaten as nuts, or they may be used as flavouring in confectionery, cakes and trifles. Almond oil, which is extracted from both bitter and sweet almonds, is used as flavouring essence, in pharmacy, and in cosmetics. The tree usually reaches some 25 feet or more in height.

Aloes. A bitter purgative drug derived from the juice of the fleshy leaves of certain species of aloe, a plant related to the lily. There are about 200 species of this plant, most of which are native to the Cape Province of South Africa. The juice of some species is poisonous.

Aloeswood *(Eaglewood)*. The timber of a tree native to eastern Asia which yields resin, and oil used in perfumery and pharmacy. Not the same tree from which aloes is obtained.

Alpaca. It is an animal related to the camel and is domesticated in the high Andean regions of Peru and Chile. It is valuable for its wool, which grows up to 2 inches in length. Other similar South American animals are the llama, guanaco and vicuña. Alpaca cloth was originally made from alpaca, but it is now more of a trade term applied to cloth made from other fibres such as mohair and wool.

Alum. A mineral salt which is the double sulphate of alumina and potash. It is widely used industrially to give permanency to dyes, in tanning, in making paper and baking powders, and as an astringent.

Alumina. (Al_2O_3). This oxide of aluminium is the most abundant of all metallic oxides, making up 15% of the earth's crust. It occurs in clay, slate and shale, and as a hard crystalline mineral called corundum in the form of rubies, sapphires and emery, which is used as an abrasive. Alumina is an important source of aluminium.

Aluminium (Al). Next to oxygen and silicon, aluminium is the third most abundant element in the earth's surface rocks, and it has been estimated that approximately 8% of the earth's crust consists of aluminium, as against 5% of iron. Aluminium never occurs as a native metal, however, and its ultimate extraction is by means of electrolysis.

Bauxite is by far the most important aluminium ore. This is a hard clay-like rock, the leading producers of which are Jamaica, Surinam, the U.S.S.R., France, the U.S.A., Guyana, and Hungary. Alumina is another source of aluminium.

The chief advantages of aluminium are its lightness and its resistance to corrosion. It is relatively soft in its pure state but can be hardened by alloying with other minerals such as copper, manganese and zinc. Among the many uses of aluminium and its alloys are: in the construction of aircraft and cars, for kitchen utensils, storage tanks, piping, electrical equipment, wrapping for foodstuffs, in the building industry, castings, bridges, flooring and costume jewellery.

The leading producers of aluminium are the U.S.A., Canada, the U.S.S.R., France, West Germany and Norway,

Amber. A fossil resin varying in colour from yellow to brown which is found mainly along the southern coast of the Baltic Sea, especially in East Prussia. It has the property of becoming charged with electricity when rubbed with a soft cloth. It is used in jewellery, for cigarette holders and pipe-stems, and in the manufacture of hard varnish.

Ambergris. Literally grey amber. A greyish wax-like substance sometimes found floating in tropical or near-tropical seas, or cast up on tropical coasts. It may be found in small pieces of less than an ounce, or in large lumps weighing nearly a hundred-weight. Ambergris has a sweet sickly smell and it forms in the intestines of some sperm whales. Its main use is in the making of perfume.

Amboina wood. A very hard and finely marked wood obtained from certain East Indian trees, highly valued as a cabinet wood.

Amethyst. A bluish-violet semi-precious stone which is a variety of quartz. It occurs in many parts of the world and is used as a gem-stone in jewellery. It is a fairly widespread mineral, but gem-stones are rare, being found mainly in Brazil and the U.S.S.R.

Amianthus *(Amiantus)*. The finest type of asbestos containing long silky fibres which can be made into fabric; some of the best deposits are in the French Alps.

Amiantus. *See* Amianthus.

Anatta *(Annatto, Anatto, Arnatto)*. A bright orange colouring substance obtained from the pulp of the fruit of a tree which grows in the Caribbean lands. It is used for colouring butter and cheese and as a dye.

Anchovy pear. The plum-like fruit of a West Indian tree which is used in chutney.

Andalusite. *See* Sillimanite minerals.

Anet. *See* Dill.

Angelica. An aromatic herb used in cooking and medicine. An oil is derived from the fruit and roots of certain species of the angelica plant which grows in cool climates (Iceland and Faroe Isles). It is used as flavouring and in perfumes. The stalks and shoots are candied.

Angora. The long silky fibre of the fleece of the angora goat, native to Anatola, which is used in the manufacture of cloth and rugs. This fibre is also known as mohair. Owing to the demand for angora, the angora goat was introduced to other parts of the world and today South Africa is the leading producer of the fibre.

Angora wool, which is used for knitwear, is the long, very silky fibre obtained from the angora rabbit.

Angostura bark. The bark of a tree which grows in the Caribbean area and from which a bitter substance is extracted for medicinal use and as a flavouring essence (Angostura bitters).

Anhydrite. This mineral is anhydrous calcium sulphate, and is often found in association with salt and gypsum. Deposits occur at Stassfurt in Germany, and in the Billingham area of County Durham, England. It is important as a source of calcium, and also in the manufacture of fertilizer and sulphuric acid.

Anil. Indigo, a deep blue dye, is made from the stalks and leaves of this West Indian shrub, but it is now largely superseded by synthetic dyes.

Animé. Various resins, originally obtained from the courbaril or locust tree which grows in the West Indies and tropical South America. It is used in making varnish and perfume.

Aniseed. The seed of the anise plant which grows in parts of southern Europe and the eastern Mediterranean lands. The seeds are used whole or ground as flavouring. The aromatic oil, which is obtained by distillation, is used in medicine, as flavouring, and in making the liqueur anisette. Star-anise (Badian), a plant which grows in north-east China, is the usual source of the oil today.

Ankerite. A mineral similar to dolomite containing iron.

Annatto. *See* Anatta.

Anthracite. *See* Coal.

Antiar. A poison used medicinally and for tipping arrowheads which is obtained from the resin of the bark of the upas tree, related to the fig tree, which grows in Indonesia, especially in Java and nearby islands.

Antimony. (Sb). A hard, brittle, bluish-white metallic element obtained mainly from the ore stibnite or antimonite. It is obtained as a by-product when refining other metals. It is chiefly important as a hardening agent in the manufacture of alloys, in combination with tin, copper and especially lead. Such alloys are used in making printing type, solder, Britannia metal which is used for spoons, forks, and other tableware. "Babbit's metal" used for bearings, pewter, and cable sheathings. Antimony is also used in semiconductors, explosives and many industrial chemicals.

Most antimony ore is produced in China and the Republic of South Africa. Other important producing countries include Bolivia, Mexico, China and Korea.

Apatite. A phosphate-bearing mineral used in producing fertilizer. Deposits occur in many parts of the world, but especially in the U.S.A., Canada, Norway, the U.S.S.R., and North Africa.

Apple. This is the most extensively cultivated fruit of the temperate zones, and there are several thousand varieties which can be divided into three main groups: dessert apples, cooking apples and cider apples. They grow in a wide range of climate, but require a long dormant period and 100 frost-free days and a well-drained soil. The largest quantities of apples are produced in France, the U.S.A., and the U.S.S.R. which together produce well over 50% of the world crop. In the southern hemisphere Tasmania is one of the places important for the growing of apples. 80% of the world's apple crop is used as fresh fruit. (*See also* Crab apple). The hard, densely grained wood is used for tool handles and for general turnery.

Apricot. The stone fruit of a deciduous tree believed to be native

7

to China. The tree is now cultivated in many parts of the world, chiefly in warm temperate climates and especially in California, the Near East, the western Mediterranean countries, South Africa, and south-east Australia. The fruit may be dried or preserved, or eaten as a dessert fruit. The tree may reach about 25 feet in height.

Aquamarine. A transparent blue-green semi-precious stone which is a variety of beryl. It is valued as a gem-stone and is found in granitic rocks in numerous countries including Brazil, the U.S.S.R. and the U.S.A.

Aragonite. A mineral form of calcium carbonate named after Aragon in Spain where it was first discovered. It is the second most common form of calcium carbonate, and is found throughout the world.

Araroba *(Goa powder)*. A drug derived from a yellowish-brown powder found in the wood of a Brazilian tree which was introduced into Goa in India. It is used mainly for certain skin diseases.

Archil. A colouring substance obtained from certain species of lichens found on trees, rocks and some soils in Angola, Cape Verde Islands, southern India and Peru. It is used in producing a fast purple dye utilized for carpets and textiles. Unlike most vegetable dyes, it cannot be equalled by coal tar dyes.

Areca. *See* Betel nut.

Argentite. An important ore of silver occurring in Mexico and Nevada (Comstock lode).

Argil. A clay, especially that used in pottery.

Arnatto. *See* Anatta.

Arnica. A tincture used for sprains and bruises, derived from the flowers and roots of the mountain tobacco, a species of the arnica plant which grows in mountainous regions in Europe and North America.

Arracacha. A tropical South American plant with edible tubers.

Arrowroot. This term is used for the edible starch obtained from the underground stems or rhizomes of a number of tropical plants. True arrowroot, however, comes from a plant native to the West Indies and other Caribbean lands. Arrowroot is produced in both the East and West Indies, South Africa, Brazil, India and Australia, and because it is one of the most digestible forms of starch it is greatly used in food for children and invalids.

Arsenic (As). This is a widely distributed element which occurs in metallic form in the ores of lead, silver and nickel. Sweden, Mexico and France are the leading producers of white arsenic, the most important form. Considerable amounts of arsenic are recovered as a by-product from the soot which occurs in the smelting of mineral ores such as gold, copper and lead. Much arsenic, a strong poison, is used in the making of weedkillers and insecticides, and in addition it is employed in the manufacture of some alloys, wood preservatives, paint and medicine.

Artichoke. The term artichoke is used for three quite different vegetables.

The Chinese artichoke is a plant native to the Far East and its tubers, somewhat resembling radishes, are used in salads or are consumed boiled or fried.

The globe or common artichoke resembles a large thistle believed to be native to Asia. It grows wild in southern France, but it is also cultivated in France and other European countries, and in the U.S.A., especially California. The edible part of the plant is the fleshy base of the scales of the flower bud which is boiled. It requires a rich soil and a mild humid climate.

The Jerusalem artichoke is a plant native to North America which is similar to the sunflower. It develops potato-like tubers which are eaten by humans and animals.

Asafetida *(Asafoetida)*. An offensive gum resin obtained from the root latex of a plant of Iran and Afghanistan. It is esteemed as a condiment in some eastern countries, and in France. The plant grows to a height of about 5 to 6 feet.

Asafoetida. *See* Asafetida.

Asbestos. A group of minerals made up of fibrous material which can be separated easily into fibres that can be spun and woven, or felted into fabric. Asbestos is valuable industrially because of its heat-resisting property, and it is used in making fireproof material utilized for theatre curtains, fire-fighting suits, brake linings, paint and roofing cement. It is also employed as a heat insulator for covering boilers and pipes. About 60% of the world's asbestos comes from Canada. The U.S.S.R. and Rhodesia are the next largest producers.

Ash. The name given to a number of deciduous trees, not necessarily related, which grow in temperate climates. The European ash yields a hard durable timber used for handles of certain sports gear, axe shafts, ladders, wheelbarrows and other agricultural equipment. The trees reach a height of about 50–80 feet.

Asparagus. A perennial plant related to the lily and of which there are over 100 species, most of which grow wild, but certain varieties are cultivated as ornamental house plants.

Garden asparagus consists of several varieties which are cultivated for use as a vegetable which may be canned, frozen, or cooked fresh. Asparagus is grown on sandy soils in temperate climates, especially in Europe and North America, as a market garden crop. The plant develops from a root stock which may last for many years, and the thick young shoots are cut for use for 8–10 weeks in spring when between 6 and 8 inches in height.

Aspen. This is a deciduous tree related to the poplar which grows extensively in the deciduous forest regions of the north temperate zone. The bark yields tannin, and its light, soft timber is used in making paper pulp, pails, casks, and matchsticks. The tree may reach 100 feet in height but usually it is less than this. It is a quick growing tree, and the shoots are sometimes used as animal fodder.

Asphalt. A black or dark-brown substance containing bitumen found in solid or semi-solid form which has resulted through the partial evaporation of mineral oil. Deposits occur in many countries, including France, Italy, Switzerland and the U.S.A., but the best-known source is the pitch lake of Trinidad. This lake has a surface firm enough to support a light railway, but soft enough for the asphalt to be removed with a pick. The holes left by the removal of the asphalt are filled in within a few days due to the upward movement of the pitch. Asphalt is put to a variety of uses such as for surfacing roads, school-playgrounds and tennis courts, and in making waterproof flooring and roofing materials, sealing compounds and insulating material. It is also obtained as a by-product of the distillation of petroleum. (*See* Plate I.)

Ass. *See* Donkey.

Atropine. A poisonous alkaloid that occurs in certain plants such as Belladonna and Henbane. It is used medicinally, especially for eyes.

Aubergine. *See* Egg plant.

Autumn crocus. *See* Colchicum.

Ava. *See* Kava.

Avocado *(Alligator pear)*. The richly flavoured pear-shaped fruit with a large stone of a tree native to Mexico and Central America. It is eaten raw or cooked as a fruit, and is also used in salads. The tree is now cultivated in other semi-tropical parts of the world including South Africa, India, the East Indies and Australia.

Azurite. An important copper ore, often found in association with malachite.

B

Babool *(Babul)*. A species of acacia, the bark of which is used in India for tanning, and the leaves and pods as fodder for camels and goats.

Babul. *See* Babool.

BAEL FRUIT

Bael fruit *(Bel fruit, Bengal quince)*. The sweet fruit of a thorny tree which grows wild, or is cultivated in tropical Asia and Africa. The unripe fruit is sometimes dried for use as a cure for dysentery.

Bagasse *(Megasse)*. The fibrous residue which remains when sugarcane has been crushed to extract its juice. It is used as fuel in the furnaces in sugar plantations.

Balata. The milky fluid (latex) of the bully tree which is native to the West Indies and tropical South America. It is a substance similar to rubber and gutta percha but less elastic, although it is sometimes used as a substitute for them. Balata is also utilized in making machine-belting.

Balsa. A tree native to tropical South America. The wood, also known as corkwood, is the lightest commercial wood and is used for life-belts, as heat-insulating material, in aircraft construction, as shock absorbers, for scale models of aircraft and boats. The soft silky hairs which cover the seeds are utilized for padding cushions.

Balsam. The term applied to certain resins obtained from a number of different trees which grow in various parts of the world such as the East Indies, South America and the U.S.A. Balsam is a thick brown or black oily substance which is used medicinally, or in the making of perfume.

Bamboo. A type of grass consisting of many different species, some of which may grow to over 100 feet in height. It is a rapid-growing plant consisting of a long slender hollow-jointed woody stem, at the top of which grow clumps of narrow leaves. Different species are widely distributed throughout the tropics, and where conditions are favourable the plant will grow in sub-tropical and even temperate regions such as in central China, Japan and the U.S.A. Bamboo is put to a wide variety of uses, particularly in the Orient. The hollow stems are used for light constructional work, furniture, boat timbers and masts, umbrella handles, walking sticks, cages, and as a receptacle for containing liquids and cooking food, and when split they are used for chair seating and

Bamboo

basket work. The young shoots of bamboo may be cooked and eaten as a vegetable; the seeds of some species are used as grain; and the stem fluid is sometimes used medicinally.

Banana. The fruit of a large tree-like herbaceous plant, some varieties of which may grow to a height of 30 feet. It has a somewhat superficial resemblance to a palm tree. There are more than 100 varieties of the plant, which thrives best in hot damp climates where the temperature does not fall below 50°F, and it grows extensively throughout the tropics, both wild and cultivated, in the West Indies, especially Jamaica, Central America, tropical South America, Africa, the Canary Islands, India, Malaya and the Indonesia. The large leaves of the plant, which may be as much as 12 feet long and 2 feet wide, are utilized for thatching, and weaving into mats.

The banana is rich in starch and is one of the leading fruits of the world in the amounts produced. As a fruit for export it is picked green, shipped refrigerated, and then ripened artificially in the importing country. Certain varieties, some of which may grow to nearly 2 feet in length, are eaten cooked, others are dried and ground into flour, and are an important item of food in the areas in which they are grown.

The tropical plantain is a species of banana.

Bang. *See* Bhang.

Baobab *(Monkey-bread)*. A tree native to tropical Africa, the trunk of which may attain a diameter of 20-30 feet. The edible pulp of its gourd-like fruit is known as monkey-bread or sour gourd and is used for making a beverage. The fibres of the inner bark of the trunk are utilized in making cloth, paper and rope. Living trees are sometimes hollowed out to make houses. (*See* Plate II.)

Barilla. *See* Glasswort.

Barites. *See* Barytes.

Barium (Ba). A metallic element derived chiefly from barytes by electrolysis. In its metallic form it is used in the manufacture of radio vacuum tubes. Its compounds have various uses. Barium sulphate in milk is sometimes given as a "barium meal" to patients who are to be X-rayed, because it leaves a deposit upon the digestive tract which is opaque to X-rays. Lithopone is a mixture of barium sulphate and zinc sulphide which is used as a substitute for white lead paint, and as a filler for paint and rubber.

Bark cloth. This material is made from the inner bark of the branches of certain trees. The outer bark is removed and the inner bark is stripped off and soaked in water, after which it is beaten to remove unwanted substances and to render the bark supple. The making of bark cloth is confined mainly to tropical and sub-tropical regions, especially in Africa and the Pacific Islands, but its use is now dying out due to the increasing use of imported cotton fabric in its place.

Barley. One of the five most important cereals used for human food. It is a temperate cereal which grows to about 4 feet in height, and it is distinguishable from wheat by the long stiff bristles which project from the ear. In general, growing conditions for barley are similar to those required for wheat, and it is cultivated extensively in many areas where wheat is grown. Barley will thrive on soils that are too poor for wheat, however, and its 90-day growing season is shorter, and because of this it is grown further north than wheat, especially in north-west Europe, but the crop is restricted to drier conditions than those required for wheat.

Barley

There are many varieties of barley and it is especially important as a fattening food for cattle and pigs. Barley is of some importance as human food, but mainly in those areas which are too cold or too dry for wheat or rye, but it does not make good bread. Malting barley has to be of very high quality and it is used in brewing of beer, and for the distillation of whisky and industrial alcohol.

The leading barley-producing countries are the U.S.S.R., China and the U.S.A.

Barwood. *See* Cam-wood.

Barytes *(Barites).* This mineral (barium sulphate) is the chief source of barium. It occurs in veins in limestone, and in ores of other minerals such as lead and zinc. Barytes is utilized as a filler for paper, textiles and leather, and in the manufacture of paint, plastics and linoleum. The leading barytes-producing countries are the U.S.A., West Germany, Canada, Mexico, the U.S.S.R. and Yugoslavia.

Basil. An aromatic herb belonging to the mint family used as a seasoning for food. Basil oil is utilized in perfumery.

Bass *(Bast).* A fibre derived from the inner bark of certain trees, especially the lime or linden. It is used for matting, baskets, table mats, and by gardeners for tying up plants.

Basswood. The American lime or linden which grows mainly in the eastern half of the U.S.A. and particularly in the region of the Great Lakes. Its timber is utilized in joinery, in the car industry, and in making pianos and furniture. The tree reaches 80 feet in height.

Bast. *See* Bass.

Bastard saffron. *See* Safflower.

Batata. *See* Sweet potato.

Bauxite. The principal ore of aluminium.

Bay. A large evergreen shrub of the laurel family which is native to southern Europe. Its dried leaves are used for flavouring fish, meat, rice and soup.

Bay rum. An aromatic liquid used in perfumery and as a hair dressing. It is prepared from the volatile oil distilled from the leaves of the bay rum tree, which is native to the West Indies (bayberry tree), mixed with alcohol and other oils. It is the chief export of the Virgin Islands.

Bdellium. A gum-resin similar to myrrh which is derived from certain African and Asian trees. It is used in pharmacy.

Bean. The name given to certain leguminous plants and their kidney-shaped seeds, and also to the bean-like seeds of other plants such as the Calabar bean and the locust of the Carob tree.

There are many varieties of bean and they are grown widely throughout the world. They may be either climbing or bush plants.

Beans are used for both human and animal food and in some instances the pods are eaten as well as the seeds. Among the different varieties cultivated are the broad bean of Europe; the kidney bean, known also as the French or haricot bean; the scarlet runner bean, so-called on account of its scarlet coloured flowers, the pods of which are sliced together with the small seeds; and the lima bean, native to Peru, which is similar to the kidney bean, and is a variety particularly favoured in the U.S.A. Beans are cultivated in climates ranging from temperate to tropical.

The world's most important bean is the soy or soya bean which is a valuable source of vegetable oil. (*See also* Soya bean.) Other beans include the Cow pea and the Mung bean.

Bêche-de-mer *(Sea cucumber, Trepang)*. A variety of marine life (sea-slug) somewhat resembling a cucumber in shape. It varies in length from a few inches to as much as 4 feet, and is found in the seas in various parts of the world, but especially in East Indian and Californian waters and on the Great Barrier Reef off the coast of north-east Australia. Bêche-de-mer is dried for use in the making of soups greatly relished by the Chinese and other Asian people.

Beech. A deciduous tree which grows extensively in the temperate zone of Europe from Russia to Britain, and in some northern areas of the Near East. It yields a hard durable timber, which although not suitable for outdoor use, lends itself well to steam bending, and it is utilized for chairs, planes, and tool handles.

The timber of the American beech, which grows extensively in eastern U.S.A., is used for similar purposes. Stunted beeches serve as hedgerows but the tree usually reaches a height of some 100 feet.

Beechmast or beech nuts, the fruit of the beech tree, have long been used as a food for livestock such as pigs and poultry.

Beech-oil is derived from beechmast, and is suitable for lighting and cooking. In some parts of France it is used as a substitute for butter.

Beechmast. *See* Beech.

Beech-oil. *See* Beech.

Beef. This is the flesh of full-grown cattle, which is an important food with a high protein content. Beef cattle are raised throughout the world in climates ranging from cool temperate to tropical. The largest numbers of beef cattle are bred in the U.S.A., the U.S.S.R. and Argentina. The carcases may be exported frozen, or chilled, which keeps the meat in good condition and preserves its full flavour. Meat may also be canned or used for making meat extracts. The leading beef-exporting countries are Argentina, Australia, Uruguay and New Zealand.

Bees. A genus of insects that produce wax and collect and store honey. Also useful for the pollination of fruit trees.

Beeswax. This is the wax secreted by bees and used in the construction of their cells. Used for polish, ceremonial church candles, etc.; much of it comes from East Africa.

Beet. This is a root crop derived from a plant native to southern Europe. It is grown in temperate regions and there are four main varieties.

Beetroot, known also as garden beet, red beet, and table beet, is a garden vegetable that is globular or conical in shape, and is usually a dark purplish red in colour. It is cultivated extensively in vegetable gardens and as a market garden crop in Europe and North America.

Sugar-beet has a conical root and white flesh, and has the appearance of a large parsnip. It is of great commercial importance as a source of sugar, and the leaves and tops of the roots are used for feeding livestock. The largest amounts of sugar-beet are produced by the U.S.S.R., the U.S.A., Germany and France. (*See also* Sugar.)

Mangolds, or mangel-wurzels, are a large variety of root crop related to a beet which provide a succulent and highly nutritious food for livestock.

Leaf beet or Swiss chard is a variety of beet the leaves of which are used as a potherb.

Beetroot. *See* Beet.

Bel fruit. *See* Bael fruit.

Belladonna *(Deadly nightshade).* A perennial plant of the order Solanaceae that grows to a height of 4–5 feet, and is native to Europe and Asia. It is a poisonous plant but is cultivated for hyoscine and atropine which are prepared from the root and leaves. Atropine is used in ophthalmics.

Dwale is a drink prepared from belladonna.

Benares hemp. *See* Sunn hemp.

Bengal quince. *See* Bael fruit.

Benjamin. *See* Benzoin.

Bensoin. *See* Benzoin.

Bentonite. *See* Fuller's earth.

Benzoin *(Gum Benjamin, Bensoin).* An aromatic resin obtained from a tree native to Java and Sumatra, and other related species. It is used as incense, medicinally and in perfumary.

Bergamot oil. The oil derived from the rind of the bergamot, a citrus fruit similar to the orange and grown in Italy. It is utilized mainly in the making of perfume.

Beryl. This mineral consists mainly of beryllium aluminium silicate and is the chief source of beryllium. It is generally light green in colour, but it also occurs in other colours such as sea-green, blue, yellow and pink, and in some instances it may be colourless. Certain varieties are used as gemstones and these include the blue or sea-green aquamarine and the brilliant green emerald.

Mozambique and Brazil together produce approximately 40% of the world's common beryl. Other producing countries include South Africa, south-west Africa, Rhodesia and the U.S.A.

Beryllium. This is a silver-white metallic element which is derived chiefly from beryl. It is a very hard strong metal with a high melting point. It is used in the construction of aircraft, space vehicles and nuclear reactors, and for hardening copper; the alloy containing from 2 to $2\frac{1}{4}\%$ of beryllium is about six times as strong as ordinary copper. It is also alloyed with nickel.

Betel nut *(Areca).* This is the fruit of the betel or areca palm, a tree reaching 40–50 feet in height and widely cultivated in southern India, Ceylon and Malaya. The nut resembles a hen's egg in size and shape. Betel nuts are masticated by very many Eastern people on account of their stimulative properties, and for this purpose the nuts are cut into small strips which, together with a small amount of lime or cardamon added for flavouring, are wrapped in betel leaves, the leaves of the betel vine. The chewing of the nuts stimulates the saliva, which becomes stained a vivid red. Betel nuts are also a source of catechu.

Bhang. The name given to a variety of the hemp plant, and also to its dried shoots and leaves prepared as a narcotic for smoking. The dried leaves are also made into an intoxicating drink by steeping them in water and then straining it off. The use of bhang is most widespread among Hindus and Muslims, especially throughout the Indian sub-continent.

Bilberry *(Blaeberry or Whortleberry)*. A very dark blue edible berry that is the fruit of a low shrub that grows in moorland and woodland areas of cool temperate regions. It is used in cooking, and is the principal food of grouse. Similar berries are the blueberry and the cranberry.

Biotite. A common rock-forming mineral found in the form of dark, easily cleaved crystals belonging to the mica group. Generally it contains more impurities than mica and for this reason it is used mainly in the form of powder as a filling material. Biotite is widely distributed; workable sheets occur in Ontario, Canada.

Birch. A deciduous tree of the north temperate zone which grows extensively in the cool temperate regions of Asia, Europe and North America. It yields a strong hard timber utilized for numerous purposes such as for making chairs, brushes, spools and bobbins, plywood, furniture, panelling, agricultural implements and wood pulp.

The bark of some birches is used in making leather, boxes and other containers, and as a roofing material. North American Indians use birch bark in the making of canoes. Some species are merely shrubs while others may reach to 50–80 feet.

Bismuth. A hard, brittle, greyish or reddish-white metallic element which is derived chiefly as a by-product in the smelting of other metals such as copper, lead and gold. Bismuth is mainly used in making medicines and cosmetics, but in addition it is also utilized for the production of alloys with low melting points used for solders, fuses, metal toys and type metal, and in nuclear reactors. The chief producers of bismuth are Korea, China and Bolivia.

Bitter apple. *See* Colocynth.

Bitumen. A dark oily hydrocarbon widely distributed in the earth's surface rocks which occurs as asphalt, or which can be extracted by distillation from coal and petroleum. It is used in the surfacing of roads, and for making wood road blocks, waterproof paints and roofing materials.

Bituminous coal. *See* Coal.

Blackberry. The small edible soft fruit of the bramble, a thorny trailing bush of the rose family. Many species grow in cool temperate regions of the northern hemisphere. A number of varieties are cultivated, such as loganberries and boysenberries. Blackberries are used in cooking and for making jam and jelly.

Blackcurrant. *See* Currant.

Black diamond. *See* Carbonado.

Black lead. *See* Graphite.

Blende. *See* Sphalerite.

Blubber. The oily, fatty layer beneath the skin of whales and seals from which oil is obtained. (*See also* Whales.)

Blueberry. It is the edible fruit of a low shrub of the Ericaceae family, native to North America. It thrives on acid moist soils. It is similar to the British species, bilberry.

Boart. *See* Bort.

Bombay hemp. *See* Sunn hemp.

Bone. A by-product of the meat industry, bone provides a material utilized for a variety of purposes. Buttons and knife handles are made from solid bone; bone meal, used as a fertilizer and animal food, consists of ground bones; bone fat is used in making soap and candles; bone gelatin is a source of glue; bone charcoal is utilized in sugar refining, and bone ash is used both as a fertilizer and in the making of bone china. More primitive uses of bone include the making of fish-hooks, needles and harpoons.

Borage. A herb that has a rough stem and bright blue flowers. The young leaves are sometimes used in salads. It is cultivated as a honey plant for feeding bees as it is bee-fertilized. It is found in many parts of Europe and North America.

Borax. Sodium borate, or borax, is a white crystalline substance found naturally in volcanic regions, and in arid regions on the bed of evaporated salt lakes. Extensive deposits occur in the Western Cordillera of North America, and California is by far the largest producer.

Borax is put to a wide range of uses. It is utilized in the manufacture of glass and enamels, in metallurgy, for water softeners and for fertilizers.

Borecole. Scotch kale that is sometimes called cow-cabbage. The curly leaves are used as a winter vegetable.

Bornite. One of the chief sources of copper, being copper-iron sulphide. It comes chiefly from Utah, Nevada, Mexico, Chile and Katanga.

Bort *(Boart)*. Small, badly coloured impure diamonds utilized mainly as an abrasive. They occur in Brazil and in South Africa.

Boxwood. The wood of the box-tree which is widely distributed throughout Eurasia. It is a very hard, densely grained wood utilized for wood-engraving blocks, measuring rules, chessmen, musical instruments, inlaying and turnery. It is a small, slow-growing tree rarely exceeding 16 feet.

Boysenberry. A cultivated variety of blackberry.

Bramble. *See* Blackberry.

Bran. The outer covering or husk of cereals. It is used as a feed for livestock and for packing. As human food it is ground into meal and used either alone or mixed with flour to make brown bread.

Brassica. The genus of plants among which are included Brussels sprouts, broccoli, cabbage, cauliflower, kale, black mustard, rape and savoy. *(See also under individual names.)*

Brazilin. The yellow colouring matter which changes to red on contact with the air derived from Brazilwood, a dye-wood from a small tree which grows in Central and tropical South America and the West Indies. Brazilin is used in making dye and red ink.

Brazil nut. The edible seed of one of the tallest trees of the Amazon forest, which may reach over 150 feet; its triangular nuts are packed together in a hard globular fruit. To obtain the nuts for commercial purpose the fruit is opened with an axe. It has not been successfully produced outside Brazil.

Brazilwood. *See* Brazilin.

Breadfruit. The large melon-like fruit of a tree cultivated within the tropics, particularly in the South Pacific. It is unsuitable to be eaten uncooked. Its high starch content makes it a staple food of the Pacific. The wood of the tree is utilized for making canoes, and the fibres of the inner bark are made into cloth. The tree reaches some 40–60 feet. (*See* Plate III.)

Brick earth. A mixture of clay and sand or loam that is used for the manufacture of bricks and is found in the alluvial deposits near London. England.

British Columbian pine. *See* Douglas fir.

Broad bean. *See* Bean.

Broccoli. It is the name given to sprouting broccoli, and to a type of late cauliflower.

Brussels sprouts. A variety of cabbage.

Buckthorn. The common name for shrubs of the *Rhamnus* order native to the northern hemisphere. The berries of the common buckthorn are of medicinal value. The alder buckthorn is used as a cathartic and the wood is of value for charcoal making.

Buckwheat. This plant is not a cereal but is related to knott-grass and the dock. It is native to Central Asia, but today is cultivated on poor soils in Europe and North America. Buckwheat grows to between 2 and 3 feet in height, and its three-sided seeds or nuts are similar in appearance to beechmast. It is grown as a green forage crop, or as green manure for ploughing in to enrich the soil. Its seeds also are used for stock feed, and in addition they provide human food for which purpose they are ground into meal and consumed in the form of groats and pancakes.

Buff. A soft brownish-yellow leather originally made from the hides of buffalo, from which the name is derived, utilized in making military coats. The term is now used for leather prepared from the hides of other animals.

Buffalo. Large animal resembling an ox but larger and more powerful. The Indian buffalo is domesticated as a beast of burden and used in the cultivation of the rice fields. The water buffalo of the Philippines is a smaller species. The buffalo is also found in southern Europe and in Egypt. It is also the name given to the North American bison.

Buhrstone. *See* Burrstone.

Bulletrie. *See* Bully tree *and* Balata.

Bullet tree. *See* Bully tree *and* Balata.

Bully tree. *(Bulletrie, Bullet tree).* The name given to certain tropical trees which are the source of balata. *(See also* Balata.)

Burrstone. *(Buhrstone).* They are siliceous or siliceo-calcareous stones whose dressed surfaces present a keen cutting texture; they used to be used as mill-stones and still are, though to a much lesser extent. The best stones are found in the Paris basin.

Butter. A dairy product obtained from the fat of cow's milk. One-third of the world's milk is used for butter making. New Zealand and Denmark are the chief producers.

C

Cabbage Crops. These consist of a number of culinary vegetables such as the common cabbage, Brussels sprouts, cauliflower, and kale, which are believed to have been developed from the wild cabbage *(Brassica oleracea)* which is to be found growing in some coastal areas of Europe. Leaves, flowers, and stem are eaten in the different varieties.

Common cabbage consists of two main types, one having a conical-shaped head whilst the other is more spherical in shape.

The leaves may be eaten raw or cooked. Cabbage requires a mild, cool climate and is frost resistant. Different varieties of the plant such as winter cabbage and spring cabbage become ready for gathering at different seasons.

Red cabbage is similar to the round-head common cabbage but its red leaves are used mainly for pickling.

Savoys are also similar in shape to the common cabbage but the leaves are completely crinkled.

Brussels sprouts are small, cabbage-shaped heads which form in a manner somewhat like a cluster of large buds on the stem of the plant, beneath the crown of the leaves.

Cauliflower is a type of vegetable cultivated for its large white or yellowish flower-heads, contained within and at the base of the leaf cluster, which form the edible part of the plant. The name broccoli is sometimes given to a type of late cauliflower. Sprouting broccoli consists of a number of similar but smaller flower-heads which may be white, green or purple.

Kale is a larger plant than the common cabbage and grows to about 2 feet in height. It has large plain or curled leaves growing from a central stem. Borecale is a Scottish variety of kale, and collards an American one.

Kohlrabi develops a turnip-like bulbous swelling in its stem just above the ground. It is cultivated for stock feed.

Cabbage crops are cultivated for both animal and human food. As animal feed they may be used as fresh green food, or made into silage. In some instances the animals may be "folded" on the crop—that is, they are enclosed within hurdles and allowed to feed on a certain area of the crop as it is growing.

Cacao. *See* Cocoa.

Cacoon. The bean of a tropical climbing plant used medicinally.

Cadmium. A bluish-white metallic element derived mainly as a by-product in the processing of zinc ores. It is used for plating iron and steel to provide a rust-proof coating, and as a hardening agent in the manufacture of alloys, and especially with copper for electric transmission cables. It is also used for control rods in some nuclear reactors. The U.S.A., South Africa, Belgium and Canada are the chief sources of cadmium.

Caesium. A soft silvery white alkali metal that is used in the manufacture of vacuum flasks.

Cainito. *See* Star apple.

Cairngorm. A yellow or reddish semi-precious stone formed by quartz coloured by iron oxide or titanic acid. It is named after the mountains in Scotland where it is mainly found.

Cajeput oil. *See* Cajuput oil.

Cajuput oil *(Cajeput)*. A greenish oil distilled from the leaves of an East Indian tree that is used for medicinal purposes.

Calabar bean. The large seed of a tropical leguminous climbing plant native to Africa, especially West Africa, from where its name was derived. It yields a strong poison utilized in the preparation of drugs used for alleviating nervous and optical disorders.

Calabash. The name of a tree, or its melon-like fruit, or the hard shell of its fruit utilized for making bowls for holding liquids, and for pipes. The tree is native to the West Indies and tropical Africa.

Sweet calabash is the edible fruit of a variety of passion fruit.

Caladium. A tropical plant of America, related to the arum, possessing edible starchy roots.

Calamander *(Calaminder)*. A valuable cabinet wood similar to ebony derived from trees native to southern India and Ceylon.

Calaminder. *See* Calamander.

Calamine *(Zincspar)*. An important mineral from which zinc is obtained. It is used in the preparation of ointments and skin lotions.

Calcedony. *See* Chalcedony.

Calcite. Crystalline calcium carbonate, an important constituent mineral of chalk, limestone and marble. It occurs in various forms—for instance, Iceland spar and aragonite.

Calcium. A silvery coloured metallic element, the compounds of which are widely distributed in the form of chalk, limestone, gypsum, etc. It is the fifth most abundant element, but must be extracted from its compounds by electrolysis. Among its uses are the making of alloys, bleaches, pottery, paints, medicines and fertilizer.

Calf. *See* Veal.

Calumba. The root of an East African plant used medicinally.

Camel. The animal used as a beast of burden in Arabia, Central Asia, North Africa and India. It is an ungulate, being well adapted to desert travel because of the structure of its wide-spreading feet and its ability to travel for up to three days without water. There are two distinct varieties, the Arabian camel with one hump and the two-humped Bactrian camel of Asia. The flesh is edible, the milk can be drunk and the hair woven into a coarse cloth.

Camel's hair. It is used in the making of blankets and carpets often mixed with other fibres. Light-coloured hair comes from China, and strong, dark fibre from the U.S.S.R.

Camomile *(Chamomile)*. A plant related to the aster, the dried leaves and flowers of which are used medicinally in the form of a tea. Grows in western Europe. A volatile oil is produced from the flower-heads.

Campeachy wood. *See* Logwood.

Camphor. A vegetable oil possessing a strong odour which is distilled from the wood and leaves of certain trees, especially the camphor tree, a type of laurel, which grows in many parts of south-east Asia (China, Japan, Formosa). It is utilized for moth-proofing fabrics, in medicine and liniments, plastics and cosmetics.

Synthetic camphor is made from the oil of turpentine.

Cam-wood *(Barwood)*. A West African tree of the order Leguminosae, that yields a red dye. The wood is used for tool handles, and when first cut is white but turns red on exposure to the air.

Candleberry myrtle. *See* Myrtle wax.

Cane. The name given to the stems of certain plants of the grass family. The strong flexible rattan canes, used for chair seating, walking sticks, baskets and cricket bats, are obtained from Malayan and East Indian climbing plants. The stems vary in thickness from $\frac{1}{8}$ inch to 4 inches and from a few feet to over 200 feet in length. Sugar cane and bamboo are also canes.

Canella. A tropical tree from the inner bark of which a type of cinnamon is obtained.

Cannabin. A toxic resin derived from an Asiatic plant from which Indian hemp is obtained.

Cannel coal. *See* Coal.

Cantaloupe. A type of musk melon which derives its name from a town of Cantalupo near Rome in the district where the fruit was first cultivated in Europe.

Caoutchouc. The elastic gum of rubber trees.

Caper. The unopened flower bud of a Mediterranean shrub which is pickled for use in sauces.

Capsicum. *See* Pepper.

Caracul. *See* Karakul sheep.

Carapa tree. A vegetable fat used in making soap. It is obtained from the kernels of the Carapa tree which is widely distributed throughout the tropics and is of a lofty height.

Caraway. This is a spicy aromatic fruit of a plant which grows in temperate climates in many parts of the world. The seeds, and the oil obtained from them by distillation, are used as flavouring in cakes, cheese, confectionery, and in making liqueurs and medicine. The plant is cultivated in Europe, especially in Holland, and also in Morocco.

Carbon. A non-metallic element widely distributed in many forms in animals, vegetation and minerals. It is present in coal, charcoal and petroleum. Diamonds and graphite are carbon in its purest form.

Carbonado. A very hard, dark, impure form of diamond, known also as black diamond, which is produced in the state of Bahia in Brazil. It is used as an abrasive and for diamond set drills.

Cardamon. This is a sweet flavoured spice derived from the seeds of a reed-like plant related to the ginger plant, and is used especially in the East as a condiment, in making curry powder, and for flavouring medicine. The seeds may be gathered from both wild and cultivated plants. There are a number of varieties of this plant, but the best cardamon comes from those grown in southern India and Ceylon, the chief producing countries.

Cardoon *(Chardoon)*. A thistle-like plant with edible stalks or chard which is native to Mediterranean countries. It is related to the artichoke.

Carmine. The crimson pigment obtained from the dried bodies of the cochineal insects of South America and Mexico. It is used in cosmetics and in making water colours.

Carnauba. A tall South American palm tree which has its leaves coated with small waxy scales that yield a pale yellow wax when boiled. This wax is used in shoe polishes and in car polishes.

Carnelian. *See* Cornelian.

Carnotite. A mineral which is one of the sources of uranium, radium and vanadium. It occurs as a yellow impregnation of sandstones in Colorado, Utah, Canada and the Caucasus Mountains.

Carob. *See* Locust tree.

Carrageen *(Carragheen, Irish moss)*. This is a type of edible seaweed utilized as a thickening agent. It is common to the seas around the British Isles and derives its name from a town in southeast Ireland.

Carrot. A root vegetable related to the parsnip and parsley and developed from the wild carrot which grows extensively in many parts of Europe. There are a number of varieties which develop small spherical- or long conical-shaped white, yellow, or orange roots. Carrots are a valuable and nutritious food for both humans and animals, and they may be cultivated as a garden or field crop. They require a deep rich soil and a cool temperate climate.

Carthamin. *See* Safflower.

Cascara sagrada. A laxative and tonic prepared from the dried bark of certain trees of the American Pacific coast.

Cashew. It ranges from a shrub in dry tropical regions to a tree 30–40 feet in height in humid areas. The tree is grown in the West Indies and in Central and South America for the sake of its nuts which are eaten raw or roasted. The wood and gum are also used.

Cashmere. The undercoat of the Kashmir goat, used as a fine textile fibre.

Cashoo. *See* Catechu.

Cassareep *(Cassaripe)*. The juice of the bitter cassava which is used in the preparation of sauces.

Cassaripe. *See* Cassareep.

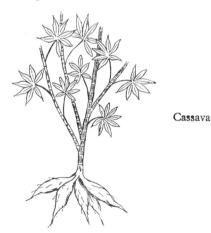

Cassava

Cassava *(Manioc, Mendioca)*. A tropical plant which grows from 5 to 9 feet in height. It is extensively cultivated in tropical South America, the West African coastlands and the Malay Archipelago.

The tubers of cassava may grow up to 3 feet in length and to 9 inches in diameter. There are two varieties of the plant, bitter and sweet, the former being the most important. The sap of the root of the bitter variety is poisonous, but after the extraction of the poison the tubers are ground into a meal, the starch content of the roots is extracted and it is from this substance that tapioca is made.

Cassia. *See* Cinnamon.

Cassiterite *(Tinstone)*. This mineral is the chief source of tin, and is worked in Malaya, Indonesia, Bolivia and Nigeria.

Castor oil. An important vegetable oil derived from the large seeds of a plant widely cultivated throughout the tropics, especially India and Brazil. This plant is also grown in some warm temperate countries. The oil is used medicinally, and in the production of Turkey-red dye, paint, varnish, plastics and cosmetics.

Catechu *(Cutch, Cashoo)*. Black catechu or cutch is extracted from the wood of two species of Indian acacia, and is used in medicine as an astringent, and as a source of dye and tannin. White catechu is obtained from some East Indian plants. A similar product is derived from betel nuts and certain mangrove barks. The tree is stripped of bark, which is split into small pieces and then boiled in water in order to obtain the catechu.

Cattle. Cattle are reared for their meat (*see* Beef), their milk, and for use as a draught animal. There are two main types of cattle: the European that are found in the temperate regions, and of which there are many breeds, and the hump-backed or Zebu cattle of tropical regions. The largest cattle population is in India, followed by the U.S.A., the U.S.S.R., Brazil, Argentina, Pakistan and China. From milk, dairy products (butter, cream and cheese) are obtained. The skin or hide is tanned into leather; the hair is used in making brushes and for upholstery; the ground bones and dried blood are made into fertilizers and animal food; glue is produced from the hoofs, and bone for knife handles from the horns.

Cauliflower. *See* Cabbage crops.

Cava. *See* Kava.

Cayenne. *See* Pepper.

Cedar-wood. The fragrant timbers of a wide variety of evergreen trees used for cabinet making, pencils and cigar-boxes. The cedar of Lebanon reaches some 50–80 feet while the Deodar is not quite so tall. The term cedar may be applied somewhat loosely to junipers, cypress, red cedar, white cedar, and others.

Celeriac. *See* Celery.

Celery. A plant of the order Umbelliferae which is cultivated for its succulent leaf stalks eaten in salads or cooked as a vegetable. A special variety known as celeriac is grown for its swollen root rather than for its stalks. The seeds may also be used as a culinary herb.

Celestite. This mineral, strontium sulphate, is a source of strontium. It is also used in sugar beet refining, and in the manufacture of fireworks.

Cellulose. The main substance of which the cell walls of many plants are composed. It is of special importance in the manufacture of paper, plastics and synthetic fibres. The main sources of industrial cellulose are cotton and wood.

Cereals. Grain crops such as wheat, oats, barley and rice, which have edible starchy seeds, that have been derived from cultivated grasses. (*See also under individual headings:* wheat, rice, etc.)

Cerite. *See* Cerium.

Cerium (Ce). This is a rare earth metal occurring in the minerals monazite and cerite. At one time it was greatly used in the making of gas mantles, but today its chief uses are in the iron and steel industry, in the manufacture of light alloys, one of which is used for the flints of gas and pocket lighters.

Cerussite. This mineral, lead carbonate, is an important lead ore, and occurs at Leadville, Colorado.

Chalcedony *(Calcedony).* A white or bluish-white gem-stone of similar nature to quartz which occurs in volcanic rocks. Workable deposits are found in Northern Ireland, Iceland and the Deccan of India. Coloured varieties are agate, carnelian, onyx and crysoprase.

Chalcocite. Copper sulphide, the second most important source of copper, usually found in association with bornite.

Chalcopyrite *(Copper pyrites).* A copper ore, of the greatest importance. Deposits in South Africa and the U.S.A. of this copper iron sulphide.

Chalk. A pure, white or greyish limestone consisting mainly of the shell fragments of minute marine life which existed during the Cretaceous period. Chalk contains a very high percentage of calcium carbonate in the form of calcite. It is used in making putty, writing chalks, Portland cement, lime, and fertilizer. Extensive deposits are found in southern England, and in the Mississippi valley.

Chalybite. *See* Siderite.

Chamois leather. A very soft, pliable leather which derives its name from the small, goat-like chamois antelope found in the mountainous regions of south and central Europe and south-west Asia. The hides of these animals were the original source of chamois leather, but the term is now applied to similar leather obtained from other animals (e.g. sheep and goats). It is used for bookbindings, gloves, window leathers, and for purse linings and pockets.

Chamomile. *See* Camomile.

Charcoal. An impure form of carbon derived from charred vegetable and animal substances such as wood and bone. It is used as a drawing material, for fuel, as a filter for purifying water, and as a decolorizing agent in sugar refining.

Chard, Swiss. *See* Beet.

Chardoon. *See* Cardoon.

Chay root *(Choy root, Shaya root).* The root of an Indian plant of the madder species used in making a red dye.

Cheese. A dairy product made from milk curds. It is widely used as a food. 20% of the world's milk production is used for cheese making. The chief producers are the U.S.A., Italy, France, New Zealand and Holland.

Cherimoya *(Cherimoyer).* A sub-tropical fruit similar to the custard apple. It is known also as the Peruvian custard apple on account of its origin, but now it is cultivated in many other parts of the world including Central America and the West Indies, California, around the Mediterranean, and in parts of Africa and India. It is a large, soft, pleasant-tasting fruit which may weigh over 5 lb and the tree itself may reach 20 feet.

Cherry. The small stoned fruit of the cherry tree, numerous varieties of which may be found wild or cultivated over many areas of the North Temperate Zone. There are two main species of cultivated cherry, sweet and sour. Sweet cherries are consumed mainly as a dessert fruit. Sour cherries are usually canned, bottled, or frozen, for use in cooking. Cherry brandy, Kirschwasser and Maraschino are cherry liqueurs. The leading producers of cherries are the U.S.A. and Germany.

Chervil. The name given to several plants of the Umbelliferae order which are cultivated to a small extent in southern Europe for the sake of the pungent-flavoured leaves which are used in salads and soups.

Chestnut. The edible fruit or seed of the sweet chestnut tree which is contained within a prickly outer husk. Chestnuts are used for both human and animal food and they may be eaten raw, boiled, or roasted, or alternatively they are ground into meal which is used as a substitute for cereal flour.

The timber of the chestnut tree resembles that of the oak and it is used for constructional work, telegraph poles, fencing posts and pit-props. The bark yields tannin. There are four main species: European, American, Japanese and Chinese. The tree grows to a height of 60–100 feet with a diameter of 3–12 feet according to the species.

Chica. An orange-red pigment derived from the leaves of a tropical South American climbing plant.

Chickens. *See* Poultry,

Chick-pea *(Gram)*. A dwarf variety of pea cultivated in warm climates, and especially in India. Used to make a porridge.

Chicle. This is obtained from the sapodilla plum, and was originally used as a rubber substitute, and later for chewing gum. The chief producers are Yucatan and Guatemala, but chicle is now largely superseded by synthetic materials.

Chicory. This is a plant related to the lettuce and of which there are both wild and cultivated varieties. It is grown quite extensively in north-west Europe, some varieties being cultivated as a fodder crop whilst others are produced as a salad crop or vegetable. Magdeburg chicory is especially grown for its roots which, when roasted and ground, provide the chicory that is sometimes blended with coffee. Chicory as a salad vegetable is grown widely in Belgium. In America chicory is known as endive.

Chile saltpetre. *See* Nitrates, Sodium.

Chili. *See* Pepper.

China clay *(Kaolin)*. A fine soft white powder which results from the decomposition of felspar in granite, brought about by ascending hot vapours or by water percolating down from the surface. The term kaolin is Chinese in origin and is derived from the word Kau-ling, a hill-ridge in China reputed to be the original source of the first china clay introduced into Europe.

Today most china clay is produced in the U.S.A., especially in the south-east, but extensive deposits of purer clay occur in Devon and Cornwall, making Britain the second largest producer.

China clay is utilized in the making of china and porcelain, cosmetics, paint and kaolin poultice, and as a filler in the manufacture of paper, rubber and textiles.

China grass. *See* Ramie.

Chinese wood oil. *See* Tung oil.

Chives. A herb of the onion family, used as a culinary flavouring.

Choy root. *See* Chay root.

Chromite. *See* Chromium.

Chromium (Cr). A very hard, whitish metallic element derived mainly from the ore chromite. It is most used in steel manufacture as a hardening agent and for producing stainless steels, but in addition it is utilized for electro-plating nickel to provide a hard, shiny, non-tarnishable coating; in dyeing and tanning; and in the manufacture of green, red and yellow paints.

The largest producers of chromium ore are the U.S.S.R., the Republic of South Africa, the Philippines, Rhodesia and Turkey.

Chrysolite. A gem-stone composed of magnesium and iron silicate of a yellowish-green colour; it is used in jewellery.

Chrysoprase. A variety of chalcedony coloured by nickel oxide to a greenish colour. Used for ornaments and in jewellery.

Cimolite. A white clay used in the manner of fuller's earth as a decolorizing agent.

Cinchona *(Peruvian bark)*. A genus of trees of the order Rubiaceae consisting of several species, some of which grow to over 80 feet. They are native to the tropical belt of the South American Andes where they grow at between 5000 and 8000 feet above sea-level. The bark of some species is the source of quinine, a substance that tends to reduce the high temperature in the human body and is therefore widely used in combating malaria, as well as for colds and influenza. Most of the world's quinine comes from the cinchona plantations of Java.

Cinnabar. This mineral, mercuric sulphide, is the chief ore of mercury, and is found in Spain, Yugoslavia and Italy.

Cinnamon. This widely used spice is obtained from an evergreen tropical shrub related to the laurel. It is made from the inner bark of the shrub which is dried and then rolled into sticks. Although used mainly as a sweet flavouring, it is also used in pharmacy and in the making of incense. The principal source of cinnamon is Ceylon but it is also produced in southern India and in both the West Indies and Indonesia.

Cassia, or Chinese cinnamon, is an inferior quality cinnamon. Canella is a tree yielding a type of cinnamon.

Citron. An oval-shaped edible citrus fruit with a thick yellow peel that has a pleasant flavour when candied.

Citronella. One of the essential oils in large supply used in the manufacture of perfume. It comes from the tropical citronella grass. It is also used in the treatment of mosquito bites.

Citrus fruits. These flourish in areas of Mediterranean climate. The fruits contain a soft yellow or orange pulp with a similar coloured rind or peel on the outside. They are edible and used in marmalades and soft drinks. (*See also under individual names,* e.g. Orange, Grapefruit, Lemon, Citron, Tangerine, etc.)

Clay. A fine-grained sedimentary material formed from the sediments produced from the weathering of rocks, and of which there are numerous kinds. Suitable clays are used in making bricks, tiles and earthenware. (*See also* China clay.)

Clementine. A small orange citrus fruit.

Clover. A leguminous plant of the cool temperate regions of the world which provides a rich animal feed as pasture, hay or silage. The distinctive characteristic of the clover plant is its leaf pattern of three small leaves growing at the end of a single stalk. There are well over 200 different species of clover but the most widely cultivated are the red and white flowering varieties. Clover may be grown on its own or mixed with grasses and other plants.

Cloves. These are the dried, unopened flower-buds of an evergreen tree native to the Moluccas in Indonesia. Used for flavouring various foods and also possess medicinal properties. The tree was introduced to other islands within the tropics, and today production is concentrated almost entirely on the East African islands of Zanzibar and Pemba, which produce nearly three-

COAL

Cloves

quarters of the world's cloves, and the Malagasy Republic. The tree grows to some 40 feet.

Coal. Coal is the main source from which man derives energy. It consists chiefly of carbon and was formed from the remains of vegetable matter, especially wood, which in the main existed in the Carboniferous period over 200 million years ago. Some coals, however, were laid down at a later period during the Tertiary era, but these are nearly all low rank coals, a classification depending upon various factors which determine the heat value of the coal. There are three main groups of coal.

Anthracite is a very hard, black, shiny coal with a high carbon content (over 90%). It gives off great heat, yields little ash, is smokeless, but is difficult to ignite. The most extensive known deposits of anthracite occur in the north-east of the Appalachian coalfield in the U.S.A. Other deposits occur in the South Wales field in Britain, the Donetz field in the U.S.S.R., and in the province of Shansi in northern China.

Bituminous or humic coal has a carbon content ranging from below 50% to over 80% according to whether it is of low, medium or high rank. Included in this group are household and cannel coals which are burnt in open grates, steam coals and coking coals. A wide range of products is derived from bituminous coal when it is carbonized, which consists of heating the coal in airless chambers. Among these products are coke, gas, and coal tar which is processed in a number of ways to produce tar, light oil, naphthalene, drugs, perfumes, disinfectants, dyes, creosote and phenols.

Lignite and brown coal are of similar nature. They are low rank coals which give off considerably less heat than anthracite and bituminous coal but they are of great value in some countries for the production of thermal electricity.

The leading producing countries of high rank coal are the U.S.A., the U.S.S.R., Britain, China, West Germany and Poland.

Cobalt (Co). A metallic element widely distributed within the surface rocks of the Earth, but only in very small quantities. Most cobalt is derived as a by-product of other mineral ores such as copper, silver, nickel and manganese, and nearly 50% of the world's cobalt comes from the copper belt of Katanga. The other leading producers are Zambia, Canada, the U.S.A., New Caledonia and Morocco. Cobalt is chiefly utilized for the manufacture of hard rust-resisting steels used for high-speed tools, safety-razor blades, permanent magnets, jet-engine and other engine parts, and electroplating. It is also alloyed with other minerals, and in addition cobalt is used as a colouring agent in the making of glass, pottery and paint.

Cobaltite. A silvery white mineral with a brilliant lustre; it is mined in Scandinavia and used in the making of jewellery and ornaments.

Cobnut. *See* Hazel.

Cocaine. *See* Coca leaves.

Coca leaves *(Cuca)*. These are the leaves of a shrub native to Peru and Bolivia, which is now cultivated in Java, India and Ceylon. The leaves are the source of the pain-relieving drug cocaine, used as a local anaesthetic in minor operations. The shrub may be 8 feet high.

Chewing coca leaves is an old-established habit among the Andean Indians, due to the property the leaves possess which gives the chewer a remarkable resistance to both mental and physical fatigue, as well as a sense of happiness and well-being.

Cochineal. A bright scarlet dye-stuff used for colouring cakes, icing and other confections. It is also used in the preparation of scarlet, crimson and orange pigments. Cochineal is prepared from the dried powdered bodies of the female cochineal insect which feeds on certain species of cactus. The insect is native to the area extending from Mexico to Peru, but it has been introduced to other areas, notably north-west Africa and southern Spain, together with the cactus upon which it feeds. The demand for cochineal has declined considerably due to the substitution of aniline dyes.

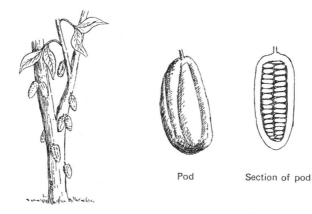

Pod   Section of pod

Cacao (Cocoa)

Cocoa *(Cacao)*. The cacao tree is the source of cocoa and chocolate. This is a tropical plant believed to be native to the Amazon Basin, and cocoa as a beverage was originally introduced into Europe from Mexico by the Spanish in the 16th century.

The tree is cultivated in many coastal areas within about 20° north and south of the equator, but the chief producing countries are Ghana, Brazil and Nigeria, which together produce more than two-thirds of the world's total supplies. Other producers include West Africa, Cameroons, Dominican Republic, Trinidad, Ecuador and Venezuela. The tree may grow to 40 feet but is pruned to 20 feet.

Requirements for the growth of the tree are a deep, rich, well-drained soil; high average temperatures (over 70°F) throughout the year, but with shade to give protection from the direct rays of the sun; a well distributed annual rainfall of over 50 inches, and an absence of strong winds which might break off the heavy seed-bearing pods.

The pods grow to about 10 inches in length and may contain as many as 50 seeds or beans. The ripe pods are cut from the trees and the beans are extracted and dried in the sun. The beans are ground to make cocoa, and a by-product is cocoa butter. Chocolate contains a higher percentage of cocoa butter than cocoa. Cocoa and chocolate are used for confectionery and drinks. (*See* Plate IV.)

Coco de mer. This is often known as the double coconut, and is native to the Seychelles. The edible fruit is very large and takes 10 years to ripen.

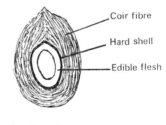

Section through a coconut

Coconut palm

Coconut. This is the fruit of the coco or coconut palm, a tree which may grow to 100 feet in height, and which is widely distributed along coastal margins throughout the tropics. The tree grows wild and is also cultivated in plantations or groves. Its fruit or nuts develop in clusters of between 10 and 20. The fruit may measure over 15 inches in length and up to 8 inches in diameter, and it consists of a thick outer layer of coarse fibre known as coir which serves to protect the coconut, within which is a very hard woody shell containing the edible white fleshy part of the nut, and this in turn serves as a container for the so-called coconut milk.

The coconut is particularly useful to man. The coarse fibre, or coir, is utilized for making door mats, matting, rope, bristles for brooms and brushes, and for upholstery, and the coir dust is used as a packing material, in making compost, and as a surface dressing in bulb culture. The hard inner shell is used for fuel, and in making charcoal, and drinking bowls.

The white edible flesh of the coconut is an important item of food to some of the inhabitants of tropical lands, but its greatest commercial value is in the oil it contains. When the flesh is dried it is known as copra, the form in which it is exported, and from which nearly two-thirds of its weight can be extracted as oil. (*See also* Vegetable oils.) The leading producers of copra are the Philippines and Indonesia. When the oil has been extracted the residue pulp is known as poonac and is used in making a rich cattle food called cattle cake. Desiccated coconut, used in cakes and confectionery, is the shredded nut flesh which is prepared from the best nuts.

The coconut palm itself is a most useful tree. Its timber is used in building houses, for furniture, for carving and as fuel. The roots are also used as fuel, are a source of an antiseptic lotion, and in addition when dried and ground the resultant powder is used for cleaning the teeth. An intoxicating beverage from which spirit can be distilled is produced from the sap. The leaves are utilized for thatching and in making mats and baskets, and brooms and fish traps are made from the mid-ribs. (*See* Plate V.)

Cod. *See* Fish.

Coffee. Although South America produces more than half the world's coffee today, the two most important types are the Abyssinia which originated in the cooler highland region of Abyssinia (Ethiopia), and the Robusta from western Africa, which is a much hardier type. Altogether there are some 20 species. Untended the coffee tree will reach 20 feet but it is

Coffee

pruned down to 10 feet on plantations in order to facilitate picking. It needs for cultivation a rich well-drained soil, a climate free from frost with moderate temperatures all the year round (between 65°F and 75°F is the most favourable), an annual rainfall of not less than 40 inches a year (over 70 inches produces the best yields) and a plentiful supply of labour for harvesting. The most favourable areas for cultivation are within the tropics, but to avoid excessive heat plantations are usually established between 1200 feet and 6000 feet above sea-level. Mocha coffee, one of the best varieties, comes from Yemen in Arabia.

Two coffee beans come from each fruit, which is red and cherry-like. The beans are dried in the sun. Brazil produces by far the largest amounts of coffee and is followed by Colombia. Other producing countries include Mexico, El Salvador, Guatemala, Indonesia, Angola and Venezuela. (*See* Plate VI.)

Cohune. A tropical South American palm the nuts of which yield oil.

Coir. *See* Coconut.

Cola nut. *See* Kola nut.

Colchicum. A drug prepared from the corms and seeds of the colchicum plant, known as meadow saffron or autumn crocus, and associated species. Overdoses of the drug can cause death, but it is used in the treatment for gout, and also in plant propagation. Belonging to the Liliaceae family, it grows wild in Britain, central and southern Europe, and the Swiss Alps.

Collards. *See* Cabbage crops.

Colocynth. A drug derived from the dried pulp of the orange-like fruit of the colocynth plant, known also as coloquintida or bitter apple. The plant is somewhat like the cucumber plant and grows in areas around the Mediterranean, the Near East, and in India and Ceylon. The drug is used as a purgative.

Colophony. *See* Rosin.

Coloquintida. *See* Colocynth.

Columbite *(Tantalite)*. This mineral is one of the two main sources of tantalum and niobium obtained chiefly from Northern Nigeria and Dakota, U.S.A.

Columbium. *See* Niobium.

Colza oil. A vegetable oil derived from the seeds of a cabbage-like plant cultivated in north-west Europe. It is used in lamps, in the manufacture of soap, and as a lubricant. After the oil has been expressed from the seeds the residue pulp provides a nutritious cattle feed.

Copal. A class of hard resins obtained from numerous different trees such as the Kauri pine of New Zealand, the East African copal, and certain South American trees. Copal is of particular importance for making varnish.

Copal balsam. *See* Sweet gum.

Copper. This is a metallic element very widely distributed in the earth's surface rocks and it is believed to have been the first metal worked by man because it is comparatively easily separated from the ore. It was probably due to the fact that copper deposits are sometimes found in the proximity of tin ores that bronze was one of the first alloys made by man. It is the most important non-ferrous metal.

Copper occurs as a pure metal; as a sulphide; as an oxide; or as other compounds. The richest known deposits of copper occur in the Rocky Mountains; the western slopes of the Andes in Chile; the copper belt of Zambia and Katanga; in the Southern Ural region and in the south of Siberia in the U.S.S.R. and in the area between the Great Lakes and Hudson Bay. These regions produce over 70% of the world's copper. Other producing countries include Australia, Japan, Mexico, the Republic of South Africa, the Philippines and Ecuador.

Copper is extracted from the ore by smelting or electrolysis. It is a relatively soft metal but is hardened by alloying with other metals, especially tin. It is a good conductor of electricity and because of this it is used extensively in all branches of the electrical industry. Approximately 50% of the world's copper is used for the manufacture of generators, electric motors, radio and television sets, transmission cables, telephone wires and transformers. Copper is also used in making ornamental ware, and today there is a tendency to use copper piping for plumbing in place of lead piping.

There are numerous copper alloys. Brass made from copper and zinc is used for metal sheeting, tubing, taps, wire, clocks, naval equipment, castings and ornaments. Bronze is the alloy of copper and tin, sometimes with the inclusion of zinc. It is utilized for making coinage, clock springs, machine bearings and mountings, pumps, valves, statues and ornaments. Nickel-copper alloys which include Monel metal are resistant to corrosion and are used for forgings, car fittings, turbine blades, tubing and coinage. Other copper alloys include aluminium bronze, silicon bronze and manganese bronze.

The chief sources of copper ore are the sulphides chalcopyrite, chalcocite and bornite.

Copra. *See* Coconut.

Coral. A rock-like substance consisting of the hard calcareous skeletons of certain marine creatures called polyps. It occurs in the form of reefs and islands in warm (65°–95°F) and relatively shallow seas (less than 300 feet deep). The Great Barrier Reef, over 1000 miles in length, lies off the north-east coast of Australia and is the most extensive of all coral deposits. There are numerous varieties of coral and they provide a source of lime. The red or precious coral of the Mediterranean Sea is used for jewellery.

Corchorus. A jute plant. (*See also* Jute.)

Coriander. The strong-smelling fruit of a European plant which is used as a spice, in medicine, and as a flavouring in curry confectionery and liqueurs. Native to south Europe and Turkey it grows to a height of 1–2 feet.

Cork. Commercially it is the very light thick outer bark of the cork oak, an evergreen tree native to the Mediterranean area, especially Spain. It grows to a height of between 30 and 60 feet. The tree lives for about 150 years and the first yield of cork is obtained when it is about 18 years old, after which the bark is removed every 8–10 years, each stripping producing a better quality cork than the one preceding.

Cork is put to a variety of uses which include stoppers for bottles and bungs for casks; lifebelts, floats, buoys, hat-linings, bath-mats, heat-insulating material, floor covering, packing material, cigarette tips and handle grips.

Corkwood. *See* Balsa.

Corn. This is a term applied to the leading cereal crop in a district. In England it is given to wheat; in Scotland and Ireland to oats; and in the United States to maize.

Cornelian *(Carnelian)*. A semi-precious stone of a red colour that is semi-transparent and used for beads and ornaments. It is a variety of chalcedony.

Corundum. A mineral consisting of the crystalline form of alumina, and which is second in hardness only to the diamond. It is used as an abrasive and for polishing, especially glass. Sapphires and rubies are transparent varieties of pure corundum. Used also as watch jewels and bearings in electrical apparatus. It is widely distributed, but Transvaal is the most important producer. The gem-stones come from Ceylon, Burma and Thailand.

Cotton. The cotton plant is a flowering shrub that grows to about 4 feet, and is grown as an annual. Cotton, the lint or fibre that serves to protect the seeds, is obtained from the boll of the plant after it has flowered. The plant is cultivated in climates ranging from temperate to tropical, and in countries experiencing frost the seed is sown after the last killing frost. The most northerly limit of cultivation is approximately the 47th parallel in the south of the Ukraine.

The general conditions for cultivating the plant are a rich soil; about 200 frost-free days; an annual rainfall of between 20 and 50 inches a year, unless the crop is grown under irrigation, with a dry period when the cotton is ripe for picking, and with average summer temperatures of 75°F or more to ripen the crop.

The quality of the cloth made from cotton depends upon the length of the staple of the fibre. Sea Island cotton, grown on the coastlands of Georgia in the U.S.A. and on the offshore islands, and in the West Indies, is the finest variety with a staple of $1\frac{1}{2}$ inches or more. Egyptian cotton is almost as good and has a staple of $1\frac{3}{8}$ inches or more. American cotton has a staple of between $\frac{7}{8}$ and $1\frac{1}{4}$ inches, whilst the staple of Asian cotton is usually less than $\frac{3}{4}$ inch.

In the production of raw cotton the leading countries are the U.S.A., which produces about 25% of the world's total production, China and the U.S.S.R. (together producing about 35% of the world total), India, Mexico, Egypt, Pakistan and Brazil. (*See* Plates VII and VIII.)

Cotton-seed oil. The oil derived from the seeds of the cotton plant which are contained within the fibres or lint of the boll. The seeds are separated from the lint by means of ginning which is done by a machine called a gin. When the seeds arrive at the oil mills they are first cleaned, after which the linters, the short cotton fibres still remaining on the seeds, are removed. The hulls are then removed from the kernels, which are then heated to facilitate the extraction of the oil. (*See also* Vegetable oils.)

Cotton-seed oil is used in making cooking fats, margarine, salad oil and dressing, cooking oils and soap. The linters are utilized as padding in upholstery, and in the manufacture of acetate, a type of rayon. The hulls are fed to livestock, and the residue pulp from the seeds is made into meal or cattle-cake which provides a rich fattening food for cattle.

Cottonwood. *See* Poplar.

Courgette. *See* Marrow.

Cow-cabbage. *See* Borecole.

Cow pea. *See* Bean.

Cows. *See* Cattle.

Crab apple. The small fruit of a deciduous tree from which the cultivated apple tree was derived. It grows in the temperate regions of the northern hemisphere. The fruit of some varieties is used for making jelly, preserving and pickling.

Crab-oil *(Carapa oil)*. *See* Carapa tree.

Crabs. *See* Shellfish.

Cranberry. The small edible red fruit of a low evergreen plant which grows extensively, both wild and cultivated, in the cooler, marshy areas of the North Temperate zone. It may be dried or canned, used as a pie fruit, or for making cordial. It is cultivated widely in the north-east of the U.S.A.

Crayfish. *See* Shellfish.

Cresol. A colourless oily liquid distilled from wood and coal used in the preparation of disinfectants and dyes.

Crocidolite. A fibrous mineral known also as blue asbestos produced in the Republic of South Africa. It is utilized mainly for decorative purposes such as for the handles of umbrellas and walking-sticks.

Croton oil. The oil derived from the seeds of a tropical plant which grows in India and Indonesia. It is used medicinally both internally, as a purgative, and externally for humans and animals.

Crottal. *See* Crottle.

Crottle *(Crottal).* A species of lichen from which a brown dye is produced and used for dyeing tweeds in Scotland.

Cryolite. At one time this mineral was the only source of aluminium but is now superseded by bauxite. It serves as a solvent for alumina in the electrolyte process of obtaining aluminium from bauxite. Also used in the making of enamel for steel and iron goods, as an electrical insulating material, as an insecticide and as a cleansing agent for metal. The only commercial source is Greenland. Synthetic cryolite has been made owing to the difficulty of supply and the high cost of it in natural form.

Cubeb. The small spicy berry of an East Indian climbing plant of the same name belonging to the pepper species. The unripe berries are picked and dried for medicinal use, and for making herbal cigarettes for the treatment of catarrh.

Cuca. *See* Coca leaves.

Cucumber. The elongated fruit of the trailing vine-like cucumber plant which is native to the warm temperate and sub-tropical regions of Asia. There are a number of varieties, some of which are cultivated under glass, whilst others are grown in the open provided there is no risk of frost. Today cucumbers are cultivated extensively in Europe and the U.S.A. both as a vegetable garden and as a market garden crop. Some varieties are sliced and eaten raw as a salad ingredient, whilst others are pickled.

Gherkins are a variety of small cucumbers used for pickling.

Cumin (Cummin) seeds. The seeds or fruit of a small herbaceous plant which is cultivated in the Mediterranean region and in the East. The seeds are somewhat similar to caraway seeds but slightly larger. They yield oil and possess a strong aromatic odour. The oil is used medicinally and the seeds are an ingredient of curry.

CUMMIN

Cummin. *See* Cumin seeds.

Curd. The thick or coagulated part of milk as distinct from whey, the watery part. It is used in making cheese.

Currant. This is the name given to the dried fruit of a species of grape-vine (*see* Grapes), and also to the small soft fruit of certain deciduous shrubs which are cultivated in the cool temperate regions of Europe and North America. These soft fruits may be black, red, or white, according to the variety of plant. Black-currants are the larger of the three types and have a high vitamin C content. All are used for making fruit pies and tarts; black-currants and redcurrants are made into jelly preserves; black-currants are also used as flavouring for throat lozenges and sweets in the form of pastiles and gums, and in the making of home-made wine. Currants are grown mainly in Great Britain.

Cuscus. The fibrous root of a species of grass native to India utilized in making baskets and fans.

Custard apple *(Annona, Sweet sop, Sugar apple)*. The edible heart-shaped fruit that is an aggregate of the individual berries of a small West Indian tree. The sweet pulp of the fruit assumes a thick custard-like consistency and appearance. It is known as cherimoya in tropical America, as sour sop also in tropical America and as squamosa in the Indonesian islands.

Cutch. *See* Catechu, Mangrove.

D

Dairy products. In general, dairying can be considered essentially an industry of the cool temperate regions, where rainfall is sufficient to provide the rich pastures necessary for dairy cattle. There are exceptions, however. Enormous quantities of milk are produced in India and Pakistan, and dairying is also being developed in other tropical and sub-tropical regions where conditions are favourable for introducing dairy stock.

Most of the world's dairy cattle are the descendants of breeds native to north-west Europe and they include the Ayrshire, Guernsey, Jersey and Holstein-Friesian.

Today the U.S.A. produces well over 25% of the world's milk. The other leading producers are the U.S.S.R., Germany, France, Britain, India, Canada, Australia, New Zealand, Holland, Denmark, Sweden, Switzerland and Argentina.

Milk may be processed into condensed or evaporated milk, or it may be dehydrated into powdered milk.

Very large quantities of milk are used in the making of butter from the cream which forms on top of the milk.

Cheese is made by adding rennet to milk, which causes it to coagulate.

Dambonite. A white crystalline substance found in a kind of caoutchouc obtained from western Africa.

Dambose is a crystallizable sugar obtained from dambonite.

Dammar resin. The resin derived from certain species of coniferous trees which grow in Indonesia, India, Australia and New Zealand. It is utilized in making varnish, in photography, and as incense.

Damson. *See* Plum.

Dandelion. A common plant of the Compositae Family with widely toothed leaves which are used in salads, and as food for silkworms. The flowers are a bright yellow.

The root when roasted is a coffee substitute.

Date. The date is the fruit of a species of palm tree which grows to a height of about 70 feet in hot arid regions, such as the Sahara Desert and Saudi Arabia, where it is the typical tree of the oases. The chief producing countries are Iraq, Saudi Arabia, Iran, Pakistan, Egypt, Algeria and Tunisia. Most of the dried dates produced for export are grown in Iraq and pass through the port of Basra.

There are many different varieties of date palm, and the fruit develops in large clusters which may weigh anything up to 25 lb and contain as many as 1000 fruits. The tree, which lives for 100–150 years, begins to yield fruit when about 6 years old, and when fully mature may be cropped from 6 to 10 times each year. Dates are especially valuable to desert peoples, forming part of their staple diet. They are eaten fresh or dried, or they may be dried and ground into meal for culinary use. They are used in the making of syrup, and a strong spirit also is obtained from them by distillation. The ground stones of the fruit provide a useful food for animals.

The tree itself is of considerable value to the desert inhabitants. Its timber is used in building houses, and for fencing, and its fibres are made into ropes, cordage, baskets and mats. (*See* Plate IX.)

Daturine. A poisonous substance obtained from the leaves and seeds of a species of the datura plant, the thorn apple, and from which the drug stramonium is derived. The drug is used medicinally to relieve asthma.

Deadly nightshade. *See* Belladonna.

Deal. This is a term applied broadly to soft whitewood timbers, especially pine. It is also used for sawn softwood boards of certain dimensions, i.e. 9 inches wide, and about 3 inches in thickness. It is exported from Scandinavia and the U.S.S.R.

Deciduous fruits. The fruits of certain deciduous trees such as the apple, peach, pear, and plum. *(See also under individual fruit headings.)*

Deciduous trees. Trees that shed their leaves every year. Also known as hardwood trees. *(See also under individual names.)*

Deodar. A sub-species of cedar found largely native in the Western Himalayas. The name is also applied in India to other trees. The valuable timber can be highly polished. Grown extensively in the Himalayas above 7000 feet.

Dewberry. A trailing blackberry. (*See also* Blackberry.)

Dhurra. *See* Durra.

Diabase. *See* Dolerite.

Diamond. This is a form of crystalline carbon and is the hardest of all known substances. Diamonds are the result of deposits of carbon which were subjected to intense heat and pressure within the molten rocks containing them. They are found in certain igneous rocks, and also in alluvial deposits which were laid down as a result of erosion by rivers and streams of the diamond-bearing rocks.

The Congo is by far the leading producer of diamonds, and is followed by Ghana, the Republic of South Africa, Brazil and Sierra Leone.

Over 75% of the world's diamonds are used for industrial purposes. These include for the cutting and drilling of glass, porcelain and metal; for making diamond set drills for cutting stone and rock, and dies through which metals such as copper and steel are drawn in the manufacture of wire; for jewel bearings; and as an abrasive and polishing material for diamonds and other gem-stones used in jewellery. (*See also* Bort *and* Carbonado.)

Most of the world's gem-diamonds are produced in the area around Kimberley in South Africa. Diamonds are greatly valued as gem-stones owing to their great brilliancy, which is due to their very high refractive powers.

Synthetic diamonds have been produced by artificial processes, but only in very small amounts.

Diatomite *(Kieselguhr, Diatomaceous earth)*. A hydrous form of silica, the deposits of which are made up of the myriads of shells of diatoms (algae). When dry it looks like chalk but is very porous, and chemically inert. It is used for filtration of crude sugar, fruit juices, mineral oils, perfumes and beverages. In a brick or powder form it is used for the insulation of furnaces and refrigerators, and for sound-proofing. In metal polishes it is used as an abrasive, and it also forms a constituent of some kinds of concrete. Sources of supply are along the coast of California, Denmark, Japan and Algeria.

Digitalis *(Foxglove)*. A genus of plants including the foxglove. From the dried leaves is made the drug digitalis used as a medicine for the heart.

Dika *(Mango)*. A West African name. Dika-bread is a cocoa-like substance prepared from the fruit of a species of mango tree.

Dill *(Anet)*. An umbelliferous annual plant, cultivated for its carminative fruits or "seeds". Native to southern Europe, Egypt and South Africa. From the small seeds oil is distilled and used in medicine, and also for gin. The leaves are used in soups and as a flavouring in cooking. The seeds are ground up to form a flavouring.

Dividivi. The curled pods of a tree of tropical South America; they are highly astringent, and much used in tanning.

Dogwood. The name given to the deciduous shrubs of the *Cornus* genus found in the temperate regions of North America. The hard wood is a useful timber.

Dolerite *(Diabase)*. A rock allied to basalt containing feldspar.

Dolomite. A mineral composed of calcium-magnesium carbonate. Dolomitic or magnesian limestones are common in Britain, while the Dolomite Alps of the Italian and Austrian Tyrol cover hundreds of square miles. Dolomite is one of the main sources of magnesium, and is also used as a building stone, as a road metal, and for lining the hearths of furnaces.

Donkey *(Ass)*. A domesticated animal of the horse family but smaller. It is a valuable beast of burden, especially in the East, Arabia, Egypt and the Middle East. Its meat and milk are also used in some countries for human consumption.

Douglas fir. A North American coniferous tree which grows extensively in the Western Cordillera region and on the coastal ranges, from British Columbia to Mexico. It is one of the tree-giants of the world, and in some instances has been found exceeding 250 feet in height. It is the most important timber tree in North America and is known under various names—British Columbian pine, Oregon pine, red fir, red pine and yellow pine—and the greatest quantities are produced in British Columbia, Oregon and Washington. The timber is put to a wide range of uses, including for constructional work of all kinds, bridges, ship masts and decking, flooring and other interior woodwork.

Doura. *See* Durra.

Dragon's blood. A dark-red resin obtained from several Indonesian plants, and from the Dragon trees which grow on the island of Socotra in the Arabian Sea and on the Canary Islands, and also from certain Mexican trees. It is used as a colouring agent for lacquers and varnishes.

Dromedary. The one-humped Arabian camel, but the name is also given to a light swift camel especially reared and trained for riding.

Ducks. *See* Poultry.

Dulse. An edible variety of seaweed found in the seas surrounding Britain, and in the Mediterranean Sea.

Dumortierite. *See* Sillimanite minerals.

Dura. *See* Durra.

Durian *(Durion)*. The somewhat unpleasant-smelling yet pleasant-tasting large fruit of a tropical fruit of the same name which grows in parts of India, the Indo-China peninsula, and in the Indonesian archipelago. The fruit is consumed raw and its seeds may be roasted. This spherical fruit may be 6–8 inches in diameter, and the tree itself may be 70–80 feet tall.

Durion. *See* Durian.

Durra *(Dura)*. A variety of sorghum.

Dwale. *See* Belladonna.

Dyer's madder. *See* Madder.

Dyer's moss. *See* Archil.

Dyes. These can be divided into two main groups—natural dyes and synthetic dyes.

Natural dyestuffs are derived mainly from vegetable sources; from the roots, stems, leaves, flowers and fruits of plants such as madder, indigo, camomile and saffron; and from the timber of certain trees, logwood, peachwood and sappan wood. Today, however, synthetic or aniline dyes tend to replace the older natural dyes.

Synthetic or aniline dyestuffs are manufactured from certain substances derived from coal-tar, from which an almost unlimited range of hues, tints, and shades can be produced. *(See also under individual names.)*

E

Eaglewood. *See* Aloeswood.

Earthnut. *See* Groundnut. It is also the name of the edible tuber of an umbelliferous plant.

Earth-wax. *See* Ozokerite.

Ebony. Hard black wood of some 15 species of tropical trees of the genus *Diospyros*. Native of Ceylon, Malagasy Republic and Mauritius, i.e. tropical distribution. Used for ornaments and piano keys (black). Some species yield dark brown or greyish timber that is used for furniture.

Egg plant *(Aubergine, Guinea squash, Egg fruit)*. An annual vegetable with an egg-shaped fruit up to a foot long, which is purple, white or yellow in colour. It is native to south and eastern Asia where it is widely cultivated. It is also grown in Florida, New Jersey and Texas.

Eggs. The eggs in commercial trade are mainly those of domestic poultry, but in the northern parts of the world especially the collecting of the eggs of sea-birds is also important. Also amongst primitive peoples the gathering of eggs for food is carried on. In addition to their use as a food, the white of eggs is used in book-binding, in the preparation of leathers and in sugar-refining and the manufacture of wines.

Eider. Eider duck is noted for down feathers on the breast, i.e. eiderdown of commerce. Down is used to line the nest and this is removed for marketing.

The birds are found in Arctic and sub-Arctic regions, e.g. northern Europe and Iceland, Siberia and Alaska.

Elder. A deciduous tree or shrub of the temperate and sub-tropical regions of the northern hemisphere. It grows to a height of about

Plate I. Trinidad. The Pitch Lake. Native workers cutting the pitch and loading it on to railway wagons. (Paul Popper Ltd.)

PLATE II. Baobab tree, Dar-es-Salaam, Tanzania. A large African tree usually from 40–70 feet in height, the oblong fruit of which is known as monkey-bread. (Aerofilms Ltd.)

PLATE III. Bread fruit, State of Bahia, Brazil. It can be fried or boiled, and forms the basic food of the native population, the large round fruit being used as a substitute for bread. (By Ewing Galloway, N.Y.)

PLATE IV. Leaves, flowers and fruit of the cocoa tree. As the pods ripen they change colour from green to yellow, dark red and purple. (Radio Times Hulton Picture Library.)

PLATE V. Coconut palm. The fruit is in clusters of between ten and twenty, and may measure over 15 inches in length. (Hunting Aerosurveys Ltd.)

PLATE VI. Coffee "cherries". The tree bears fragrant white flowers which give rise to the bright red "cherries" each containing two seeds or beans. Coffee is made from the beans after they have been dried and husked and then ground into powder. (Radio Times Hulton Picture Library.)

PLATE VII. Cotton boll open showing the fibre or lint from which the cotton thread is made. (Empire Cotton Growing Corporation.)

PLATE VIII. Cotton bush in Thailand, about 4 feet in height, showing the bolls split open exposing the fluffy white mass of lint. (Cotton Research Corporation.)

20 feet. The dark purple berries arc used for wine making. Elder flower water may be distilled from the blossoms, and is used in flavouring confectionery, and also for perfume. The wood is used for mathematical instruments and toys. The leaves yield a green colouring matter.

Elemi. A pale yellow resin from various trees used in plasters, ointments and the manufacture of varnishes.

Elm. About 18 species of trees and shrubs which are found throughout Europe, North Africa and northern Asia. They grow to about 100 feet. The wood is difficult to polish, but is free from knots and very durable. It is used for flooring, boxes, crates, furniture and in shipbuilding.

Emerald. Green variety of beryl, used as a gem-stone. The finest stone is mined in Colombia, others in the Urals, Australia, Austria and the U.S.A.

Emery. A dull bluish-black mineral of impure alumina or corundum that contains varying quantities of iron oxide. It is a hard substance and is used in polishing metals, plate glass and precious stones.

Endive. An annual plant of the Compositae family, native to Europe, North Africa, India and Pakistan. It is also cultivated in America. It is a salad vegetable similar to lettuce. One variety has curled narrow leaves. Another variety, used in stews or soups, has flat broad leaves.

Epsom salt. A white crystalline solid that is magnesium sulphate heptahydrate and used medicinally as a purgative. It is found in sea-water and also at Seidlitz and in America. Originally found at Epsom in England, hence its name.

Ermine. An animal of the weasel tribe found in northern countries, called in England a stoat, whose fur in summer is reddish brown, but in winter wholly white except for the tip of the tail which is always black. The fur is used for trimming robes of peers and judges.

Esparto grass

Esparto grass *(Halfa, Alfa, Spanish grass)*. A feathery perennial grass native to North Africa and southern Europe, especially Spain. The leaves, which may be 2–10 feet long, are fibrous and are used in the manufacture of paper, ropes, cordage and sandals. The young stalks are fed to cattle.

Essential oils. This is the term given to aromatic volatile vegetable oils that are used as essences and perfumes. Many of these are now produced synthetically.

Eucalyptus. The gum tree native to Australia and New Zealand and planted in California and other parts of the world. Resin from the trunk of the Australian red gum tree is used in medicine. Some trees reach 300 feet.

Eucalyptus oil is distilled from resin of Australian blue gum tree and used medicinally. The bark is used in tanning and in some species for paper. Timber is very strong and used for fences and shipbuilding.

Euonymus. *See* Spindle tree.

F

Feathers. Goose feathers and those from the eider duck are used for bedding and cushions, as also are swan and poultry feathers.

Feathers are also used in millinery for decorative purposes, for brushes and for flyhooks in fishing.

Feldspar *(Felspar)*. A very abundant mineral in the earth's surface, being found in igneous rocks. Feldspars consist of the aluminium silicates of potassium, sodium and calcium. The chief commercial producers are the U.S.A., Canada, Sweden and Norway. Its chief use is in the manufacture of glass, especially that used in bottles, plate glass and window glass, though much is used for ceramics, enamels for household goods, and for scouring soaps.

Felt. A kind of cloth or stuff made of wool, or of wool and fur or hair, fulled or wrought into a compact substance by rolling and pressure, with lees or size.

Fennel. A perennial umbelliferous plant native to North Africa, western Asia and Europe. It grows to a height of 4 feet. The blanched roots are eaten; the dried seeds yield an aromatic oil. Seeds and leaves are used for flavouring soups, sauces and stews.

Fescue grass. Several species of pasture and fodder grasses grown in cool temperate regions. In northern regions red fescue is grown, while in mountainous areas, such as the Himalayas and the Western Cordillera, sheep's fescue is grown.

Fibres. This is the general term given to animal and vegetable substances which are thread-like and a component part of the tissue. They may be used in the manufacture of textiles, e.g. wool silk, cotton, linen; or for paper, e.g. esparto grass, wood pulp; or for brushes, e.g. hairs of bear, squirrel, camel; or for stuffing upholstery, e.g. kapok; or for ropes, e.g. abaca. *(See also under individual names.)*

Fig. The fig belongs to the same family as the mulberry, and is native to southern Europe and western Asia. The fruit is eaten either dried or fresh. The chief fig-producing countries are Spain, Algeria, Italy, Turkey, Portugal, Greece and the U.S.A. Some fig leaves are used as fodder.

Filbert. *See* Hazel.

Fir. The name given to a number of coniferous trees, of different genera. Widely distributed in cool and cold temperate regions. Used for paper pulp, turpentine and in varnishes. The timber is inferior to pine.

Fire-clay. A kind of clay capable of sustaining great heat and used in making fire-bricks, crucibles, and gas-retorts. Often found on or near to coalfields.

Fish. Since about three-quarters of the earth's surface is covered with water, fish have always been a very important source of food for mankind, both salt and fresh water fish. The chief fishing grounds of the world are in the North Atlantic Ocean, but the Pacific Coast fisheries of North America, the fisheries of Japan and the Mediterranean are also important. The principal fish caught are cod, herring, hake, mackerel, haddock, whiting, pilchard, plaice, sardine and halibut. Salmon are important in the rivers and are chiefly canned. Much of the fish caught is packed in ice for transit, while some is canned or frozen, or dried, or cured.

Flax. Annual plant of temperate (cool and warm) regions but also

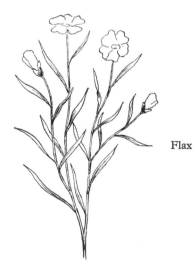

Flax

sub-tropical. The seeds yield linseed oil used in paint, linoleum, oilcloth and printer's ink. The residue after extraction of oil is used for cattle food. Seed flax is grown in the U.S.A., Argentina, the U.S.S.R. and India. If fibres are required for linen, the whole plant is pulled up, retted in ponds, dried, spun, woven and bleached. Three-quarters of the world's supply comes from the U.S.S.R.; other producers are Northern Ireland, Poland, Holland and Belgium.

Flint. A hard stone of a grey colour, found in roundish nodules usually covered with a whitish incrustation. It is one of the purest native forms of silica. Found in horizontal bands in chalk, it is occasionally used as a building stone. In prehistoric times knives, arrows and axes were made of it.

Fluor. A generic name for a class of minerals, resembling gems, but readily fusible and useful as fluxes in smelting.

Fluorite. *See* Fluorspar.

Fluorspar *(Fluorite)*. Mineral form of calcium fluoride which is the commercial source of fluorine. The crystals may be white, yellow, green or blue. It is used as a flux in the steel industry and in smelting gold, silver, copper and lead and opal glass and in enamels and as an electrolyte. Very widespread distribution.

Fodder. Feed given to farm animals. There are many forage crops, including hay, clover, lucerne, mangolds, turnips and swedes.

Forage. Food for horses and cattle, especially dry winter food as opposed to grass.

Foxglove. *See* Digitalis.

Frankincense *(Olibanum)*. An aromatic gum resin yielded by certain trees grown in Sudan, Southern Arabia and Somalia. It is used for burning as incense and as a perfume base. It was formerly used medicinally.

Fuller's earth *(Bentonite)*. The name given to various soft clays of a fine texture that contain alumina, and hydrated silica. Used in purifying oils and fats, and cleansing cloth.

Furs. The dressed skins with fine soft hair of various animals which flourish in the colder regions of the world. Cat, squirrel, seal, rabbit, hare and muskrat furnish the largest numbers of furs, but are the least valuable. Mole, sable, ermine and, especially, mink are among the more highly valued furs. They are used for coats and for trimming clothing.

Furze *(Gorse, Whin).* There are some 20 species of this shrub which belongs to the Leguminosae family. It flourishes in central and western Europe, and in north-west Africa. It bears sharp thorns and grows to about 2–6 feet. The flowers are yellow and very attractive to bees, being scented. The young shoots when chopped up are used as winter fodder for horses and cattle, as well as for sheep. It is also cut for fuel, and when burnt the alkaline ashes form a valuable fertilizer.

Fustic *(Yellowwood).* The wood of a tree that grows in Jamaica, Cuba and Brazil that produces a dye that is used particularly in dyeing wool shades of brown, olive and yellow.

G

Galena. This mineral is composed of lead sulphide, and is the chief source of lead. It is widely distributed and is worked commercially at Broken Hill in New South Wales, British Columbia and Burma. It is important in the electronics industry.

Gall. A swelling produced on the trees by the eggs of insects or mites it yields a juice that is used in tanning, in the manufacture of ink, and as a dye.

Gallium (Ga). A soft bluish metal that is easily melted and is present in zinc and aluminium ores. When added to copper it increases its hardness though it lowers its conductivity. Widely distributed, but only occurs in minute quantities; especially associated with zinc blende and bauxite.

Gambier. An earthy kind of substance that is produced from the leaves of a Malayan shrub and used for dyeing and tanning.

Gamboge. A gum resin that comes from trees that are native to Thailand and Cambodia. It is a bright yellow colour and is used as a pigment and in varnishes.

Ganister. A close-grained hard sandstone that is used for lining furnaces.

Garancine. *See* Madder.

Garden beet. *See* Beet.

Garlic. A bulbous-rooted plant that has a very strong onion-like smell and taste. It is used as a flavouring in cookery. Native to Siberia, it is grown commercially in California.

Garnet. A gem-stone that is of a deep red colour and transparent. It is a silicate mineral. Used in jewellery.

Geese. *See* Poultry.

Gems. The name given to minerals that can be cut and polished and used in jewellery. It is usually an inorganic mineral, e.g. diamond, ruby, emerald, but it can be of organic origin, e.g. pearl, amber, coral. (*See also under individual names.*)

Gentian. A plant of which there are about 500 species that grows in mountainous areas of the northern hemisphere and has deep blue flowers. A liqueur is made from it in Switzerland, and the root is used in pharmacy.

Gherkin. *See* Cucumber.

Gingelly. *See* Sesame.

Ginger. This spice consists of the dried underground stem or rhizome of a small reed-like tropical plant native to southern Asia. India and China are the chief producers but other sources include Jamaica, Sierra Leone and Mauritius. It is used as a flavouring, but in addition it may be preserved in sugar syrup or candied with sugar.

Gingili. *See* Sesame.

Gingko. *See* Maidenhair tree.

Ginseng. There are two species of this herbaceous plant that

GLASSWORT

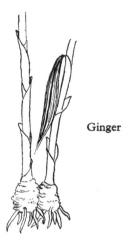

Ginger

grows in northern China and in the east of the U.S.A. to a height of about 2 feet. The root is used medicinally.

Glasswort *(Marsh samphire)*. An annual plant with leafless fleshy stems, native to western Asia, North America, North Africa and Europe. Formerly it used to be burnt in order to get soda from the ashes which was used in glass manufacture.

Goa powder. *See* Araroba.

Goats. In Europe goats are chiefly kept for their milk, but elsewhere they are reared for their skins and meat. Goats with their ability to eat young trees, shrubs and bark have to be tethered if widespread damage is to be avoided. The chief goat-rearing countries are India, Turkey, China, the U.S.S.R., Pakistan and Brazil.

Gold. This mineral is rarely found in its pure form and often contains other metals, especially silver. It occurs in veins or lodes, and in some river gravels where it has been deposited by running water. About 60% of the world's gold is mined in the Witwatersrand (the Rand) in the South African Republic. Other important producing countries include Canada, the U.S.A., the U.S.S.R., Australia, Ghana and Rhodesia.

Gold is the most malleable and ductile of all metals and owing to its softness it is alloyed with other metals such as copper, silver and nickel to harden it. A carat is a 24th part and the term is used to denote the amount of gold in the alloy. The metal is greatly valued for its decorative appearance and considerable quantities are used in making jewellery and in gilding. It is also used in making fountain pen nibs. Its principal use, however, is in the form of ingots (bullion) which are used as the basis of some monetary systems.

Gooseberry. The edible fruit of a prickly shrub that is deciduous and grows in Europe and northern Asia. The fruit may be green, purple or yellow when ripe and is about 1 inch in diameter. There are about 50 species, and they are used mainly for jam, but are also bottled and canned, and used in pies.

Gorse. *See* Furze.

Gourd. The name is given to various annual climbing or trailing plants which grow in warm temperate or tropical countries. The fruit or gourd may vary from a few inches to over 5 feet in length, and the shape also varies greatly. The dried gourds are used as containers, especially by primitive peoples.

Gram. *See* Chick-pea.

Granadilla. *See* Passion fruit.

Granite. A rock composed chiefly of feldspar, mica and quartz, usually grey in colour but can be pink, red, green or yellow. It is quarried for use in building, as a road metal, and also for kerbstones and pavements as well as for ornamental mason work, e.g. tombstones. Among the areas quarrying granite for commerce are Aberdeen in Scotland, Cornwall and Cumberland in England, British Columbia and California.

Grapefruit *(Shaddock, Pomelo).* A citrus fruit about 4 inches in diameter that grows in clusters on an evergreen tree that is commercially grown in South Africa and the U.S.A. as well as in other Mediterranean climatic regions. The rind is yellow. The fruit is eaten raw, or canned, or processed as a juice.

Grapes. *See* Vine.

GRAPHITE

Graphite *(Plumbago, Black lead)*. Graphite is a pure carbon deposit which has been subjected to intense heat and pressure. It is found mainly in metamorphic rocks in pockets, veins or flakes. It is a soft black mineral used for making crucibles, paints, stove polish, brushes for electric motors, dry storage batteries, and as the lead of pencils for which purpose it is mixed with fine clay.

The chief sources of graphite are: the U.S.S.R., Australia, North Korea, Mexico, Republic of Malagasy, West Germany and Ceylon.

Grass. Plants of the family Gramineae. Grass is the chief and most nutritious food for cattle, sheep and goats. When dried, grass forms hay which can also be used as fodder. Grass can be chopped and artificially dried for use as cattle meal. The tropical varieties include bamboo.

In farming the term grass may also include clover and all green plants growing in a field.

Grass wrack. A perennial sea plant that grows around the coasts in temperate regions and is usually submerged at low water. It is used as a stuffing for cheap upholstery, and for packing. It has grass-like leaves.

Great millet. *See* Sorghum.

Greengage. The round green fruit of a deciduous tree related to the plum that grows in southern Europe chiefly, though it also grows in Great Britain. May be eaten raw or made into jam.

Groundnut *(Peanut, Monkey-nut, Earthnut, Manilla nut, Pistache de terre)*. The groundnut plant derives its name from the fact that,

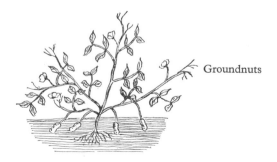

Groundnuts

after flowering, the head of the flower buries itself in the ground where the seed develops into the fruit. The term peanut is used alternatively on account of the plant's pea-shaped flower. Although native to the West Indies and South America, today it is cultivated extensively in many other parts of the world in climates ranging from warm temperate to tropical. Groundnuts are especially valuable as a source of vegetable oil of which they yield over 40%. In addition, the residue pulp is a very nutritious cattle food, as well as being a source of protein from which in recent years synthetic fibre is manufactured.

The most important groundnut-producing countries are India, China, U.S.A., and the countries of West Africa.

In North America an entirely different plant, the Indian potato, is also called groundnut. Both plants belong to the Leguminosae family.

Groundsel. An annual plant of the Compositae family that grows to about 6–15 inches in height and bears small yellow heads of tubular florets. It flourishes in temperate climates where it ranks as a weed. It flowers throughout the year and provides food for cage birds. Groundsel is native to Europe.

Guaiacum. *See* Lignum vitae.

Guanaco. *See* Alpaca.

Guano. This is the name given to the excreta of birds that has accumulated on the shores and islands off shore of South America. It is very valuable as a fertilizer being rich in ammonia and phosphates. Bats' guano is obtained from New Zealand.

Guava. An evergreen tree that grows in the West Indies and bears a pear-shaped edible fruit that has a yellow rind, containing a yellow or red pulp that is made into guava jelly.

Guinea corn. *See* Sorghum.

Guinea Squash. *See* Egg plant.

Gum. *See* Eucalyptus.

Gum arabic. *See* Acacia.

Gum Benjamin. *See* Benzoin.

Gumbo *(Okra)*. An annual plant that grows in tropical countries. The pod of the unripe fruit is some 4–10 inches long and is used in pickles and soups. The seeds are ground and used as a coffee substitute. The leaves and immature fruit are used in the East as a poultice. The plant is grown commercially chiefly in the area of Istanbul, but also in tropical and sub-tropical regions.

Gum tragacanth. It comes from Iran and from countries around the shores of the Mediterranean Sea and is the product of species of *Astralagus*. The gum is used in the printing of calico (a cotton cloth) and for pharmacy. It is the second most important gum.

Gutta-percha. From certain trees that grow in Malaya comes latex, a milky juice that when dried resembles rubber but is less elastic, and cannot be easily vulcanized. It is used for the outer covering of golf balls and as an insulator. It is now largely replaced by synthetic products.

Gypsum. It is a mineral form of calcium sulphate and is quarried in England, France, Italy and the U.S.A. It is used as a fluxing agent, a fertilizer, and in the paper industry. When heated it becomes a white powder known as plaster of Paris which is used in pottery, cement, paints and for building plasters.

H

Hackberry. The coarse-grained greyish wood from this American tree is used for boxes, furniture and ornaments. A dye from the roots is used in the dyeing of linen. The tree is found in the eastern part of the U.S.A. and in Canada.

Haddock. *See* Fish.

Haematite *(Hematite)*. An important iron ore (Fe_2O_3). It is found in Cumberland and the Forest of Dean in Britain, also in Spain and the Lake Superior area.

Hafnium (Hf). A metallic element that occurs with zircon and is used in tungsten filaments in electric lamps. The highest hafnium content is found—up to 35%—in cyrtolite, alvite, malacon, baddeleyite, and zivkelite, and the lowest content in Brazil in zircons in nepheline syenites.

Hake. *See* Fish.

Halfa. *See* Esparto grass.

Halibut. *See* Fish.

Halite. *See* Salt.

Hardwood trees. Deciduous trees produce hard timber. They can be divided into two groups: where the annual rainfall exceeds 20 inches and the temperature is between 40°F and 65°F are the temperate hardwoods; tropical hardwoods are limited to regions that receive well over 20 inches of rain a year and are frost free with an annual temperature of between 60°F and 75°F.

Haricot. The name given to various species of dried bean seeds that are widely cultivated in Europe, India, the Far East and South America for use as a food.

Hashish or **hasheesh.** The top tender leaves of common hemp are dried and used for smoking or chewing in the East and are known as hasheesh. It has a narcotic effect. *See* Hemp.

Hawthorn *(Whitethorn, May).* A member of a large group of trees and shrubs that grow to a height of about 20 feet. The small scarlet fruit is known as a haw. Native to Europe, they also grow in Australia, North America, North Africa and western Asia. The wood is a yellowish-white colour and is used for the handles of tools and for engraving. The root wood is used for tobacco pipes.

Hay *(see also* Grass). A fodder for cattle consisting of grass that is dried naturally; also contains clover and other plants that are edible to animals.

Hazel *(Filbert, Cobnut).* A deciduous tree that bears a sweet edible nut in a hard shell. Native to the temperate regions of Europe, but found also in Asia and in North America. The trees bear catkins which are wind pollinated.

Heath *(Heather, Ling).* Evergreen shrub of the family Ericaceae that grows widely in Europe and northern Asia and bears purple or white flowers in spikes. Its height is only about 2 feet. It is used as fuel when other dry resources are lacking and also for making brooms. The flowers yield much honey.

Heather. *See* Heath.

Helium. An inert gas that occurs in the atmosphere, but its greatest source is in natural gases found especially in Texas, Kansas, Utah and New Mexico. On account of its lightness and being non-inflammable it is used as a lifting gas, e.g. in radio-sonde balloons and formerly in airships. Mixed with oxygen it is used medically.

Hematite. *See* Haematite.

Hemlock. A coniferous tree of some 9 species that is native to North America. The reddish bark is used for tanning. This is a tall tree growing to some 60–80 feet and bearing dark green leaves.

Hemlock is also a poisonous plant of the Umbelliferae family with small white flowers used medically as a sedative.

Hemlock stork's-bill. *See* Pin clover.

Hemp. The term used often for fibres that come from plants that are not connected with the hemp plant. True hemp is an annual plant; from the inner bark of the stem come the fibres that are used for making rope and cloth. The seeds yield an oil that is used in varnish, and as an oil food for cage birds. It is grown in north-eastern U.S.S.R., northern China, India, Arabia and North Africa. *See also* Abaca (Manila hemp); Agave; Bhang; Henequen; Phormium (New Zealand hemp); Sisal; Sunn hemp (Indian hemp).

Henbane. An annual plant with dull grey leaves that have a very unpleasant smell. The dried leaves yield the drugs atropine and hyoscyamine used medicinally. Grows in Europe, north-west Asia and North Africa.

Henequen. A fibre that is closely related to sisal, both being species of Agave of Central American origin. Grows in dry tropical climates as a perennial crop. The fibres are in the long fleshy leaves. It takes from 4 to 7 years for a new plant to yield fibre which is used for string and cordage, especially in combine harvesting machines. The chief producers are Mexico, Cuba and Haiti.

Henna. A small shrub the dried leaves of which when powdered yield the yellow dye with reddish and golden tints that is used by the Arabs as a nail dye and in Europe and North America as a hair dye. It is also used for dyeing skins and leather. The Mohammedans use the powder in the form of a paste to dye their hands and feet. Cultivated in India, Ceylon and Australia.

Herring. *See* Fish.

Hides and skins. The raw or dressed skins of cattle and other animals before tanning to form leather. Exported mainly from Argentina, Brazil and India.

Holly. An evergreen tree that bears dark red berries used at Christmas as a decoration, with spiky dark green leaves. The hard white wood stains well and is used for furniture. The leaves are used as winter fodder. The tree, which may attain 80 feet, flourishes in west and southern Europe, and in western Asia as well as in Great Britain.

Honey. Collected as nectar from flowers and changed by the honeybee into honey which is used as a preserve and sweetener. Australia, New Zealand, Canada, and the U.S.A. are leading producers.

Hop. A perennial twining plant that grows in temperate countries and is related to the mulberry family. There are both male and female plants and it is the female plant that develops the bracts that develop into cone-shaped heads which are the hops of commerce. A resinous substance which is used to give flavour to beer is secreted at the base of each cone. Hops are harvested when ripe and dried in kilns or oasts, then cooled and cured before use in brewing. The U.S.A. leads world production of hops, followed by England, Germany and Czechoslovakia. (*See* Plates X and XI.)

Hornbeam. A deciduous tree with a hard timber that is used for turnery for cogs of wheels, and also for charcoal. The inner bark yields a yellow dye. The leaves are used for animal fodder. The tree may grow to a height of 40–70 feet, but it is used mainly for hedging as the timber polishes poorly and is hard and tough to work.

Horse chestnut. A handsome deciduous tree that bears white or pink flowers arranged on the tree-like "candles" and is native to Europe and Great Britain. The nut-like fruit is encased in a prickly cover and is used as food for cattle and pigs after the bitterness has been removed.

Horseradish. An edible rooted perennial that flourishes in Europe. The white root is grated and used as a condiment and sometimes in medicine.

Horses. These animals are used mainly for carrying goods and people and for drawing farm implements and carts in less developed lands. In some countries their meat is used for human consumption as well as for food for dogs. Horses are reared in the largest numbers in the U.S.S.R., Argentina, Brazil, the U.S.A., Mexico and Poland.

Humic coal. *See* Coal.

Hyoscine. *See* Belladonna.

Hyoscyamine. *See* Henbane.

I

Iceland agate. *See* Obsidian.

Iceland moss. A lichen that grows easily in mountainous areas of the northern hemisphere. It is about 4 inches long and ribbon-like. In Norway and Iceland it is ground into a powder that is used as flour for bread or boiled with milk for a jelly. A brown dye is sometimes extracted from it. Not of very great commercial importance even in these two countries.

Iceland spar. A pure glass-like variety of calcite that at one time came entirely from Iceland, but now much comes from South Africa, Spain and New Mexico, U.S.A. The spar has strong double refraction and is used for polarizing light in optical instruments.

Ilmenite. This is one of the chief ores of titanium and is usually associated with basic igneous rocks. It comes from Scandinavia and the U.S.A.

Indian corn. *See* Maize.

Indian cress. *See* Nasturtium.

Indian hemp. *See* Sunn hemp.

Indian millett. *See* Sorghum.

Indian potato. *See* Groundnut.

Indian rice. *See* Wild rice.

Indigo. A blue dye which can be obtained from several types of plant, chiefly in Bengal. Cultivation has almost ceased now as it has been superseded by synthetic dyes.

Indium. A silver white shining metal that is very soft and ductile. It is used for silver-plating as it reduces tarnishing and takes a high polish; also for plating copper-lead bearings as it resists oil corrosion. It is generally associated with zinc blende and tin and lead ores.

Iodine (I). A non-metallic element that does not occur free in nature, but is widely distributed in the form of its compounds. Sodium iodate is an impurity in sodium nitrate, large deposits of which are found in the Atacama Desert of South America. It is also present in sea-water. Tincture of iodine has antiseptic properties.

Ipecac. *See* Ipecacuanha.

Ipecacuanha *(Ipecac).* A substance obtained from the dried roots of a perennial plant grown in Brazil, Nicaragua and Columbia. It is used as a powder in medicine, especially in cough mixtures.

Iridium. A chemical element of precious white hard brittle metal that is used as an alloy with precious metals for fountain pen nibs, fine bearings and standard weights and measures. Usually obtained as a by-product of refining nickel and copper.

IRISH MOSS

Irish moss. *See* Carrageen.

Iron (Fe). This is the second most common metal known to man and the most important iron ores can be divided into four groups.

1. Magnetite is the richest ore and may contain over 70% of its weight in iron. Although found in small quantities in many parts of the world, the greatest amounts are produced by open cast mining around Gallivare and Kiruna in northern Sweden.

2. Haematite ores are red in colour and may contain as much as 70% of iron. The most notable deposits are those which are worked to the west and south of Lake Superior in the U.S.A. Other important deposits occur in the U.S.S.R., at Krivoi Rog in the Ukraine, and in the Cantabrian Mountains in northern Spain near Bilbao. This type of ore is also found in Britain in Furness in north Lancashire, and in west Cumberland.

3. Limonite ores are yellow-brown in colour and the richest may yield up to 50% of iron. The mining of these ores is especially important in Lorraine in France.

4. Siderite ores are the lowest grade and the yield of iron may be less than 30%. They are found in many areas of the world, and are the most extensive iron deposits in Britain where they are worked in the limestone uplands extending from Northampton-shire to the Cleveland Hills in north Yorkshire. An admixture of these ores is sometimes found in coal measures.

Pure iron is relatively soft and is of greatest value to man when converted to steel. This process is achieved in the Bessemer converter, and in open hearth and electric furnaces. The quality and nature of the steel produced depends upon the admixture of iron with small quantities of other minerals such as manganese, chrome, tungsten and nickel.

The major iron ore producing countries in order of importance are the U.S.S.R., the U.S.A., France, China, Canada, and Sweden.

The leading steel producers are the U.S.A., the U.S.S.R., West Germany, Britain, Japan, China, and France.

Ironwood. A name given to several different kinds of timber all of which are of very hard dense wood that sinks in water. Used for timber work that has to stand much water, especially salt water, hence it is used for ships' blocks.

Isinglass. A thin edible gelatine that is used for clarifying wines, spirits and beer and for making jellies and preserving eggs. It comes from drying the swim bladder of large fish, especially sturgeon. Chief exporting countries are Russia, Brazil and Canada.

Ivory. Comes mostly from Africa though some comes from Asia. It is the tooth substance or tusk of some animals, e.g. elephants (male), walrus and hippopotamus. Used for piano keys, billiard balls, knife handles, toilet accessories. Ivory dust is used as a polishing substance and for making Indian ink.

Vegetable ivory is the seeds or nuts of two species of palm trees that can be used for small articles because the nuts are hard.

Ivory nut. *See* Tagua.

J

Jade. A white to emerald green mineral used for jewellery and carved ornaments. It is the name commonly given to jadeite. It comes chiefly from Burma, China, Tibet and New Zealand.

Jalap. A drug from the tuberous root of a Mexican climbing plant of the convolvulus family. The plant is rich in resin.

Jamaica pepper. *See* Pimento.

Jarrah. A large Australian eucalyptus tree that is used for telephone poles and road blocks, as well as for railway sleepers as it is a heavy wood that resists insect attacks, including white ants.

Jasmine *(Jessamine).* It may be a shrub or a climbing plant for there are about 100 species; they all bear fragrant white flowers. These flowers have the ability to perfume grease by what is known as the enfleurage process. In China a species is cultivated for its flowers which are used to make jasmine tea.

Jasper. An impure variety of quartz that is reddish brown in colour and may be streaked with other colours. It takes a high polish and is used as an ornamental stone. The main sources are the Libyan Desert and the Nile Valley.

Jerusalem artichoke. *See* Artichoke.

Jessamine. *See* Jasmine.

Jet. A kind of hard coal that takes a high polish. It is used for jewellery and ornaments. Whitby in Yorkshire is the best known source.

Jubblepore hemp. *See* Sunn hemp.

Jujube. A sub-tropical small tree that bears spines; it is cultivated in western Asia and southern Europe. The red or black fruit is fleshy and may be round or oval, and is used as a flavouring in sweets. When processed in syrup the fruits are known as Chinese dates.

Juniper. Forty species of coniferous trees and shrubs, the cones of which are used to flavour gin. The wood is aromatic and is used in the manufacture of the so-called "cedar" pencils, and also for chests for storage, telegraph poles and fencing. From the wood comes, too, oil of cedar-wood. Oil of juniper, which is used medicinally, comes from the tree. The berries may be dried and used as a flavouring for meat.

Jute. Grown mainly in the delta of the Ganges but also produced in Brazil. It needs a fertile soil and a hot damp climate. The stems are retted in order to remove the fibres which are used in the manufacture of hessian, backing for linoleum and carpets, sacks, tarpaulin, upholstery and string. In its usefulness as a fibre jute comes second only to cotton.

K

Kainite. It is a mineral, potassium chloride and magnesium sulphate, and is used as a fertilizer as well as a source of potassium. The chief deposits are at Stassfurt in Germany and in the Carpathians.

Kale. *See* Cabbage crops. A cultivated variety of cabbage.

Kangaroo grass. Native to Australia, this perennial grass grows to a height of 3 feet and is used as cattle fodder. Grown also in South Africa.

Kaoliang. Form of sorghum grown in N. China and Manchuria. Alcohol is distilled from it, and the grain is ground into flour. Stalks are used for thatching, as a fuel and for weaving into mats.

Kaolin. *See* China clay.

Kapok. There are about 54 species of this evergreen tree that may grow to a height of 100 feet, and is cultivated in Java, Ceylon and Malaya. The seeds, wrapped in hairs, are contained in a pod. These hairs are known as the kapok of commerce. They are almost waterproof and are used for filling life-jackets, life-belts, life-saving rafts, as well as for cushions and pillows. From the seeds comes kapok oil which is used for soap and in cooking.

Karakul sheep *(Caracul).* This is a native Asiatic breed of sheep, and it is also the name given to the fur prepared from the skins of the very young sheep of this breed. The fur when dressed resembles that of Astrakhan but has a flatter and looser curl. The fur is used for coats, hats and as a trimming. (*See* Plate XII.)

Karri. The native name of an Australian tree of the eucalyptus group, one of the "blue gums" that yields a hard red wood used for paving blocks.

Kauri pine. A coniferous evergreen tree that grows chiefly in New Zealand. The resin, known as kauri gum, is used for varnish. The timber, which is durable and of a light yellow colour, is used for shipbuilding and furniture. The straight trunk, which may reach 80–150 feet, has a thick resinous bark which is of particular value for ships' masts and telegraph poles.

Kava *(Cava, Ava).* Belonging to the pepper family, it is a tropical climbing plant of Indonesia from the root of which is made an intoxicating beverage.

Kelp. No longer of great commercial importance, it was once valued as a source of iodine and potassium. It is the ash that is produced when seaweed is burnt, and the industry was carried on in Brittany, the Highlands of Scotland and the Scilly Isles. Kelp is also the popular name for several large kinds of seaweed.

Kermes *(Lac, Cochineal)*. A red dye obtained from the dead bodies of certain insects that were found in Asia and southern Europe.

Kidney bean. *See* Bean.

Kieselguhr. *See* Diatomite.

Kingcup. *See* Marsh marigold.

Kino. A reddish gum similar to catechu that is obtained from the bark of the dhak tree. It is used in medicine, and for tanning and dyeing.

Kohlrabi. *See* Cabbage crops.

Kola nut *(Cola nut)*. Seeds of this evergreen tree are in pods and are eaten by the natives of West Africa. The nuts or seeds when dried are exported to manufacture into drinks, e.g. Coca Cola, as they contain caffeine.

Kumquat. The fruit of a tree native to China, and grown widely in eastern Asia. The yellow fruit, like a small orange, is dried and crystallized for export.

Kyanite. *See* Sillimanite minerals.

L

Labradorite. A rainbow coloured mineral of the feldspar group that is found in many igneous rocks but particularly in Labrador. It is used as an ornamental building stone.

Lac. In India the bo-tree is cultivated for the lac insect which lives on it. The twigs covered with the resin exuded by the lac insect are known as sticklac. These are washed free from dye to form seedlac. When melted and strained to form thin sheets, this resin is the shellac of commerce. It is also used in paints and varnishes, and a red dye is also obtained, although this is now largely superseded by synthetic dyes.

Lamb. *See* Mutton.

Lapis lazuli. A deep blue mineral consisting of sodium aluminium silicate and sodium sulphide which occurs in crystalline limestone.

Used as an ornamental stone for it polishes well. When powdered, it is used for ultramarine pigment. The main deposits are in Afghanistan and in the Andes of Chile, as well as near Lake Baikal, U.S.S.R.

Larch. An evergreen coniferous tree of which there are about 10 species which grow in cool temperate regions. The wood is very durable and is used for buildings, railway sleepers and boats. Where the summers are fairly warm the larch produces very clear turpentine. Larch trees which may grow to a height of 140 feet abound in the Alps, the Carpathians, Canada, Alaska, and in Oregon, U.S.A.

Latex. The milky juice secreted by many types of plants and usually white. Contains mainly gums, proteins, salts and tannin as well as carbohydrates. Used commercially as a source of rubber.

Laurel. The name given to several evergreen trees and shrubs. From the variety known as bay, an aromatic oil is distilled. Common laurel yields oil of bitter almonds by distillation and prussic acid. The laurel leaf can be used with caution as flavouring in confectionery.

Lavender. An evergreen shrub that grows in mountainous areas and in western Europe, cultivated in Great Britain. From the mauve flowers is distilled the essential oil of lavender that is used in the manufacture of perfume. Dried lavender flowers are used in the making of perfume sachets.

Laver. An edible marine algae of a red or purple colour that is common around the coasts of Great Britain.

Lead (Pb). A metallic element that is usually associated with other ores but does occur pure in Sweden. The chief ore is galena and the chief lead-producing countries are the U.S.A., Australia in the Broken Hill area, Mexico and Canada. Lead is the basis of most solders and is alloyed with other metals to form type and shot metals. It is soft and easily worked, used for roofing, service pipes, red lead and lead foil. Lead arsenate is used as an insecticide especially for fruit trees. Lead absorbs radio-activity.

Leaf beet. *See* Beet.

Leather. This is the term given to animal skins or hides that have been preserved by tanning after the hair and flesh have been removed. After tanning the skin or hide is rubbed with oil and then dyed and dressed. Leather is used for upholstery, suitcases, handbags, footwear, footballs, netballs, gloves and harness. The chief hides and skins used are those of cattle, calves, kids, sheep and goats. The U.S.A. and India are important producers of cattle skins.

Leek. A bulbous biennial plant that is edible and grown in Great Britain. The whole plant except the roots is used in soups and stews as a vegetable; it has an onion-like taste.

Lemon. An edible citrus fruit with a yellow rind and of an oval shape that is widely grown in countries with a Mediterranean type of climate. Over half the world's production comes from the U.S.A., especially California; other leading countries are Italy, Spain, Australia, Greece and Algeria. The fruit comes from an evergreen tree that is a prolific fruiter. Lemon juice from the pulp of the fruit is used as a soft drink and is rich in vitamin C. Lemon oil is used in flavouring and in perfumery; this is obtained from the rind. Citric acid is also produced as a by-product. The pulp can be candied.

Lemon grass. This grass is native to Asia and has lemon-scented leaves which are distilled to produce the aromatic oil that is used in perfume as oil of verbena, and also medicinally.

Lentil. The seed of a leguminous plant grown for food and of special importance in India. It is sometimes grown mixed with barley, and may be used as human food or for milch cows.

Lepidolite. A pink litha-mica often associated with rubellite composed of basic aluminium, potassium lithium fluosilicate. In colour it is greyish-white or mauve, and from it is extracted lithium salts.

Lettuce. An edible annual vegetable that grows widely in Europe and other cool temperate regions and that is used chiefly in salads. There are two main varieties, cos and cabbage lettuces, the former being erect and crisp, and the latter, as the name implies, being cabbage-shaped.

Lichens. This is the term given to a colony of algae and fungi that each supply the needs of the other and are widely distributed, being especially plentiful in marshy areas, in the tundra and in mountainous districts. A few species are edible while others yield dyes or drugs.

Lignite. *See* Coal.

Lignum vitae *(Guaiacum)*. This tree that grows to a height of 40 feet is native to the West Indies and has a very hard, heavy, greenish timber that is used for bowls, pestles, rulers and ships' blocks, while from the tree comes a resin used medicinally. The wood of the tree is of sufficient density to sink in water.

Lima bean. *See* Bean.

Lime. This is a fruit rather like a lemon but smaller and green and comes from an evergreen tree about 8 feet high that is not so resistant to frost as other citrus trees. Lime juice and citric acid are prepared from the fruit, the former being useful in the prevention of scurvy. The chief producing countries are the West Indies, Mexico, and the southern states of the U.S.A.

Also a deciduous tree that is native of Europe, northern Asia and North America and may grow to a height of 100 feet. There are about 100 species, all in the north temperate region. The American species known as basswood provide the wood for the manufacture of kitchen furniture and cheap furniture that is stained or painted but not polished. From the inner bark of the tree comes the fibre known as bast that is used for mats. The wood can also be used for paper-pulp. Known also as a linden tree. (*See also* Coral; Limestone.)

Limestone. A rock that is white when free from impurities and is chiefly made up of calcium carbonate, deposited as the remains of sea-creatures in shallow water many millions of years ago. Rain water dissolves limestone and therefore its use as a building material is not very satisfactory. It is burned to produce quicklime which is used as a neutralizer to the acidity of soil, and in chemical manufacture as well as that of glass and soap. Magnesian limestone is known as dolomite.

Limonite. An important iron ore which is found in the English Midlands, Lorraine and Cuba.

Linden. *See* Lime.

Ling. *See* Heath.

Linseed oil. *See* Flax.

Liquorice. The peeled root of various species of a perennial leguminous plant that grows in the warmer parts of Europe and in California. The crushed root is used for making the liquorice of commerce which is of a black-brown colour and is used in the manufacture of sweets and for medicine.

Litchi. *See* Lychee.

Lithium (Li). A chemical element similar to sodium and potassium and is the lightest of all the metals, and its silvery white appearance tarnishes very quickly. It is used for light alloys, it increases the strength of aluminium and is used also as a hardener for some stainless steels and for silver solders.

Lithocarpus. An evergreen oak-like tree of which there are some 100 species. Native to Asia it belongs to the beech family. Species in Oregon and California yield bark that is valuable for tanning, and these species are sometimes known as tanbark oak.

Lithographic stone. A compact limestone used in lithography and comes chiefly from Bavaria. The blue and black varieties being the hardest are the best. It is also obtained from Canada, and Missouri, U.S.A.

Lithopone. *See* Barium.

Litmus. A colouring matter that is obtained from certain lichens found in the Levant and used to impregnate absorbent paper which is used to indicate whether a liquid is acid (paper red), alkaline (paper blue) or neutral (paper purple).

Llama *(Alpaca* and *Vicuña)*. This animal belongs to the camel family but it is smaller than a camel and has no hump. It is found only in South America where it is domesticated. Its white wool is valuable, but it is also used as a beast of burden, and as a producer of milk and meat. (*See* Plate XIII.)

Loadstone. *See* Lodestone.

Lobsters. *See* Shellfish.

Locust tree *(Carob tree)*. The pod of this evergreen tree is purple and about 4–8 inches long and contains brown seeds which are ground up and fed to animals. It grows in Mediterranean regions and in some species the pod is also edible.

Lodestone *(Loadstone)*. A form of magnetite which is used as a magnet in a mariner's compass.

Loganberry *(Logan blackberry)*. A plant that is a cross between a raspberry and a blackberry that bears deep red edible berries. Flourishes in cool temperate regions.

Logwood. This is the name given to the heart wood of an evergreen tree that grows in Central America and the West Indies. The wood chips produce a dye that gives purple, blue and black colours. It is also known as Campeachy.

Loofah *(Luffa)*. Used as a bathroom loofah, it is the skeleton of the fruit of a climbing plant that is shaped rather like a cucumber and is native to Africa.

Lucerne. *See* Alfalfa.

Luffa. *See* Loofah.

Lychee *(Litchi)*. The fruit of a tree that is native to the south of China and sub-tropical regions. The tree grows to a height of 40 feet but needs a cool winter in order to produce prolific fruit. The fruit, which is oval with a reddish skin, grows in clusters and it is the white pulp which is edible.

M

Macaroni. *See* Wheat.

Mace. *See* Nutmeg.

Mackerel. *See* Fish.

Madder *(Dyer's madder, Munjeet)*. Obtained from various species of plants of north-east Asia and Indonesia. The roots yield the dye which is used largely by physiologists as it dyes bone structure.

Magnesite ($MgCO_3$). The principal ore of magnesium which comes mainly from the U.S.S.R. and the U.S.A. It is also used in the making of refractory firebricks for steel furnace linings.

Magnesium $(Mg)_3$ This silvery metal occurs in dolomite, serpentine, asbestos, magnesite and other silicate minerals. There are large deposits in the U.S.S.R., Greece, Austria and Czechoslovakia. It is used in the manufacture of fireworks, flashlights, and medicinally as magnesium salts. It is used as a strong light alloy with zinc and aluminium in aircraft.

Magnetite (Fe_3O_4). A valuable iron ore, but often cannot be worked until the phosphorus content has been removed. The chief producers are Sweden, the U.S.A. and the U.S.S.R.

Mahogany. The timber used as a cabinet wood, it is a rich red-brown colour. It grows widely in Central America, especially Honduras, and in South America, also in Uganda and Nigeria, and may reach 100 feet in height.

Maidenhair tree *(Gingko)*. A deciduous tree with an edible fruit that is like a plum. It grows in China and Japan.

Maize *(Corn, Indian corn, Mealies, Sweet corn)*. A very important cereal of the grass family that under good conditions grows to 20 feet. It grows through a range of latitude of 58°N to 40°S and includes many varieties. It requires 150 frost-free days and summer rainfall. It is the chief American food plant and is very important in the U.S.A., Argentina and Brazil. It is used as human food, as fodder for animals (especially pigs), for the extraction of corn-syrup and sugar, and the stalks are used in the manufacture of paper.

Malachite. A common copper ore, this mineral is the basic carbonate of copper found chiefly in the Ural Mountains. It is a

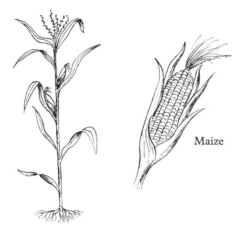

Maize

fine green colour and can be easily cut and polished and is therefore used for ornaments and jewellery.

Malt. *See* Barley.

Mamey. *See* Mammee apple.

Mammee apple *(Mamey, Saint Domingo apricot).* The yellow
fruit of this deciduous tree is eaten raw or made into jam. The
resin is used in medicine, and from the flowers is distilled an
aromatic liqueur.

Mandarin orange. *See* Orange.

Manganese (Mn). A metallic element which is widely distributed.
By far the largest deposits of its ores (e.g. pyrolusite) are located
in the U.S.S.R. India is the second largest producer, and extensive
deposits also occur in China, South Africa, Brazil, Ghana,
Morocco, the Congo and the U.S.A. It is largely used in metallurgy
and especially in steel making where it is important as a purifying
agent. Between 1 and 12% of manganese are added to steel to
increase its strength and hardness. The metal is also used in
small quantities in the chemical industry, and in the manufacture
of paints and varnishes.

Mangel-wurzel. *See* Beet.

Mango. The fruit of an evergreen tree that grows widely in Indonesia and other tropical countries. It varies in size and colour and has an edible, juicy yellow pulp. The unripe fruit is used for chutney and in preserves, but the ripe fruit does not travel well.

Mangold. *See* Beet.

Mangosteen. Native to Malaya, this deciduous tree has a purple, round, highly valued, edible fruit that is also rich in tannin.

Mangrove. The wood of these trees is hard and durable, the fruit is edible and the bark, known also as cutch, is used in tanning. The trees flourish in tropical regions in salt marshes and mud near to the coast.

Manila hemp. *See* Abaca.

Manilla nut. *See* Groundnut.

Manioc. *See* Cassava.

Manna. A food which comes from the sweet juice of several kinds of trees or shrubs and may be caused by the puncturing of the bark of the tree by an insect as in the case of the tamarisk tree. The juice is obtained by making cuts in the bark.
Used as a laxative.

Maple. The name of deciduous trees of the genus *Acer* which are widespread in North America and Europe. They yield valuable timber, and the sugar maple is tapped for maple syrup and sugar, especially in New England, U.S.A.

Marble. A metamorphosed limestone made up of calcite that can be polished; the colours in the marble come from the impurities that are present. In a dry atmosphere marble is durable but weathers very easily. It is used for statues and ornamental interior work. There are marble quarries in France, Italy, Spain and Belgium as well as in the U.S.A., India and Algeria.

Marcasite. A form of iron pyrites sometimes used as a gem-stone.

Marjoram. An aromatic herb of the mint family that grows in Europe and western Asia, and the leaves are used as a flavouring in cookery.

Marl. A mixture of lime, clay and sand that is used to improve the fertility of peaty soils. Some is used in the manufacture of Portland cement and as an insulator as it may contain over 80% calcium carbonate.

Marram grass. A perennial grass that flourishes near the coast in Europe and North Africa. It is used to stabilize sand dunes as it has long straggling roots which bind the sand together.

Marron. *See* Chestnut.

Marrow. An annual plant of the gourd family that may trail or be bush-like. It is cultivated in Britain. The fruit is cylindrical and is usually white, green or yellow and weighs up to 50 lb. There are many varieties, called squash, pumpkins and gourds in America. Zucchini or courgettes are a dark green variety.

Marsh gas. *See* Methane.

Marshmallow. A perennial herb or shrub-like biennial that grows near the sea on marshy land. It is about 3 feet high and has pink flowers, and from the root comes a sticky substance used in confectionery.

Marsh marigold *(Kingcup)*. Grows widely in the northern hemisphere in damp places; the buds are pickled and used as a substitute for capers, while the young shoots and leaves can be used as a vegetable.

Mastic *(Mastich)*. The name given to a resin that comes from the bark of evergreen trees of the Mediterranean region; it is obtained by cutting the bark. On contact with the air the resin solidifies into yellow lumps. Used for varnishes.

Maté *(Yerba maté, Paraguay tea)*. The leaves of a small shrub of the holly family are dried and used for tea that has a stimulating effect and that has the advantage of retaining its flavour even when exposed to dampness. It is grown mainly in Paraguay and southern Brazil.

Matico. The dried leaves of a shrub belonging to the pepper family grown in South America are infused for tea that is mainly used as a tonic.

May. *See* Hawthorn.

Meadow saffron. *See* Colchicum.

Mealies. *See* Maize.

Medick. *See* Alfalfa.

Medlar. Grown in western Asia and Europe the deciduous tree bears fruit that is brown when ripe and eaten when almost rotten. Used in jellies. It is a small tree rarely above 25 feet.

Meerschaum *(Sepiolite)*. This mineral comes mainly from Greece and Turkey and is associated with magnesium carbonate and is a whitish-grey colour. When exposed to heat it hardens and is used for tobacco pipes, cigarette holders, as a soap substitute and for building purposes.

Megasse. *See* Bagasse.

Melon *(see also* Cantaloupe; Muskmelon; Watermelon). A member of the cucumber family that is of trailing habit and bears an edible fruit that may be 8 inches in diameter containing many seeds and a soft pulp. It is grown in regions with a Mediterranean climate.

Mendioca. *See* Cassava.

Mercury *(Quicksilver)* (Hg). A metallic element liquid at normal temperatures. Most of the world's mercury comes from cinnabar which is found in sedimentary and igneous rocks. The chief producing countries are Spain, Italy, the U.S.A., China, Mexico, Japan and Yugoslavia. In its pure form mercury is most widely used in the making of electrical apparatus such as rectifiers and contact breakers. It is also used in the extraction of gold, for street lighting, and in barometers and thermometers. Its compounds are used in the manufacture of fungicides, drugs and paint, and in dentistry.

Metal. Most metals possess certain characteristics; they are often of a grey colour, they melt when heated, conduct heat and electricity, and are usually contained in ores though some are found in a pure state, e.g. gold. At normal temperatures most metals are solid, opaque, and can be polished.

PLATE IX. Date Palm, Laguna Beach, California, U.S.A. The date palm has a stem rising to some 70 feet and crowned with large feathery leaves, the female palm bearing the bunches of dates. (By Louis Tager from Ewing Galloway.)

PLATE X. Hops in Kent. Picking the crop in the hop gardens in September. (Central Office of Information.)

PLATE XI. Hops on the "bine". The plant has rough lobed leaves, and the green "cones" of broad scales are borne by the female plant on the climbing stem that is known as a "bine". It is the ripened cones that are used for imparting the bitter flavour to beer and other malted liquors. (Radio Times Hulton Picture Library.)

PLATE XII. Karakul Sheep, South-west Africa. The young have a black fleece and the adults a grey or brown fleece. (State Information Office, Union of South Africa.)

PLATE XIII. Llamas at the railroad station in the town of Morococha, Peru. Llamas are native to the Andean regions of South America and are raised mainly as beasts of burden, though the coarse wool is spun and woven into blankets. (By Ewing Galloway, N.Y.)

PLATE XIV. Orange trees, Nelspruit, East Transvaal, South Africa. The trees are evergreen and are cultivated widely in warm temperate and subtropical regions. The flowers are white and sweet smelling and the fruit is large, round, and many-celled with a juicy pulp and a tough outer rind or peel of a bright orange colour. The rind from the bitter oranges is dried and candied and used as a flavouring in cakes, etc. (The State Information Office, Pretoria.)

PLATE XV. Oranges from a citrus farm at Rustenburg, Pretoria, South Africa (The South African Information Service, Pretoria.)

PLATE XVI. Pampas grass. Argentina. It grows to a height of 12–14 feet and has silvery-coloured silky clusters on the stalks. (Radio Times Hulton Picture Library.)

PLATE XVII. Peat cutting in County Wicklow, Eire. Peat is used as a fuel in Ireland and in the Scottish Highlands. (Bord Fáilte Photo.)

PLATE XVIII. *Hevea brasiliensis* in a Malayan plantation. Sloping cuts being made in the bark to provide a channel down which the latex flows to the cup fixed at the lower end of the cut. The cups are emptied each day and taken to the collecting station. (Dunlop Rubber Co.)

Methane *(Marsh gas).* Formed by rotting vegetation in swamps, and found also in coal mines, this gas is odourless and colourless, and is the chief constituent of natural gas.

Mica. A common rock-forming mineral of which there are several varieties but the most widely used is the white variety known as muscovite. It occurs in the form of crystals which may measure as much as 12 inches in diameter, with a thickness of anything up to 2 inches. Crystals have been found measuring several feet in diameter but these are very rare, however. Owing to its structure mica is easily divided into very thin sheets which are very flexible, transparent, and heat resisting, with a very high resistance to electricity. On account of this latter property its greatest use is in the electrical industry as an insulating material. Its transparent and heat-resisting qualities make it suitable for use in the small windows of heating appliances such as ovens and stoves. Ground mica is utilized in the manufacture of some roofing materials, wallpapers, paint and rubber.

The chief source of mica is the U.S.A., which is by far the largest producer. The U.S.S.R. and India are next in importance and other producing countries include Norway, the Republic of South Africa, Brazil and Rhodesia.

Microline. A type of feldspar of commercial value for its use in the manufacture of ceramics.

Milk. *See* Dairy products.

Millet. The term millet is used to cover a wide variety of small-grained cereals which are cultivated in drier climates ranging from warm temperate to tropical. The grain, when ground into flour, is used extensively as human food in Africa and Asia, but as grain it is often used for feeding poultry. In some countries, especially the U.S.A., millet is cultivated for use as animal fodder. In some instances different millets are known collectively under the terms sorghum and durra.

China and India, followed by West Africa, are by far the largest producers of millet.

Millet

Mineral oil. *See* Petroleum.

Mint. There are about 25 species of this plant which belongs to the family Labiatiae and which grows in temperate regions. The leaves are aromatic, and amongst the species are peppermint, spearmint, and pennyroyal which yields an oil used in medicine. Mint is used as a flavouring in confectionery and cooking.

Mispickel. The chief ore of arsenic which is found at Butte, Montana, and in Australia and Brazil.

Mohair. This is the hair of the Angora goat of Asiatic origin. It is long and silky and used for the manufacture of cloth. South Africa is the chief producer.

Molybdenite. This is the chief ore of molybdenum, being composed of molybdenum disulphide. It occurs in crystalline rocks, e.g. granite. The chief producer is the U.S.A. It is used in the making of steel, and in the electrical industry and dyeworks.

Molybdenum. A soft white metallic element that looks like silver and is produced chiefly in the U.S.A. and Chile. It is used in ferrous alloys for high-speed cutting steels, die steels and in structural steels.

Monazite. It is the chief source of cerium and thorium, and is a phosphate of cerium with a little thoria. It is produced in south-west India, Brazil, Indonesia, and the U.S.A. Formerly it was of use in the manufacture of incandescent gas mantles.

Monkey-bread. *See* Baobab.

Monkey-nut. *See* Ground nut.

Moonstone *(Water opal).* A semi-precious stone of bluish white colour, a form of feldspar that comes chiefly from Ceylon.

Mulberry. There are 12 species of this deciduous tree that thrive in the north temperate region; they bear edible fruit rather like a loganberry. The leaves arc fed to silkworms. In Japan a paper mulberry tree has bark that is used in the production of paper.

Mule. The offspring of a male ass and a mare, it is very strong and sure-footed and is bred for use in mountainous areas as a pack-animal.

Mung bean. *See* Bean.

Munjeet. *See* Madder.

Muscatel. *See* Raisin.

Muscovite. *See* Mica.

Mushroom. A delicately flavoured edible fungus. It grows wild, and is also cultivated, very often in darkened cellars.

Musk. From the abdominal gland of the male musk deer, native to Central Asia, comes a secretion that is dried and used as a means of giving permanency and strength to perfumes. It is now also made synthetically.

Muskmelon. Cultivated in the warm temperate regions of the world, it belongs to the cucumber family. The fruit varies in shape, size and colour, and the plant grows well in many types of soil provided they are damp and fertile. Fruit is edible. Cantaloupe is a type of muskmelon.

Mustard. An annual plant the seeds of which are ground and mixed with flour and yellow colouring matter to form the mustard of commerce, which is used as a flavouring, for baths and as an emetic. Black mustard seeds are used as a condiment while the seedlings of white mustard are used with cress in salad. White mustard is also used as a forage crop. Oil may be extracted from the seeds.

Mutton. Chilled and frozen mutton and lamb is exported mainly from New Zealand and Australia. Mutton and lamb together constitute over two-thirds of the meat export trade. The sheep are reared chiefly in the cool and warm temperate regions of the world.

Myrobalans. The dried fruit of different species of the Terminalia tree and used by dyers and tanners. Comes from India and Indonesia.

Myrrh. Used in perfumes, incense and as a mouth wash, it is the gum resin of species of Commiphora trees that are native to Arabia and Somaliland.

Myrtle. An evergreen tree that is native to the Mediterranean regions, the purple berries are edible, while the white scented flowers yield an essence that is used in perfume. This tree, some 12 feet in height, is abundant in southern and eastern Europe.

Myrtle wax. Used in the making of gramophone records and varnishes, it comes from a shrub, the candleberry myrtle, that grows in North America.

N

Nasturtium *(Indian cress)*. A perennial climbing plant the leaves of which are eaten in salads, while the young fruits are pickled in vinegar as a substitute for capers.

Natural gas. The chief producers are the U.S.S.R. and the U.S.A. The gas almost always occurs in association with oil borings and consists largely of methane. It also contains ethylene and other gases of the olefin series of hydrocarbons. It is collected and used for the lighting of towns and also as a source of heat.

Nectarine. A variety of the common peach but having a smoother skin and a firmer pulp.

Neodymium (Nd). A metallic element that occurs in monazite and cerite, and is a silvery white metal that easily tarnishes. Its salts are used to give a mauve colour to glass and porcelain.

Neon (Ne). An inert gas present in the atmosphere, and used in a variety of electric lamps.

Nephrite. A commoner type of jade, found in China, Mexico and New Zealand.

Nettle. A genus of plants usually regarded as weeds that have their leaves covered with fine stinging hairs which contain an acrid and caustic fluid. When young the leaves can be cooked and eaten as a vegetable, and are also used for brewing nettle beer. Found chiefly in the cool temperate regions.

Nettle tree. A deciduous tree of the elm family with leaves like those of a nettle but without the sting. It grows in Europe and has a sweet fleshy stone fruit that is edible. The timber is also useful.

New Zealand flax. *See* Phormium.

Nickel (Ni). A metallic element that is silvery white with a bright sheen that is resistant to corrosion. 80% of the world's nickel comes from Canada, the rest from the U.S.S.R., Greece, Norway, Burma, the U.S.A., Brazil and Morocco. Nickel steels are very strong and are used in the manufacture of cars, ships, locomotives, and also as stainless steel. Nickel silver is used for electro-plating and also for chromium plating. Nickel is the basis of all heat-resistant steels, and is used in coinage.

Nicotine. A volatile liquid that comes from the leaves of the tobacco plant. It is used as an insecticide, and when pure and colourless is a deadly poison.

Nightshade. *See* Belladonna.

Niobium (Nb). A grey metal, formerly known as Columbium, that is often found in association with tantalum. The chief ore is columbite, and it is mined in Nigeria and the U.S.A. It is used for hardening steel, stainless steel, and high-speed steels, as it is highly resistant to corrosion.

Nitrates. Potassium nitrate (Nitre) is found as a mineral deposit in Peru, Iran, Bolivia and India, while Chile saltpetre or sodium nitrate is found in Chile, Peru, Bolivia and Egypt. Used as fertilizers and for explosives.

Nut. The name given to a fruit consisting of a kernel encased in a hard shell; many are of great commercial value, and enter into international trade. *(See also under individual names.)*

Nutmeg. The evergreen nutmeg tree is native to the East Indies, and nutmegs are the dried kernels of its pear-shaped fruit. Indonesia is the largest producer of nutmegs today, but appreciable quantities are also produced in the West Indies (especially Grenada) where the tree was introduced. It reaches about 25 feet in height.

Mace is the spice obtained from the dried inner fibrous covering of nutmegs, the fruit being orange-coloured.

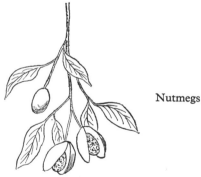

Nutmegs

Nux vomica. A deciduous tree that is grown in South-East Asia, it bears orange berries that contain the seeds that yield the poisonous drug that in small quantities acts as a tonic.

O

Oak. There are over 300 species of this tree that flourishes not only in the north temperate regions but also in North Africa, the Andes, Himalayas, and in Indonesia. The fruit, the acorn, is sometimes used as food for pigs, the bark is used for tanning, while the hard-grained timber is important as a cabinet wood, for furniture and shipbuilding.

The British oak is noted for its use in shipbuilding, the Holly oak has timber and bark that are used in tanning, the Cork oak, as the name implies, supplies cork, while both the White or Quebec oak and the Turkey oak have useful timber. An oak tree may reach 130 feet with a girth of some 60 feet.

Oak moss. A lichen that contains oleoresin that is used in perfume both for its fragrance and for its fixative properties. It grows on the trunks and branches of trees in mountainous areas in the northern hemisphere. It is a pale green colour and appears in tufts that may reach 3 inches long. Canada, the U.S.A., France and Yugoslavia are the chief producers.

Oats. The climatic requirements of oats are similar to those of wheat, but crops can be produced in areas too damp and too cool for wheat, and the northern limit of cultivation lies just within the Arctic Circle. Oats are grown primarily as animal fodder, ranking second to maize in this respect, and although enormous quantities are produced very little enters world markets due to the fact that the crop is of greater value to the producer as animal food rather than as an item of trade. As human food oats are eaten as porridge, oatcakes and groats.

Oats which grow to a height of 2–5 feet are cultivated extensively

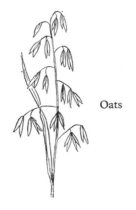

Oats

in nearly all European countries, and in Canada, but more than half the world's supplies come from the U.S.S.R. and the U.S.A.

Obsidian. When lava that is rich in silica cools rapidly a natural glass is formed that is obsidian, and may be black, grey or green in colour. It is known as Iceland agate when polished and used as a gem-stone. Often used by primitive tribes as a material out of which to fashion their weapons. Occurs in many parts of the world.

Ochres. Native earths containing hydrated iron oxide and clay; if yellow contains ferrous oxide, if red then ferric oxide. The best ochres for use in paints and pigments come from South Africa, France and India.

Oil. This is a general term that is given to an organic liquid that will not mix with water. Mineral oils come from hydrocarbons derived from petroleum, coal or shale.

Animal oils are fats if they are solid, e.g. butter, lard.

Fatty oils come from vegetable sources, e.g. palms, olives, groundnuts.

Essential oils are volatile and have a definite smell and come from plants.

Oil palm. This West African palm which is now cultivated throughout the Tropics needs a temperature between 75°F and 80°F

Oil palm

Fruit

for the best palms to be produced. The rainfall must be at least 40 inches a year and preferably 60–80 inches. The oil comes from both the fruit pulp and the kernels; usually the latter are exported for the process of extracting the oil. The chief producing countries are Nigeria, the Congo, Sierra Leone, Cameroons and Indonesia.

The oil is used for margarine, soap, and as an edible oil in cooking.

Oil plant. *See* Sesame.

Oily grain. *See* Sesame.

Okra. *See* Gumbo.

Olibanum. *See* Frankincense.

Olive. An evergreen tree 20–30 feet high of the genus *Olea* which flourishes in a Mediterranean climate, being especially important in Spain, Greece, Portugal and Tunisia. The small fruit grow in clusters, and oil, which is its main value, is expressed from the fruit, the oil being used in salads and for cooking, and table use generally. Olives can also be pickled.

Onion. Grows in a cool temperate climate, the bulbous part, which is really the thickened bases of the leaves, being edible and used as a vegetable or as a flavouring.

Onyx. An agate with alternate striped black and white bands that comes from South America and India. When polished it is used as an ornamental stone and for jewellery.

Opal. A form of amorphous silica that is coloured by impurities, and widely distributed throughout the world though the finest stones come from Australia. The changing of the colours in the gem-stone is due to the different water content of the thin layers in which the fragments of silica were deposited.

Opium. A species of poppy needing a tropical climate with not too abundant rainfall. The seeds of the opium poppy when unripe yield the juice that is the commercial opium used as a drug to relieve pain. Its sale is regulated by international agreement.

Orange. The edible citrus fruit of a deciduous tree that flourishes in Mediterranean climate areas. It is round and yellow-orange in colour when ripe. It is widely used as a dessert fruit and for juice as it has a high vitamin C content. The chief producers are the U.S.A., Brazil and Spain. Seville oranges are bitter and are used for marmalade making. Tangerines and mandarin oranges are smaller varieties of oranges. (*See* Plates XIV and XV.)

Orchella weed. *See* Archil.

Ore. The name that is given to a naturally occurring mineral that contains one or more metals. Whether or not they are exploited commercially depends upon the amount and value of the metal, and the ease of working.

Oregon myrtle. A member of the laurel family, it is a North American tree that grows to 90 feet, and bears a dark purple fruit rather like an olive. The wood is valuable for cabinet making.

Oregon pine. *See* Douglas fir.

Oregon tea tree. A member of the buckthorn family that grows in North America along the west coast. It grows to a height of some 10 feet and the smooth leaves are used as a tea.

Orris root. The rhizome of a kind of iris grown in temperate and in tropical regions, the dried root giving off the scent of violets. Used in cosmetic and dentistry preparations.

Orthoclase. A type of feldspar.

Osier. This is the general name given to any member of the genus *Salix* or willows which have been cut back so that the shoots are long and slender enough for their use in the manufacture of baskets and bags. The shoots of the purple osier are used for fine baskets and bags.

Osmiridium. This naturally occurring alloy of osmium and iridium is very hard wearing and is used for fountain pen nibs, instrument pivots, and watches. It occurs in gold dust as pale steel grey grains.

Osmium (Os). A metallic element of the platinum group of metals that is used as a catalyst and as a filament for electric lamps. Occurs also as the alloy osmiridium in gold dust.

Oxen. Used as draught animals drawing carts and ploughs, especially in the Tropics, southern Europe and Asia.

Oysters. *See* Shellfish.

Ozokerite *(Earth-wax, Ozocerite).* A native wax that occurs in Germany, near the Caspian Sea, and in Poland and Australia. From it is obtained a wax which is used in the making of candles, as an adulterant of beeswax and combined with rubber as an insulating material. It is a greenish wax that is found in bituminous beds of coal measures.

P

Pagoda tree. Native to China and Korea, it is a deciduous tree that bears clusters of yellow flowers that are used to yield a yellow dye used especially for the dyeing of silk in China. The tree belongs to the Leguminosae family and may reach a height of 80 feet.

Palladium. Metallic element of the platinum group that occurs with platinum but the largest part comes from the copper-nickel ores of Canada. Harder and stronger than platinum, it is used in telephone electrical contacts and for jewellery. In photography palladium salts are used for toning.

Palm *(see also under individual names).* About 150 species of an evergreen tree that flourishes in the tropical regions and grows to a height of about 150 feet. The leaves may be fan-shaped or feathery and are used for baskets, thatching, matting. Many palms are of commercial value, e.g. date palm, coconut palm, oil palm.

Pampas grass *(Cortarderia argentea).* This native grass has given its name to the vast treeless plains that stretch from Argentina across to the Andes. It grows to a height of some 12–14 feet and has silvery silky clusters on the top of the strong stalks. In Argentina it is now replaced by grass suitable for grazing, but it has been introduced into European gardens as an ornamental decorative grass, and the silvery clusters are dyed and sold for decoration. (*See* Plate XVI.)

Papais. *See* Paw-paw.

Paprika. *See* Pepper.

Papyrus. A plant of the sedge family that lives in or close to water. Used by the ancient Egyptians as a form of writing material by pressing the soaked papyrus stems that had been cut into strips and drying them.

Paraguay tea. *See* Maté.

Parsley. Hardy biennial that grows in temperate latitudes and is used in cooking especially as a flavouring and for garnishing.

Parsnip. A biennial plant grown in temperate regions for the sake of its edible large root which is eaten as a vegetable.

Passion fruit *(Sweet calabash).* A perennial climbing plant that grows in the West Indies and in the tropical regions of South America, and in Australia. The jelly-like yellow fruit, which is known sometimes as granadilla, is edible and used as a flavouring for ice-cream. Sweet calabash is a variety of passion fruit.

Paw-paw *(Papais).* A shrub which is native to North America and which belongs to the custard apple family. The fruit is edible and has a banana flavour if it is orange coloured, but inedible if it is white or pale yellow. The fruit does not travel well, so is only eaten where it is grown.

Pea. Annual climbing leguminous plant with pods that contain edible seeds that are used as a vegetable either fresh, frozen or canned. Split dried peas are used in soups, and a variety known as sugar peas have pods which are also edible. Peas require a cool temperate climate, and are best grown in England.

Peach. It is next in importance to the apple as a deciduous fruit. The tree, which grows to 25 feet, requires mild winters, but with a definite cool period. The fruit is about 3 inches in diameter and has a soft downy skin which is yellowish-red when ripe. The edible pulp is yellow or white, and is eaten fresh or canned. The chief producing countries are the U.S.A., France, Italy and South Africa. The nectarine is a smooth-skinned variety of the peach.

Peanut. *See* Groundnut.

Pear. The edible fruit of a deciduous tree that grows in the temperate regions, particularly important in Europe, Japan, South Africa, Australia and New Zealand. Fermented pear cider known as perry is manufactured. The fruit can be eaten raw, canned, dried or preserved.

Pearl. This is a precious stone that is found inside the shells of molluscs, particularly oysters. When a foreign body enters the shell the creature covers it with layers of calcium carbonate which is the same material as its shell. Cultured pearls are formed by the deliberate placing of foreign matter within the shell. In rivers the pearls produced by the mussels are known as seed pearls and are very small. Found in Scotland, Ireland, China, the U.S.S.R. The chief pearl fisheries of the world are off the Philippine Islands, the coast of Queensland, and Ceylon where the pearls are collected by divers. From the Bahamas come pink pearls while the rare black pearl comes from oysters of the South Sea Islands.

Peat. Peat is really an early stage in the formation of coal and is formed by the accumulation of decayed vegetation in swamps. It only possesses about half the heat of coal but is nevertheless used as a fuel when it is dried. Some peat is dug into the ground to increase fertility. Peat is important in the U.S.S.R., Canada, Finland, Sweden and Ireland. (*See* Plate XVII.)

Pecan. A round or oval edible nut that is the fruit of a tree cultivated in North America, especially in the southern states. The tree may be as much as 180 feet tall.

Pennyroyal. Belonging to the mint family, this is a scented herb that yields a volatile oil that has stimulating properties, and was formerly used medicinally.

Pentlandite. Nickel iron sulphide from which nickel is obtained.

Pepper. This is one of the oldest and most widely used spices. It is produced from the berries of a tropical climbing plant native to southern India and Ceylon. White pepper is obtained from the dried seeds contained in the ripe berries or peppercorns. Black pepper is produced from the unripe whole fruit which is dried and then ground. Oil of pepper is used in the manufacture of some perfumes. The chief sources of these peppers are Indonesia, India, Sarawak and Malaya.

Pepper

Red peppers are derived from ground capsicums, known also as paprika, and chillies. These are the red seed pods of numerous varieties of small shrubs which grow in both temperate and tropical climates. The large pods, about 1½ inches long, are known as capsicums, and the small pods which produce the hottest peppers, including cayenne pepper, are called chillies. These seed pods are

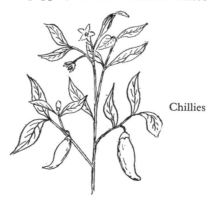

Chillies

also used for pickling, flavouring food, and for medicinal purposes. The chief producing countries are India, East and West Africa, and tropical South America.

Peppercorns. *See* Pepper.

Peppermint. Grown in the U.S.A. and Europe this is a perennial herb of which there are two varieties—white, the oil of which fetches the highest price, and black, which yields more oil and is therefore more widely cultivated. The volatile oil is widely used as flavouring and in medicine.

Peridot. A pale greenish-yellow, rather soft kind of chrysolite that is used in jewellery. The name is also applied to a yellow variety of tourmaline found in Ceylon, and to a yellowish-green variety of tourmaline found in Brazil.

Peruvian bark. *See* Cinchona.

Petroleum. A naturally occurring mineral oil found in sedimentary rocks. There are large deposits in the U.S.A., Iraq, Iran, Arabia, Venezuela, the U.S.S.R., Canada and Mexico. Petroleum is formed by the decayed animals and plants of the sea which aeons ago sank to the bottom, were acted upon by bacteria, and were changed into a thick greenish-black oil that is usually obtained by drilling. Lubricating and diesel oils are obtained from petroleum as well as paraffin waxes, motor fuel, asphalt and, in addition, the basis of many synthetic chemicals.

Phormium *(New Zealand flax or hemp).* This is a vegetable fibre which is obtained from the leaves, which may grow up to 8 feet in length, of a species of lily. This plant is native to New Zealand and for many centuries the Maoris have used its fibre for making cloth. It is also utilized in the making of ropes, twine and fishing nets.

Phosphates. This sedimentary rock, which comes mainly from North Africa, Germany, the U.S.S.R. and the U.S.A., is usually found with limestone and shales. It is used as a fertilizer and for matches and chemicals. The main constituent of the rock is apatite.

Pigs. Pigs have a very widespread distribution, not being affected by climate. The chief producers are China, the U.S.A., the U.S.S.R., Brazil, Germany, France and Poland. The pig acts as a scavenger, and is often fed on food such as skimmed milk, small potatoes, and on grain unsuitable for milling. The main products are pork, lard, bacon and ham.

Pilchard. *See* Fish.

Pimento *(Allspice, Jamaica pepper).* The pimento, a member of the myrtle family, is also known as allspice because its flavour tends to resemble that of a mixture of nutmeg, cinnamon and cloves. It is made from the small dried unripe berries of a West Indian shrub, which are also a source of oil used as a flavouring and in the manufacture of cosmetics and soap. Almost all pimento is produced in Jamaica.

Pin clover *(Hemlock stork's-bill, Red filaree, Pin weed).* An annual plant of the geranium family. It grows widespread and is naturalized in North America, especially along the west coast from Texas to California where it is used as a forage plant.

Pine. An evergreen coniferous tree with needle-shaped leaves of which there are some 76 species all of which yield resin. The Scotch pine is important also for timber, as are the Red and Corsican pines. In the Landes region of France the Cluster pine, which grows very quickly, is used for binding the sand together and preventing the further spread of the sand inland. The Stone pine that flourishes in Italy has edible seeds. The height of the trees varies according to species, but the Scotch pine may reach between 70 and 120 feet.

Pineapple. The perennial plant which needs a sub-tropical climate and sandy soil and which is widely cultivated in Hawaii, Mexico, Brazil, the Philippines and Cuba. The stiff sword-like leaves yield a fibre that is used by the Philippine natives to form a cloth. The fruit is eaten raw, canned, frozen, made into jam or the juice extracted. It may weigh as much as 6 lb, and has a tough yellowish outer skin.

Pin weed. *See* Pin clover.

Pipe-clay. This white clay is used for making clay pipes, for whitening, and for coarse pottery. It is found where kaolin has been washed away and then redeposited.

Pistache de terre. *See* Groundnut.

Pistachio. This edible nut is the fruit of a tree that needs a Mediterranean or sub-tropical climate. The fruit is small and hangs in clusters. The single seed contained in each fruit is used in confectionery as a green colouring agent.

Pitchblende. This ore that occurs naturally is uranium oxide and is the chief source of radium and uranium which it contains in small quantities. There are deposits in the Congo, Canada, Bohemia and Germany.

Pitch. *See* Asphalt.

Plaice. *See* Fish.

Plantain. *See* Banana.

Platinum. This is a heavy silvery metal that is harder than silver and has a high melting point. It is also very resistant to tarnishing. It is found in alluvial deposits in the Ural Mountains, Ethiopia, Colombia and Canada. Used for jewellery, alloyed with other precious metals, electrical contacts and dentistry.

Platinum metals. All have very similar properties to platinum and have much the same uses; they are ruthenium, rhodium, palladium, osmium, iridium, and platinum.

Plum. Plum is the edible stone or drupe fruit that may be yellow, purple, red or blue in colour when ripe. It is grown in Europe, North America, China and Japan. Plums are used for jam, dried to form prunes and eaten raw. Varieties include the greengage, yellow egg plum and damson.

Plumbago. *See* Graphite.

Plutonium (Pu). This element is derived from uranium and is radioactive; the chief uses are for nuclear reactors, and atomic bombs.

Pomegranate. In the eastern part of the world this is a very important fruit that comes from a small deciduous tree or bush.

POMELO

The fruit looks like an orange but has a very tough rind and the juicy pulp is full of seeds. Among the chief producers are the U.S.A., Chile, India and Mediterranean countries.

Pomelo. *See* Grapefruit.

Poplar. There are 30 species of this tree that has a soft and easily worked timber. In some cases the wood is used for paper-making. The tree flourishes in the cool temperate regions of the northern hemisphere. In the American continent these trees are also known as cottonwoods. These cottonwood trees, which grow up to 150 feet, are often planted as shade trees.

Poppy. This plant may be an annual or a perennial and is widely cultivated. The tiny seeds are crushed in order to obtain the oil which is used in paints as a drying agent. In France and Germany the oil is used in salads. Other uses of the oil include soap, lamp oil and varnishes. The residue is used as cattle feed. Poppy seeds may also be used as a herb with a nut-like flavour. One variety of poppy yields opium.

Potash. *See* Potassium.

Potassium (K). A silvery white alkali metal with a brilliant lustre that very quickly dulls. It is found in combination with aluminium and silica. The chief potash deposits are at Stassfurt in Germany, and others are in the Urals, in Spain and in California. Potassium compounds are used for soap manufacture, glass, fertilizers, explosives, and in tempering steel. About 90% of the total production is used as a plant fertilizer. It is usually applied in conjunction with other plant nutrients—for example, nitrates and phosphates. The chief ores are sylvite, carnallite and kainite. Potash is also present in the water of salt lakes.

Potato. The potato is the edible tuber of a plant of which there are many varieties. It is greatly used as a vegetable and is widely cultivated as it can be grown on any soil; the cooler areas produce the best seed potatoes. Potatoes are used in crop rotation. They are a source of starch and alcohol.

Poultry. More poultry are kept than any other animal, the chief countries being the U.S.A., China, the U.K., France, Canada and Italy. Chickens are kept for both egg production and for meat. They are the commonest form of poultry. Ducks are also reared for meat, as are turkeys and geese. Poultry feathers, and especially those of the eider duck, are an item of commerce.

Precious stones. *See* Gems.

Prickly pear. The pear-shaped fruit of a cactus, of which the pulp is edible. There are some 250 species. Some varieties are free from prickles. It has been introduced into Australia in order to provide fodder for animals in time of drought, but it spreads so rapidly that it can become a pest.

Prune. *See* Plum.

Puff-ball. A round fungus that is edible only when young and white.

Pulque. The juice of a species of agave which is fermented and used as a drink by the natives of Mexico; very nutritious.

Pulse. This is the collective name for peas, beans, lentils, and other plants that belong to the leguminous family.

Pumice. Very light and porous stone that is formed of volcanic lava which contains many small bubbles. It is used for the removal of stains from the skin, as an abrasive, and as a packing agent for vinegar generators. It is only found in lands where there has been comparatively recent volcanic activity, e.g. Iceland, Hungary, and New Zealand and in Nevada, U.S.A.

Pumpkin. A variety of gourd grown in Europe and North America, this annual plant, which may be of a climbing or bush habit, has a round yellowish fruit that may weigh up to 20 lb. The pulp is edible and is also used for feeding livestock.

Purslain. *See* Purslane.

Purslane *(Purslain)*. A plant used in salads and for pickling.

Pyrethrum. A member of the chrysanthemum genus. The flower heads of some species are powdered to yield pyrethrum, which is an important insecticide.

Pyrites. This is iron disulphide that occurs naturally as a yellow mineral that develops a metallic lustre on exposure to the atmosphere. It is used in the production of sulphuric acid, sulphates and sulphur dioxide. Important producers are Spain, Tasmania, Germany, Portugal, Japan, the U.S.A., Italy and Norway. It often contains copper, nickel, cobalt and gold in commercial quantities.

Pyrolusite. A source of manganese which is mined in the U.S.S.R., Germany, Brazil, India, Cuba and the U.S.A. It is used in the manufacture of steel, glass and paint.

Pyrrhotite. The most important nickel ore, although it is composed largely of iron sulphide. It is found at Sudbury, Ontario, and in Finland and Sweden.

Q

Quartz. Quartz is a natural crystalline form of silica. It is the commonest mineral and is the chief ingredient of sand and sandstone, and is very widely distributed throughout the world. It varies in colour according to the impurities that are present and may be a semi-precious stone, e.g. amethyst. Quartz sand is used as an abrasive, a building stone, in cement manufacture, in glass and porcelain, and in foundry moulds. If the crystals are pure they may be used for lenses and prisms, and in the radio and television industries.

Quassia. A deciduous tree that yields medical quassia, a bitter tonic. It grows to a height of about 60 feet and is native to the West Indies. It is also used as a substitute for hops, and as an insecticide.

Quebracho. A tree that grows in Paraguay and Argentina with a very hard wood, hence its name which means "axe-breaker". An extract from the tree is used for tanning leather.

Quicklime. This is calcium oxide obtained by heating calcium carbonate.

Quicksilver. *See* Mercury.

Quince. A small deciduous tree that bears a roundish fruit that is golden coloured when ripe. If eaten raw it is bitter, and usually the fruit is made into jams and jellies, becoming pink in colour when cooked.

Quinine. *See* Cinchona.

Quinoa. A grain native to the Andes of South America, it is cultivated by the natives as a food, the small seeds being either ground into flour or cooked like rice. The green parts of the plant are used as a vegetable.

R

Radish. This annual or biennial plant possesses a swollen red or white root that may be round or oval in shape, which is edible and used in salads. It grows in the temperate parts of Europe and Asia.

Radium. (Ra) A chemical element that is very radioactive and occurs in pitchblende and uranium deposits. It is mined chiefly in the Katanga region of the Congo, near Great Bear Lake, Canada, and in Czechoslovakia. It is a source of atomic energy, and is also used in medicine, particularly in the treatment of cancer, and also in the luminous dials of watches, clocks and meters.

Raffia. From the inner bark of the raffia palm which grows in Japan and Madagascar comes the fibre that is used by gardeners for tying plants and also for coarse embroidery, as well as for baskets.

Raisin *(see also* Grapes). A raisin is a dried grape that is used in cookery and as a dessert fruit. The grapes may be dried in an oven though the sultana raisins are dried in the sun; so are the small black seedless grapes that form currants. From the muscatel grapes come the large muscatel raisins. They are the products of Greece, Anatolia and Spain and the Mediterranean-like regions of Australia and California.

Ramie *(Rhea, China grass)*. The stems of a perennial plant contain the ramie fibres which are the strongest natural fibres known and are non-stretchable and non-shrinkable. They are woven into material and nets and used for incandescent mantles. The plant grows chiefly in south-east Asia where it may reach 6 feet in height.

Rape. Rape is widely used as a fodder crop, especially for sheep, and there are both winter and summer varieties. Winter rape seeds when crushed yield an oil that is used as a lubricant and as an oil for lamps; the seed that has been expressed for oil is then used in cattle cake manufacture.

Raspberry. A shrub that is found in Europe, northern and western Asia and North Africa with prickly stems that produces red, yellow or black fruit that is eaten raw, or made into wine and jam.

Rattan cane. *See* Cane.

Realgar. A mineral composed of arsenic mono-sulphide that is used in fireworks and as a red pigment. It is also a source of arsenic and arsenious oxide or white arsenic. Usually occurs with ores of silver and lead. Nevada is the main producer.

Red filaree. *See* Pin clover.

Red fir. *See* Douglas fir.

Red pine. *See* Douglas fir.

Redwood. *See* Sequoia.

Resin *(see under individual names)*. The name given to a large number of substances which are sticky at certain temperatures, and are usually exuded from trees, hardening in due course. Used in the manufacture of paints and varnishes. Fossil resin is known as amber and is used for jewellery.

Rhea. *See* Ramie.

Rhodium. (Rh) This is one of the platinum metals and is used for plating silver in order to prevent tarnishing. Also used in the preparation of a "silvered" surface that serves as a reflector in mirrors. Alloyed with platinum.

Rhodochrosite. A mineral containing manganese carbonate that is a source of manganese. It usually occurs in sedimentary rocks and crystalline masses. Colorado, U.S.A., is one of the suppliers.

Rhodonite. A red mineral composed of manganese metasilicate that is used ornamentally. It is chiefly mined in the Urals and in California.

Rhubarb. A perennial plant that is widely cultivated in the cool temperate regions of Asia and Europe, especially in Great Britain. While the leaves are poisonous the juicy, pink stalks are edible. Rhubarb is cooked, and is used for jam and wine. The dried powdered root of Turkey rhubarb is used in medicine.

Rice. This cereal is second only to wheat in the total amount produced. It is the staple food of South-East Asia. Its water requirements during growth are greater than for any other cereal. The general conditions necessary for its cultivation are a rich alluvial soil which will retain water on and below the surface of the ground; an annual rainfall of 50 inches or more unless the crop is grown under irrigation; temperatures of over 75°F during the growing season, and a large labour force for cultivating and harvesting the crop.

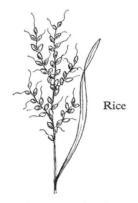

Rice

The seed is sown under water in the mud of nurseries, and when about 6 inches high the young plants are transplanted under water in the main paddy fields. The plant grows quickly and when mature the water is drawn off and the ground dries out in readiness for harvesting. Under ideal conditions as many as 5 crops have been obtained in a year.

In Eastern countries rice is known as paddy and although there are numerous varieties of the plant they are divided broadly into two main classes: (a) lowland or swamp rice; (b) upland or hill rice.

The monsoon lands of Asia are particularly suited to the cultivation of rice with China and India together producing more than half the world's total supplies. Other regions of production include the Mediterranean countries, the tropical coastlands of South and Central America, Central and West Africa, Egypt, the Gulf Coast lands of the U.S.A. and California.

In the West rice is polished prior to its sale whereas in the East the grain is merely husked and ground.

Rice-paper plant. This is really misnamed for it is an evergreen shrub from the stems of which a white pith is used to make rice-paper. This paper is used in the manufacture of paper and artificial flowers. It is a native of Formosa in the wet forested regions.

Rice, wild. *See* Wild rice.

Rocksalt. *See* Salt.

Root crops. Crops whose roots are important vegetables for human or animal consumption—for example, carrots, potatoes, turnips, sugar-beet. They form an important part in crop rotation.

Rosemary. This shrub with scented leaves and small mauve flowers is cultivated for the oil which is obtained by the distillation of the leaves, and used in perfume. Though native to the Mediterranean, it is widely cultivated in temperate regions. It is also used as a culinary herb with a strong, bitter taste.

Rosewood. South America, Central America, and Jamaica are important sources of this deep reddish timber which is used as a cabinet wood and especially for pianos. When the wood of this tree, which reaches up to 50 feet, is being worked it gives off a rose-like smell from its essential oils.

Rosin *(Colophony)*. It is a resinous substance obtained by the distillation of turpentine and is left when the oil of turpentine has been removed. The chief producer is the U.S.A. but it is also exported from Portugal and France. It is used in the manufacture of varnish, soap, paper and inks.

Rubber. The bulk of the world's rubber comes from plantations in Malaya, Indonesia and Ceylon. It is obtained from the whitish sap, latex, that exudes from certain trees found in the tropical regions but especially from *Hevea brasiliensis* that is native to the Amazon region. Crepe rubber is made by adding formic acid to the latex while foam rubber is made by making the latex frothy by means of a gas. Rubber has manifold uses amongst them being tyres, waterproofing, shoes. Rubber can also be manufactured synthetically.

Rubellite. A red variety of tourmaline used as a gem-stone and obtained from Siberia, Burma, the U.S.A. and the Urals. A pink variety is also known. The colour is due to the presence of manganese.

Rubidium (Rb). A rare element used in the manufacture of photo-electric cells and in microchemistry as a compound. This metallic element is often associated with mica and feldspars and is obtained from Europe and America.

Ruby. Occurring in crystalline limestone the ruby is the most valuable gem-stone and is a variety of corundum. It comes from Burma, Ceylon and Thailand. Poorer quality stones are used as bearing jewels in watches.

Rue. A herb with bitter strong scented leaves used as a flavouring.

Runner bean. *See* Bean.

Rutile. One of the chief ores of titanium found only in a few areas, the largest deposits being in Virginia, U.S.A.

Rye. An important cereal in the cool temperate regions. It can be grown as far north as the Arctic Circle, and on very poor dry sandy soils. It is important in Scandinavia, Germany, the U.S.S.R., Canada and Argentina. It is used as a fodder crop, and for the making of bread. The straw is used for thatching, animal litter, hats and paper. Vodka and rye whisky are distilled from it.

113

Rye

S

Safflower *(Bastard saffron)*. A scarlet dye is obtained from the flowers of this plant native to Indonesia, and cultivated in India. This dye was formerly an important commercial dye or rouge. Oil is extracted from the seeds.

Saffron. This substance is used as flavouring and as a yellow dye. It is produced from the dried stigmas of the purple saffron crocus which is cultivated in some Mediterranean countries, and in Iran and Kashmir.

Saffronhout. *See* Saffron wood.

Saffron wood *(Saffronhout)*. A South African tree which provides valuable timber and is found in tropical regions.

Sage. Native to southern Europe, it is a perennial plant with aromatic leaves that are dried and used as flavouring in cookery.

Sago. A starchy substance obtained from the pith of certain varieties of palm trees, but the chief source is the Metroxylon palm, or sago palm, which is native to the East Indies. Sago is obtained by splitting the stem of the palm, extracting the pith and grinding it into powder. This is mixed with water and then strained to separate the starch from the fibre. To produce the small grains of sago, the starch is mixed to a paste and rubbed through fine sieves. Indonesia, especially Borneo, is the main source of sago, which grows in low marshy areas to a height of about 25 feet.

Saint Domingo apricot. *See* Mammee apple.

Salmon. *See* Fish.

Salsafy. *See* Salsify.

Salsify *(Salsafy)*. Growing to a height of about 3 feet the plant has a white edible root that has an oyster-like taste. It is cultivated in the Mediterranean region, the U.S.A. and Canada but is found also in cool temperate areas.

Salt. Originating from the evaporation of sea water, salt occurs widely in the earth's crust as rock salt or halite deposits. Important sources of supply are the U.S.A., the U.K., China, India, Germany and France. Common salt (sodium chloride) is used as a preservative in fish-curing, meat-packing, and in curing hides, as a condiment, as a flux in metallurgy, and in the glass and soap industries. It forms an important constituent in the manufacture of baking powder, caustic soda, and washing soda, and is used in bleaching. It is one of the most important raw materials for the chemical industry.

Saltpetre. *See* Nitrates.

Samphire. Found along the rocky coasts of the Mediterranean and Black Seas and the North Atlantic, this plant is used in salads and in pickles. The leaves are thick and fleshy and have a salty flavour.

Sand. This is the term given to small particles of various minerals, but especially to mica, feldspar and quartz, and is the product of rocks that have been weathered by the agents of erosion. Sand's many uses include pottery, glass and as an abrasive, concrete, cement and in the building industry as mortar.

Sandalwood. An evergreen tree the fragrant wood of which is repellent to insects. It is used especially for ornamental woodwork and for specimen cases for insects. Oil is obtained by distillation from the wood and is used in perfume manufacture. It is native to Indonesia.

Sandarac. A resin obtained from a coniferous tree that grows in Australia, Africa and North America as well as in Morocco. It exudes from the bark and is used in the making of varnishes and for incense. The tree has valuable timber.

Sandstone. A common type of rock consisting mainly of quartz grains cemented together. It is used in the manufacture of silica bricks which are used to line furnaces, and also as a building stone, but it is not very resistant to weathering.

Sapan *(Sappan wood)*. A tree that grows in tropical regions of Asia and yields a red dye wood.

Sapodilla plum. An evergreen tree with a soft edible fruit with yellow edible pulp. Chicle, the gum obtained from the bark, is used in the manufacture of chewing gum. Important in the West Indies and Central America. The timber is very durable.

Sappan wood. *See* Sapan.

Sapphire. A blue variety of corundum which contains iron and titanium, hence its colour. The chief mining areas are Ceylon, Thailand, Rhodesia, Australia and Upper Burma where it is found in alluvial deposits.

Sardine. *See* Fish.

Sardonyx. A variety of onyx used as an ornamental stone in jewellery.

Sarsaparilla. A drug obtained from the roots of several species of smilax.

Sassafras. This deciduous North American tree yields a stimulant from the root (used to make root beer), and from the boiled leaves a substance that is used for thickening and flavouring soups. The fruit contains an oil that is used in perfume and a yellow dye comes from the bark and root. The tree grows to about 80 feet.

Satin walnut. *See* Sweet gum.

Savory *(Savoury)*. An annual plant of two varieties, summer and winter savory; the leaves of both kinds are used in cookery as a flavouring, particularly in soups and sauces. It is native to southern Europe, and seldom reaches more than 12 inches.

Savoury. *See* Savory.

Savoy. *See* Cabbage crops.

Scarlet runner. *See* Bean.

Scheelite. One of the chief ores of tungsten, coming mainly from California and Nevada.

Scorzonera. It is a perennial fleshy rooted edible plant native to central and southern Europe. It is shaped like a turnip and the white flesh is boiled and eaten as a vegetable.

Sea cucumber. *See* Beche-de-mer.

Sea kale. A hardy perennial that is cultivated in Europe as a vegetable for its blanched roots.

Seaweed. *See* Dulse.

Seedlac. *See* Lac.

Selenium (Se). An element which is sulphur-like, and though widely distributed rarely occurs native. Used with sulphur in the vulcanization of rubber; other uses include photo-electric cells and rectifiers, as a glass decolorizer, the dioxide as an oxidizing agent, and as an addition to copper and stainless steel in order to improve their machinability. Usually occurs as selenides of lead, copper, silver and mercury. Most of the world's supply comes from Canada, the U.S.A. and Zambia, with the latter contributing only a very small quantity.

Semolina. *See* Wheat.

Senna. A leguminous perennial plant or shrub that is grown in Nigeria and the Sudan. The flat seed pods and dried leaves are used medicinally as a purgative.

Sepia. From the ink sacs of the cuttlefish comes this dark brown dye that is used as a water colour.

Sepiolite. *See* Meerschaum.

Sequoia. A genus of conifers that include the giant redwoods which may reach over 300 feet. Found in Oregon and California. The timber is very strong and durable and resistant to pests.

Serpentine. A crystalline green mineral that is composed of magnesium silicate, and is used in the manufacture of ornaments as it can be highly polished. Some is mined in Cornwall.

Service tree. A deciduous tree that is found in warm temperate and Mediterranean regions. The greenish oval berries are used for making jellies. The fruit is edible when allowed to become over-ripe, and follows the mass of creamy white flowers which this 80-foot-high tree produces.

Sesame *(Gingelly, Gingili, Oil plant, Oily grain)*. A widespread annual plant that is native to India and Pakistan, the small seeds of which yield an oil that can be used as a substitute for olive oil. The seeds are also used as a spice on bread, etc.

Sesame

Shaddock. *See* Grapefruit.

Shale. This is a rock that consists of hardened clay. The softer shales are used for firebricks, the limestone shales in the manufacture of Portland cement, and the iron shales in paint; the alum shales yield alum, and the bituminous shales yield oil.

Shallot. Perennial edible plant with a bulbous root that belongs to the onion family, and is usually pickled.

Shantung. *See* Silk.

Shaya root. *See* Chay root.

Shea nuts. Grown in Ghana and Dahomey and yield a fatty substance known as shea butter. It is also used in the manufacture of soap.

Sheep. Sheep are bred either for their wool or for meat generally, but in some regions of southern Europe they are kept for their milk which is made into cheese. Sheep skins are an important export from many tropical countries. The largest number of sheep are kept in Australia, followed by the U.S.S.R., Argentina, India, the U.S.A., New Zealand and South Africa.

Shellac. *See* Lac.

Shellfish. These are molluscs or crustaceans whose external covering consists of a shell, e.g. oysters, crabs, lobsters, crayfish. Many are edible.

Siderite *(Chalybite)*. An important iron ore.

Silica. Consists of silicon dioxide and is found abundantly and in a fairly pure form in the earth's crust. The chief crystalline form is quartz. When pure it is colourless, but takes various colours according to the impurities contained in it, e.g. amethyst. Uses include lenses, the cutting and grinding of glass or stone, foundry moulds, furnaces and in the building of roads and buildings.

Silicon. (Si) A non-metallic element that is very commonly found in the earth's crust but almost always in combination with oxygen as silica. Acid-resistant steels are made by alloying it with iron, as are steels with special magnetic properties. Used widely in industries such as glass, china, porcelain, tiles and ceramics.

Silk. The fibre from the cocoon of insects, especially the larvae of the mulberry silk moth that feeds on mulberry leaves and produces white or yellow silk. From the wild silk worm that feeds on oak leaves comes the silk known as shantung that is coarser and of a brownish hue. Japan, China and Italy are the chief silk-producing countries.

Sillimanite. *See* Sillimanite minerals.

Sillimanite minerals. These are the aluminium silicate minerals, andalusite, kyanite, sillimanite, and dumortierite. They are important in the manufacture of high-grade refractories as they can withstand very high temperatures. Porcelain made from them is used for sparking plugs, laboratory ware and refractory bricks. Sillimanite minerals are obtained from Assam, California, Nevada and Transvaal. Occasionally gem quality minerals are found.

Silver. (**Ag**) A precious metal that is sometimes found native, but the bulk of the world production comes from deposits occurring in association with other minerals. Argentite is the chief ore and is usually found with the lead ore, galena. More than half the silver produced is obtained as a by-product in the refining of lead, copper and zinc. In addition, it is also found in appreciable amounts in association with gold.

Silver is a relatively soft and very malleable and ductile metal. Owing to its softness it is usually alloyed with copper, and in some instances with small percentages of zinc and nickel. Its chief use is for coinage. Many so-called "silver" coins, however, contain very little silver and some none at all. Other uses of silver include for making special solders, jewellery, silverware, electroplate and the backing of mirrors. It is also used in the photographic, glass and electrical industries.

Mexico, the U.S.A. and Canada are the largest producers of silver, but other sources include Peru, Australia, Bolivia and the Congo.

Silverberry. A North American shrub ranging from 6 to 12 feet with silvery olive-like fleshy fruit that encloses a nut. The fleshy part is edible.

Silver fir. An evergreen coniferous tree that bears cones about 6 inches long that is native to southern and central Europe. The tree may reach 150 feet and is an important timber tree. The name comes from the silvery appearance of the leaves. Turpentine is also obtained from this tree.

Sisal. A species of Agave, from which a hard fibre is obtained. It is native to Mexico and Central America, but is widely cultivated in East Africa, Indonesia, Haiti and Hawaii. The plant grows to a

PLATE XIX. Drying sisal in Tanzania. The fibre is extracted from the leaves by machines that beat and break the unwanted tissues of the leaves which are scraped away from the fibres. It is used in making mats, carpets, ropes, and for upholstery.

PLATE XX. Sisal cutting, Africa. The leaves are thick, sharp pointed about 5 feet long and 6 inches wide. (J. Allan Cash.)

PLATE XXI. Tea plant in Ceylon showing the flowers, seed pod and the leaves. The plant is carefully pruned so that it will grow into a bush of convenient size and shape for the "plucking" of the leaves. (By Ewing Galloway, N.Y.)

PLATE XXII. Tea pluckers at work in Ceylon. Each "plucking" is known as a "flush" and the work needs both skill and speed. After "plucking" the leaves are "withered", and then after rolling and crushing they are allowed to ferment. (Ceylon Tea Centre.)

PLATE XXIII. Tobacco, Kentucky, U.S.A. The crop of tobacco is ripe and ready for cutting. After harvesting the picked leaves are strung and allowed to wilt in the sun before they are cured. Curing is a form of drying in the sunshine or in specially built heated sheds. (From Ewing Galloway.)

PLATE XXIV. Specimen leaves of tobacco, Southwick, Massachusetts, U.S.A. Tobacco is related to the potato and tomato plants. The leaves grow from the main central stem. There are numerous varieties of tobacco plant some of which grow to a height of 7 feet. Tobacco flourishes best in a warm sunny climate. (By Ewing Galloway, N.Y.)

PLATE XXV. Vineyards near to Spiez on the Lake of Thun, Switzerland. (Paul Popper Ltd.)

PLATE XXXVI. A vineyard in the Paarl Valley, Cape Province, South Africa. (State Information Office, Union of South Africa.)

PLATE XXVII. Grapes being harvested. The bunches or clusters of grapes are carefully packed into hampers, ready for sorting and grading. (State Information Office, Union of South Africa.)

height of about 20 feet. The fibre is used for binder twine and ropes. Henequen is a similar variety, also known as Yucatan or Cuban sisal. (*See* Plates XIX and XX.)

Slate. A rock that is metamorphosed shale. It is capable of being split into thin sheets in accordance with the cleavage planes. It is used as a roofing material, and in powdered form for cement, bricks and pottery. It is quarried chiefly in North Wales, Ireland, Belgium, Scotland and Germany.

Soapbark. The inner bark of a tree of the rose family that grows mainly in Chile, and is powdered as a substitute for soap.

Soap plants. Included under this name are many herbs, trees and shrubs which contain some saponium which lathers in water but is also poisonous.

Soapstone. *See* Talc.

Soapwort. The leaves and root of this perennial of the pink family, which is widespread in its distribution, contain saponium. It can be used for washing materials.

Sodium (Na). A chemical element which does not occur naturally, but is common in combination with other elements. Common salt (sodium chloride) deposits are found in Cheshire, in Stassfurt, Germany, and in Poland. Borax is sodium borate, Chile saltpetre is sodium nitrate—both are important commercially. Sodium peroxide is used in bleaching and dyeing; other sodium salts are used in medicine; sodium sulphate is used as a food preservative. Sodium thiosulphate and sulphite are used in photography. Sodium carbonate is used in the manufacture of mineral waters. Sodium vapour is used for street lighting.

Sorghum *(Great millet, Indian millet, Guinea corn)*. There are many varieties of this grain with various names. The plant may be 3–15 feet high, the pith may be juicy, dry or sweet. In hot dry lands it is an important food crop, for example in South Africa, India and China (Kaoliang). The grain is made into starch and alcoholic drinks, while from some varieties a syrup is extracted. It is also cultivated in the U.S.A. It is sometimes erroneously called millet.

Sorrel. Grown in the northern hemisphere in the temperate zone it is a perennial plant that is used in sauces, soups and salads.

Sour sop. *See* Custard apple.

Soya bean. The soya bean comes from a leguminous plant native to the Far East, and although cultivated in China for over 3000 years it was not introduced into western countries until about the beginning of the 19th century. From the seed or bean a highly nutritious flour is produced, but in the west the soya bean is most valued as a source of vegetable oil of which it yields about 15%. The plant is cultivated extensively within the warm temperate regions between latitudes 25°N and 45°N, and also within the tropics, especially in Java. The greatest quantities of soya beans are produced by the U.S.A., China and Manchuria.

Spaghetti. *See* Wheat.

Spanish grass. *See* Esparto grass.

Spearmint. A kind of mint that is used in cooking and especially in the canning of peas. Chief grower is the U.S.A.

Spermaceti. A wax obtained from the head of the sperm whale and used for candles, ointments and in the dressing of cloth.

Sperm oil. Used as a lubricant, it comes from the thick outer cover of the blubber of the sperm whale.

Soya beans

Sphalerite *(Zinc blende, Blende)*. The chief ore of zinc, a sulphide occurring often with galena.

Spices. These are vegetable substances possessing distinctive flavours and aromas which are used for seasoning or flavouring food, in medicines, and in the manufacture of soap, cosmetics and perfumes. In general, they are the produce of tropical countries and are derived from various parts of plants such as the bark, roots, flowers and seeds. *(See also under individual names.)*

Spinach. Eaten as a vegetable, it is grown for the sake of its young leaves in cool temperate regions.

Spindle tree *(Euonymus, Wahoo)*. A small deciduous tree of some 20 feet, the wood of which was formerly used for spindles, hence its name. It is native to North Africa and Europe, and is used for charcoal making and in joinery.

Spinel. A mineral composed of magnesium and aluminium oxides. Gem-stones are often found in association with sapphires and rubies, and are often confused with the latter.

Sponge. Many species of this lowly water creature live in salt and fresh water, and are of various sizes and shapes. They are used for toilet and household purposes generally.

Spruce. About 40 species of this coniferous evergreen tree grow in cool temperate regions. Red and white spruces are used for wood-pulp; black spruce for paper pulp; Norwegian spruce yields the best timber as it may reach 170 feet in height with a diameter at the base of the trunk of 5 feet. The timber is used generally for pit-props, ships' masts and constructional work.

Squash. The American name for many varieties of marrow.

Star-anise. *See* Aniseed.

Star apple *(Cainito)*. An evergreen tree that grows in tropical America and bears edible fruit that is apple shaped. When unripe the seed cells form a star shape, hence its name. The fruit may be 4 inches in diameter.

Statite. *See* Talc.

Steatite. *See* Talc.

Stibnite. The chief ore of antimony, which is mined in China, Bolivia and Mexico.

Sticklac. *See* Lac.

Stoat. *See* Ermine.

Stramonium. *See* Daturine

Straw. The name given to the dried stalks of various cereals which is used for bedding and fodder for cattle. It is also used for the manufacture of strawboard, hats, baskets and for thatching.

Strawberry. A plant grown in temperate climates that bears a juicy sweet fruit with the seeds on the surface. Used as a dessert fruit, for preserving and as a flavouring.

Strontianite. This mineral, composed of strontium carbonate, is the principal source of strontium. It is used in the refining of sugar, and in the manufacture of fireworks. It occurs in limestone regions of California, the lead mines of Scotland, and in the Westphalian region of Germany.

Strontium. (Sr) A metallic element that occurs in strontianite and in celestite. It is distributed in small quantities in many different rocks and soils. Present in fall-out of nuclear fission.

Succinite. *See* Amber.

Sugar. This is obtained from the sweet juice that is extracted from some palm trees, the sugar maple, but more commonly from sugar-beet and sugar-cane.

Sugar apple. *See* Custard apple.

Sugar-beet. Sugar-beet thrives best in a cool temperate climate with summers averaging 70°F, a dry autumn in order to consolidate the sugar content, and rain during the growing season. It is an important source of sugar, which is extracted from the bulbous root. The residue is used as cattle fodder. It is cultivated widely on the northern plain of Europe, north and central U.S.A., and in Canada.

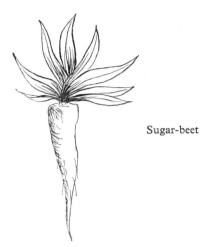

Sugar-beet

Sugar-cane. A giant grass with a solid stem of $\frac{1}{2}$ inch or so diameter that grows to over 20 feet in height. Needs a temperature of 80°F, over 40 inches of rain, and a rich fertile lowland soil. Cuba, India, Brazil, Hawaii, and the Philippines are important producers and exporters of sugar-cane. The chief source of sugar. The molasses are used as cattle food.

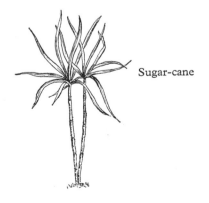

Sugar-cane

Sugar maple. *See* Maple.

Sulphur(S). A non-metallic mineral or element which occurs naturally in the volcanic areas of Sicily, Italy, Japan and Chile as well as in the oilfields of the U.S.A. Used for making sulphuric acid, as an insecticide, in medicines, as well as a means of making paper and wood more resistant to atmospheric conditions. In combination with other minerals it is found generally as a sulphide or as a sulphate. Sulphur dioxide is used as a bleach, and in the making of wood-pulp.

Sultanas. *See* Grapes, Raisin.

Sumac. A small deciduous tree that grows in warm temperate regions. From the resin that exudes from the bark varnish is made. One species yields a yellow dye from its leaves and twigs, and another has leaves used for tanning leather.

Sunflower. It is the double sunflower with a large yellow head that is of importance commercially. The flowers yield a yellow dye, the leaves are used as fodder, while the seeds are used for feeding to livestock. Cultivated in the U.S.S.R., Europe generally, Argentina, Egypt, India and Pakistan. Seeds when crushed yield oil.

Sunn hemp *(Indian hemp)*. An annual plant of the Leguminosae family and not related to true hemp. Used in the U.S.A. and India for canvas and cordage, and in some places for use as a green manure as well. It is also known as Bombay hemp, Jubblepore hemp and Benares hemp.

Swede. *See* Turnip.

Sweet calabash. *See* Passion fruit.

Sweet chestnut. *See* Chestnut.

Sweet corn. *See* Maize.

Sweet gale. A small shrub that grows in the north temperate zone. The leaves can be used for making tea of a medicinal nature.

Sweet gum. A North American tree with a rough bark that grows to over 100 feet and has a hard red-brown wood that is used in furniture making as satin walnut. A gum resin comes from the tree known as copal balsam.

Sweet potato *(Batata)*. Grown extensively in the U.S.A. and Japan as well as in the Pacific Islands. It is a plant with edible tubers which may weigh as much as 10 lb each. They are sometimes called yams.

Sweet sop. *See* Custard apple.

Swiss chard. *See* Beet.

Sycamore. A deciduous tree with large leaves, the timber of which is used for furniture. The Eastern sycamore or American plane is probably the largest hardwood tree in the eastern U.S.A. and may reach some 150 feet.

T

Tagua *(Ivory nut)*. From a tree that grows in Ecuador. Used in the manufacture of buttons.

Talc. A soft mineral composed of magnesium silicate that is widely distributed. In a compacted form it is known as soapstone or statite, a greasy stone used for carving and for utensils. French chalk used in tailoring is a granular variety. It is heat-resistant and is used for stoves and firebricks.

Tallow tree. Cultivated in south-east Asia though native to China the seeds are thickly coated with a white greasy substance that is known as vegetable tallow and used for the making of candles, and also for dressing cloth. A tree of the same name in Sierra Leone has a fruit with a thick yellow greasy juicy flesh which is used as a butter substitute.

Tamarind. A deciduous tree that is widespread in tropical lands. Apart from the use as timber, the leaves yield a yellow-red dye, and the bean pods are used medicinally.

TAMARISK

Tamarisk. The name given to small trees or shrubs that have the ability to withstand barren and salty soils and that can grow where nothing else is able to grow. They are often used as windbreaks. The branches are feathery and the leaves are very small.

Tanbark oak. *See* Lithocarpus.

Tangerine. *See* Orange.

Tannin. This is the general name given to vegetable products containing tannic acid which are able to change raw hide into leather. Much comes from the galls that form on oak and some other trees. Tannin is also used in medicine and in dyeing. *(See also under names of individual tannin-producing plants.)*

Tantalite. *See* Columbite.

Tantalum. (Ta) An element with similar properties to columbium with which it is usually associated. Due to its anti-corrosive properties it is used in sheet form for the manufacture of protective containers for substances that are corrosive. A hard greyish white metal. It is used for surgical and dental instruments and in nerve and bone surgery. Chief sources of supply are Nigeria, the Congo, Brazil, Norway, Mozambique and Malaya.

Tapioca. The starchy food made from the long, thick roots of cassava. The roots are washed and pulped. In tropical Africa and Brazil it forms a staple item of food. Elsewhere it is used for puddings. It is exported from Indonesia.

Tarragon. A herb used in cooking, and in the preparation of tarragon vinegar.

Tea. Tea is produced from the dried leaves of an evergreen shrub native to South-East Asia. To facilitate picking the leaves the tea bush is kept to a height of 3–4 feet by pruning. The best conditions for cultivating the plant are to be found in the monsoon areas of Asia. The shrub requires an annual rainfall of 40 inches or more, a warm damp growing season, and a deep rich well-drained soil. Good drainage is essential, and because of this tea

Tea

plantations are usually established on hill slopes. In addition an abundance of skilled labour must be available for picking and processing the leaves.

About 75% of the world's tea is produced by India, Ceylon and China. Very little China tea enters international trade for it is mostly consumed by the home market. India and Ceylon are the chief exporting countries and Britain is the major importer.

Tea production in China is widespread. In India production is concentrated mainly in the north-east, in Assam, but the region of the Nilgiri Hills in southern India is also a tea-producing area of some importance. In Ceylon tea is produced in large quantities at about 5000 feet in the highland area around Kandy.

Other tea-producing countries include Japan, Indonesia, Pakistan and the U.S.S.R. (*See* Plates XXI and XXII.)

Teak. A deciduous tree native to South-East Asia. It is one of the world's most valuable timber trees, the wood being very hard and resistant to weathering. It is used for shipbuilding, furniture, fences and railway carriages. The oil content prevents the rusting of iron. The tree may reach 150 feet. It is exported chiefly from Siam and Burma.

Teasel. A plant with a very prickly stem, and flower heads that when dry have stiff hooked and barbed bracts which are used for raising the nap on cloth. Grown in Great Britain.

TELLURIUM

Tellurium. (Te) Chemical element that is grey, metallic and a poor conductor of both heat and electricity. It occurs with other metals, e.g. copper, lead and iron, as a telluride. Mined in North and South America, Europe and Zambia, but there is little demand for the element. Used in stainless steel to improve machinability and also in aluminium to improve ductibility.

Thorium. (Th) A soft white chemical element that is radioactive. It is obtained chiefly from monazite sand and is used as an alloy with nickel, lead, aluminium and many other metals, and in the making of gas mantles.

Thorn apple. *See* Daturine.

Thyme. An aromatic shrub with small leaves, native to Mediterranean regions. It yields the essential oil, thymol. The dried leaves are used as a flavouring in cooking.

Timber. The prepared wood of over 6000 varieties of trees. It can be divided into softwood, the timber of coniferous trees, and hardwood, that of deciduous trees.

Tin. (Sn) This metal has been used by man since prehistoric times, and its main ore is cassiterite. Over two-thirds of the world's tin comes from Malaya, Bolivia, Indonesia and China. Other producing countries include the Congo, Thailand, Nigeria, Burma and South Africa. The greatest amounts of tin are derived from alluvial and detrital deposits by means of dredging and hydraulic mining, but in some localities, especially in Bolivia, it is found in rich veins and lodes.

The metal is extracted by smelting and it is used chiefly for tin-plating. This consists of immersing thin sheets of low grade steel in molten tin to give a coating which prevents rust. The various branches of the canning industry are the largest consumers of tinplate. Other uses of tin include for the manufacture of alloys such as brass, bronze and gun metal, tin foil, bearing metals and household utensils.

Tinstone. *See* Cassiterite.

Titanium. (Ti) A hard white metallic element that is ductile and resistant to corrosion. It is always found in combination with oxygen, the chief ores being ilmenite and rutile. It is mined chiefly in India, Scandinavia, North America, Australia and the Urals. It is used as an alloy with aluminium, the dioxide as a white pigment, and as a carbide for high-speed cutting steels. Titanium tetrachloride is used for smoke screens. Titanous chloride is used in the removal of iron stains from cloth. It is also used in the ceramics industry for yellowish glazes.

Tobacco. An annual plant native to North America, three species of which are used commercially. The leaves, 2–3 feet long, are harvested when green, dried, fermented and aged. Cigars are rolled from the whole leaves. Pipe tobacco is coarsely shredded and pressed, and cigarette tobacco is finely cut. The leaves are ground for snuff. The largest producer is the U.S.A., and other important growers are China, India, Japan, Brazil and Turkey. (*See* Plates XXIII and XXIV.)

Tomato. Classified as a vegetable because of its usage but actually the fruit of a plant that though a perennial is always cultivated as an annual. The fruit may be red or yellow, round or oval, and is eaten raw, canned, as a sauce or canned as a juice. Native to South America it is cultivated in most warm and cool temperate lands.

Topaz. A mineral usually occurring in granite and often associated with mica, cassiterite and tourmaline. It is used as a gem-stone, and is obtained from Brazil, Peru, Ceylon and the U.S.A.

Tortoise-shell. The yellowish-brown epidermic plates of the hawksbill tortoise. It is used for ornaments, and the best varieties come from Indonesia, West Indies and Brazil.

Tourmaline. A boro-silicate mineral found naturally; if it contains iron it is black, if magnesium then brown. When transparent used as a gem-stone, and known as Brazilian emerald (green), indicalite (blue) and rubellite (pink). Found in the Urals, Ceylon and Madagascar.

Tragacanth. A sticky substance obtained from the bark of a shrub. It is used as a base for medicines.

131

Travertine. A compact limestone which is an attractive decorative stone when polished.

Trepang. *See* Bêche-de-mer.

Truffle. Name given to several kinds of edible fungi that are native to Europe, and are found about a foot below the surface. Pigs, dogs and goats are trained to hunt them out by scent in the woods where they are usually found, as there is no indication on the surface of the presence of truffles.

Tumeric. *See* Turmeric.

Tung oil *(Chinese wood oil).* The chief producing countries are China, the U.S.S.R., Argentina, the U.S.A., Brazil and Paraguay. The oil comes from the fruit of two trees of Chinese origin. Both trees need a cool season when they are dormant and a rainfall of about 40 inches a year that is distributed throughout the year. The oil dries very speedily and is therefore very useful in paints and varnishes as a drying oil.

Tungsten (W). A metallic element mainly obtained from its ores, wolframite and scheelite. China produces 40% of the world's production of tungsten. Other producing countries are Tasmania, Korea, the U.S.A., Bolivia, Portugal and Brazil. The chief use of tungsten is in the steel industry for producing a very hard steel from which high-speed cutting tools are made. Such steel is also used for hack-saw blades, razor blades, grinding tools, knife blades and armour plate. Tungsten is also used for making filaments in light bulbs and radio valves because of its high melting point.

Turkeys. *See* Poultry.

Turmeric. A yellowish powder rather like a pepper that is used widely in curries and also as a dye. Comes from the tuberlike rhizome of a plant of the ginger family that grows in the tropics.

Turnip. A biennial plant with a white juicy root that is eaten by humans and animals. The leaves can be used as a vegetable. Many varieties grouped according to shape and colour. Swede turnip is very nutritious and keeps well. Grown in cool temperate regions, sometimes in rotation with cereals.

Turpentine. It is a resin obtained from some species of coniferous trees. It is used as a solvent and also as a drying agent in paints and varnishes. It can also be used medicinally, and as an antiseptic. It can be separated into rosin and spirit of turpentine (turps).

Turqoise. A blue-green semi-precious stone that is hydrous aluminium sulphate, coloured with a copper or iron sulphate. The best stones come from Iran.

Tussore. A silk produced by the larvae of two species of silkworm that are found in China and India. The silk is strong, but rather coarse, and of a cream colour.

U

Ugly. A mottled green citrus fruit that is produced by crossing a tangerine and a grapefruit.

Umber. A natural earth pigment consisting mainly of the hydrated oxides of iron and manganese. When calcined it is a warm rich brown colour and is known as burnt umber. It can be ground in water, oil or turpentine or mixed with other pigments.

Upas. From the cut bark of this deciduous tree of the fig family that is native to Indonesia comes a poison which is used by the natives for their arrows. It grows to a height of 60 feet or more before bearing branches.

Uranitite. A uranium ore.

Uranium (U). A greyish-white metallic element that is obtained chiefly from pitchblende mined near Great Bear Lake (Canada), Katanga (Congo) and from carnolite mined in the U.S.A. It is used for nuclear energy and atomic power.

V

Vacoua. *See* Vicua.

Valerian. A herbaceous perennial plant that is grown in Holland, Germany and the U.S.A. especially. The dried root contains a volatile oil used medicinally.

Valonia. The acorn cups of a species of oak that grows in Anatolia and is used for dyeing and tanning.

Vanadium (V). A metallic element that is widely distributed in the earth's crust in combination with other elements. Small amounts are recovered from the ashes of asphalt, coal and oil. 75% of the world's vanadium ores are mined in the U.S.A., and the other important producing countries are South-West Africa, the South African Republic and Finland. It is used almost entirely in steel manufacture as a hardening and purifying agent. The steels are used for high-speed tools, automobile and machine parts and springs. Vanadium compounds are used in the printing of fabrics, in medicines, and in paints.

Vanilla. The dried seed pods of several species of orchids widely cultivated in Java and the Seychelles. It is used as a flavouring for confectionery, ices, and in perfume. The best varieties are the very dark pods, but most of the flavouring is now made synthetically.

Veal. The name given to calf flesh when killed for table use.

Vegetable. A general term that can be applied to any form of plant life but is usually applied to plants that are edible to human beings, or for feeding cattle or other animals, e.g. potatoes, carrots, cabbages, etc.

Vegetable marrow. *See* Marrow.

Vegetable oils. Oils that are derived from plants, and may be obtained by crushing the seeds, e.g. flax seeds, give linseed oil, or by crushing the fruit itself, e.g. olives, yield olive oil. These oils are used for cooking purposes, in the manufacture of margarine, and for soap. (*See also under individual names.*)

Venison. The flesh of various members of the deer family that is used for human consumption and includes reindeer.

Verbena. A perennial or annual plant native to tropical America. From the leaves and flowers of the lemon-scented verbena comes the oil of verbena used in perfume.

Vermicelli. *See* Wheat.

Vermiculite. This is the name given to biotite micas which when heated swell to more than ten times their original volume. One of the main uses of vermiculite is for the insulation of walls, for fire-proofing, as a sound deadener, and for the covering of pipes and in refrigerators. The main deposits are to be found in the U.S.A., in Montana, in Tanzania, and the Urals.

Vetch. Native to Europe and Asia it is a leguminous plant that is cultivated to enrich the soil and as fodder. It grows in a great variety of soils and is often grown with another crop such as rye that will give support to its climbing or trailing stems.

Vicua *(Vacoua).* The name given to fibres from the screw pine that grows in South-East Asia and the islands of the Pacific; the fibres are woven into sacking. The coarser fibres from the outside of the stem are used for brushes.

Vicuña. The fleece of a kind of llama that is native to the Andes of Chile and Peru. The long soft silky wool is used in worsteds and woollens.

Vine. Widely cultivated in Africa, the U.S.A. and the Mediterranean regions of Europe. The fruit grows in clusters on the vines and is known as grapes. The skin may be purple or green when ripe. The fruit is eaten raw, or fermented into wine, or dried into currants, raisins and sultanas. The vine with its long roots can withstand frost and periods of drought, but the main conditions for its growth are a hot dry summer, an autumn temperature of about 60°F to mature the grapes for wine making, and a porous soil. Vines are often cultivated on south-facing slopes in order that the ground does not become too wet, and that sufficient sunshine may be obtained. France is the leading wine producer and her wines include champagne, claret and burgundy. Italy and Spain are also important, the latter being famed for sherry; Germany, California, Algeria, Australia, Hungary, and South Africa are of growing importance.

Vines are particularly susceptible to the disease *Phylloxera* caused by a genus of aphids which are very destructive. Some years ago the French vines were destroyed by this pest. (*See* Plates XXV, XXVI and XXVII.)

W

Wahoo. *See* Spindle Tree.

Walnut. A deciduous tree about 60 feet high which is widely cultivated, especially in France and Spain. The timber is used as a cabinet wood. The nuts are edible and are brown when ripe; if gathered green they are used for pickling. The shells of the nuts yield a brown dye.

Watercress. An aquatic perennial plant that may be a floating or creeping variety, and is found in Asia and Europe, usually in clear, running shallow water. Used in salads.

Watermelon. Native to tropical Africa it is an annual plant that is now widely grown in tropical countries. The edible fruit is spherical or oblong, with a green rind containing a yellow or red pulp. May weigh as much as 20 lb.

Water oats. *See* Wild rice.

Water opal. *See* Moonstone.

Wattle. *See* Acacia.

Waxes. These are plastic substances of low melting point and may be of mineral, vegetable, or animal origin and are dealt with under their individual names.

Whales. Two kinds of whale are hunted commercially: the sperm whale and the hump-backed whale. They are widely distributed, generally moving towards tropical waters during the winter months. Commercial whaling is now confined to antarctic waters. Norway is the leading exporter of whale oil, closely followed by Britain. Other producers are South Africa, Japan, the U.S.S.R., Holland and Germany. The chief whale products are whale oil, spermaceti, whalebone and ambergris.

Wheat

Wheat. This is the most widely cultivated cereal. It is grown in nearly all countries within the temperate zones where average summer temperatures are over 60°F, and where conditions are suitable it may be grown within the tropics. The general conditions necessary for its cultivation are a cool damp early growing season; 90 frost-free days; a rainfall of 15-30 inches annually; a warm dry sunny period for ripening, and a well drained soil sufficiently firm to support the long thin stem with its heavy ear. Wheat grows to a height of some 2–5 feet.

The largest quantities of wheat are produced on the temperate grasslands such as the prairies of North America and the Ukraine, and in addition the North China Plain. Yield per acre varies considerably. In the U.S.A., Canada, Australia and Argentina it may be less than 18 bushels, whereas on the more intensely farmed lands of north-west Europe yields may be twice as much, or even more.

Of the many varieties of wheat the bread wheats are the most important. They may be either hard or soft grained and there are two main classes, winter wheat and spring wheat.

Winter wheat is sown in autumn and harvested the following summer. About 75% of the world's total wheat production consists of winter wheat.

Spring wheat is sown in spring. It is a quick-growing variety which can be harvested within 4 months of sowing.

Hard grained wheat is used for making bread and wheat paste, from which macaroni, spaghetti, vermicelli and semolina are made. Soft grained wheat may be mixed with hard wheat for the making of bread, and it is also used to make biscuits and cakes. Wholemeal flour is produced by grinding the husk with the grain.

The leading wheat-exporting countries are the U.S.A., Canada, Australia and Argentina. Britain is the leading importer.

Whin. *See* Furze.

Whitethorn. *See* Hawthorn.

Whiting. *See* Fish.

Whortleberry. *See* Bilberry.

Wild rice *(Indian rice, Water oats)*. A coarse annual grass that provides food for the American Indians and is grown in damp muddy places, especially in the southern states of the U.S.A.

Willow. A small tree or shrub belonging to the *Salix* genus and containing much tannin in their bark. The wood of some species is used for cricket bats, basket work and charcoal. Salicin used in medicine is extracted from the bark.

Wine. *See* Vine; Grapes.

Wintergreen. A herb-like plant of the heath family that grows in cool temperate regions. An oil is distilled from the shiny leaves and it is used externally for muscular pains. The fruits are edible.

Winter's bark. An evergreen South American tree of the magnolia family the bark of which is used for the treatment of scurvy.

Witch hazel. A deciduous shrub from the small oval leaves of which is extracted a liquid used both as a lotion and as a tonic.

Witherite. This mineral, composed of barium carbonate, is mined in north-west England. It is the chief source of barium, and is used in the manufacture of glass and porcelain.

Wolfram. *See* Wolframite.

Wolframite *(Wolfram)*. This mineral is the chief source of tungsten, a brownish-black ore that contains iron, tungsten and manganese. Occurs chiefly in Peru, north-west Spain, Bolivia, China.

Wool. The soft hair, which is usually short and may be curled, that is found on some mammals. The minute scales which overlap one another interlock and hold the wool fibres together. It is the curliness of wool that gives it the ability to stretch. The name is applied usually only to the wool of the domestic sheep, but other fibres from alpacas, Angora goats, Cashmere goats and vicuñas are so like wool that the term is often applied to these fibres as well. Australia is the world's largest producer of wool, but other producers include Argentina, New Zealand, South Africa, the U.S.A. and the U.S.S.R.

Wrack. *See* Grass wrack.

Y

Yam. A perennial climbing plant which is found in tropical areas. It is cultivated as a staple food in Central and South America and

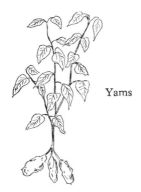

Yams

in West Africa. The thick tubers weigh up to 50 lb. and are used as a vegetable. Some varieties are known as sweet potatoes.

Yellow-wood. *See* Fustic.

Yerba mansa. A herb found in damp marshy places near to the sea in Mexico and along the Pacific coast of the U.S.A. The capsule-like fruit is used as a medicine.

Yerba maté. *See* Maté.

Yew. An evergreen tree with needle-shaped leaves and bearing a single seed in a cup-like berry. The wood is used for cabinet making. It has a thick rugged trunk and rarely exceeds 50 feet in height. The wood was formerly used for making long-bows.

Ylang-ylang. A tree of the custard apple family found in South-East Asia. The flowers yield a perfume that is valued amongst the natives.

Z

Zedoary. A broad-leaved plant that grows in Indonesia with a rhizome that is used for food and as a condiment. It is rather like ginger.

Zinc. (Zn) This mineral is not found in its free state and the chief ore, zinc blende, usually occurs with other minerals such as silver and lead. Zinc is extracted from the ore by smelting or by an electrolytic process if ample electric power is easily available.

The chief use of zinc is for galvanizing iron, whereby the iron is coated with zinc to give it a protective covering against rust. Galvanizing is achieved by immersing the iron in molten zinc; by spraying; by electro-galvanizing; or by Sheradizing which consists of covering the article with zinc powder and then submitting it to a temperature of about 375°C. Zinc is also used in the manufacture of alloys, especially brass, roofing material, storage batteries, die castings and engraving plates.

Zinc oxide is utilized in making paint pigment, cosmetics, ointments and dental cements.

The largest producers of zinc ore are the U.S.A., the U.S.S.R., Canada, Mexico, Australia, Poland, Japan, Peru and Italy.

Zinc Blende. *See* Sphalerite.

Zincspar. *See* Calamine.

Zircon. Common zircon (zirconium silicate) is an opaque mineral, but those used for gem-stones are transparent. The latter are found in alluvial gravels in South-East Asia, New Zealand and New South Wales. The stone resembles a diamond, but can be coloured red, orange or yellow.

Zirconium (Zr). A metallic element that can be recovered from beach sand and is also found in brazilite, zirkelite and baddeleyite in Brazil. It is used in electrical appliances, refractories, and in nuclear energy piles because of its low absorption of neutrons. Photoflash bulbs use powdered zirconium, and zirconium carbide is used as an abrasive for cutting glass.

Zucchini. *See* Marrow.

APPENDIX

ANIMALS
Buffaloes
Camel
Caracul
Donkey
Dromedary
Ermine
Goat
Horse
Karakul sheep
Llama
Mule
Oxen
Pigs
Poultry
Sheep
Whales

CEREALS
Barley
Buckwheat
Maize
Millett
Oats
Rice
Rye
Wheat
Wild rice

DYES AND TANNIN
Alizarin
Alkanet
Anatto

Anil
Aniline
Brazilin
Carmine
Carthamin
Catechu
Chay root
Chica
Cochineal
Crottal
Crall
Hackberry
Henna
Indigo
Madder
Mynobalans
Pagoda tree
Quebracho
Safflower
Saffron
Senna

ELEMENTS
Aluminium
Antimony
Arsenic
Barium
Beryllium
Bismuth
Cadmium
Calcium
Carbon
Cerium

Chromium
Cobalt
Copper
Gallium
Gold
Hafnium
Indium
Iodine
Iridium
Iron
Lead
Lithium
Magnesium
Manganese
Mercury
Molybdenum
Neolymium
Neon
Nickel
Niobium
Osmium
Palladium
Platinum
Platinum metals
Plutonium
Potassium
Radium
Rhodium
Rubidium
Selenium
Silicon
Silver
Sodium
Strontium
Sulphur
Tantalum

Tellurium
Thorium
Tin
Titanium
Tungsten
Uranium
Vanadium
Zinc
Zirconium

FIBRES
Abaca
Alpaca
Angora
Bark cloth
Camel's hair
Cane
Cotton
Cuscus
Eider
Feathers
Felt
Hemp
Indian Hemp
Jute
Kapok
Mohair
Phormium
Raffia
Ramie
Rice paper plant
Silk
Straw
Tussore
Vicuña
Wool

APPENDIX

Prickly pear
Quince
Raisin
Raspberry
Rhubarb
Silverberry
Star apple
Strawberry
Tallow tree
Ugly
Vine
Watermelon

GAS
Helium

GEMS
Agate
Almandine
Amethyst
Aquamarine
Chalcedony
Chrysoprase
Cornelian
Emerald
Garnet
Jade
Jasper
Jet
Lapis lazuli
Moonstone
Obsidian
Onyx
Opal
Pearl
Rubellite

Ruby
Sapphire
Topaz
Tortoise-shell
Turquoise
Zircon

GRASSES
Alfalfa
Clover
Esparto grass
Fescue grass
Grass
Pampas grass
Pin clover
Vetch

HERBS
Basil
Bayleaf
Caper
Caraway seed
Chervil
Cinnamon
Cloves
Dill
Fennel
Marjoram
Mint
Parsley
Peppermint
Rue
Sage
Sorrel
Spearmint
Thyme
Vanilla

APPENDIX

LEATHER
Buff
Chamois

MEDICINAL
Angostura bark
Antiar
Arnica
Atrophine
Belladonna
Cacoon
Calabar bean
Calumba
Camomile
Cinchona
Coca leaves
Colchicum
Colocynth
Daturine
Digitalis
Gentian
Ginseng
Hashish
Henbane
Ipecacuanha
Jalap
Nux vomica
Opium
Pennyroyal
Quassia
Sarsaparilla
Sassofras
Senna
Sweet gale
Valerian
Wintergreen

Winter's bark
Witch hazel
Yerba mansa

MINERALS
Alabaster
Alum
Alumina
Amianthus
Andalusite
Anhydrite
Ankerite
Apatite
Aragonite
Argentite
Argil
Asbestos
Asphalt
Barite
Beryl
Biotite
Bitumen
Borax
Bornite
Bort
Caesium
Cairngorm
Calamine
Calcite
Carnotite
Cassiterite
Celestite
Cerussite
Chalcocite
Chalcophrite
Chalk

Charcoal
China clay
Chrysolite
Cinnabar
Clay
Coal
Cobaltite
Columbite
Coral
Corundum
Cryolite
Diamond
Diatomite
Dolerite
Dumortierite
Emery
Epsom salt
Feldspar
Fire-clay
Flint
Fluorspar
Galena
Graphite
Gypsum
Iceland spar
Ilmenite
Kyanite
Labradorite
Magnesite
Malachite
Meerschaum
Mica
Microcline
Molybdenite
Monazite
Osmiridium

Pentlandite
Petroleum
Phosphate rock
Pitch
Pitchblende
Pyrites
Pyrolusite
Quartz
Realgar
Rhodochrosite
Rhodonite
Rock salt
Rutile
Salt
Scheelite
Serpentine
Silica
Sphalerite
Strontianite
Talc
Torbernite
Tourmaline
Vermiculite
Witherite
Wolframite

NUTS
Almond
Beechmast
Betel
Brazil
Cashew
Groundnut
Kola nut
Pecan

Pistachio
Walnut

OIL
Angelica
Aniseed
Bergamot
Cajuput
Camphor
Castor
Cohune
Colza oil
Cotton seed
Croton
Oil palm
Poppy
Rape
Sesame
Sperm oil
Tung oil

ORGANIC CHEMICALS
Acetic acid
Alkali
Benzene
Casein
Cellulose
Litmus
Methane
Natural gas
Nicotine
Nitrates

PERFUME
Musk
Myrrh

Oak moss
Orrisroot
Rosemary
Verbena
Ylang-ylang

PLANTS
Agave
Bhang
Borage
Cassava
Dandelion
Dulse
Flax
Furze
Glasswort
Gourd
Groundsel
Guttapercha
Heath
Hop
Horseradish
Iceland moss
Jujube
Kava
Lichens
Liquorice
Marram grass
Marsh marigold
Mustard
Nasturtium
Nettle
Pyrethrum
Soapbark
Soapwort
Sunflower

Teasel
Tobacco

RESINS
Amber
Ambergris
Amine
Asafetide
Balsam
Benzoin
Chicle
Dammar
Dbellium
Dragon's blood
Elemi
Frankincense
Gamboge
Mastic
Rosin
Rubber
Sandarac
Shellac
Sticklac
Sumac
Turpentine

ROCKS
Brick earth
Burrstone
Cimolite
Granite
Limestone
Marble
Marl
Ochres
Ore

Peat
Pipe clay
Pumice
Sand
Sandstone
Shale
Slate

SPICES
Canella
Cardamon
Coriander
Cubeb
Cumin
Ginger
Nutmeg
Pepper
Pimento
Turmeric

TREES
Acacia
Aloes
Amboina
Ash
Aspen
Balsa
Bamboo
Baobab
Basswood
Beech
Birch
Boxwood
Buckthorn
Calabash
Cam wood

Canella
Cedar
Chestnut
Coconut
Cork
Deal
Deodar
Dogwood
Douglas fir
Ebony
Elder
Elm
Eucalyptus
Fir
Fustic
Hardwoods
Hawthorn
Hazel
Hemlock
Holly
Hornbeam
Horse chestnut
Ironwood
Jarrah
Juniper
Kauri
Larch
Laurel
Lavender
Lithocarpus
Logwood
Mahogany
Maidenhair tree
Mangosteen
Mangrove
Maple

Myrtle
Nettle tree
Oak
Olive
Oregon myrtle
Oregon tea tree
Osier
Palm
Pine
Poplar
Rosewood
Saffron wood
Sandalwood
Sapan
Sequoia
Service tree
Soapbark
Spindle tree
Spruce
Sweet gum
Sycamore
Tamarind
Teak
Willow
Yew

VEGETABLES
Arracacha
Artichoke
Bean
Borecoal
Cabbage
Caladium
Cardoon
Carrot
Celery

Chick-pea
Chicory
Cucumber
Egg-plant
Garlic
Haricot
Leek
Lettuce
Okra
Onion
Parsnip
Pea
Potato
Pumpkin
Radish
Salsify

Scorzonera
Sea kale
Shallot
Spinach
Sweet potato
Tomato
Turnip
Watercress
Yam

WAX

Beeswax
Carnauba
Ozokerite
Spermaceti
Tallow tree